THE CAPITAL YEARS
Niagara-on-the-Lake, 1792-1796

Richard Merritt,
Nancy Butler, and
Michael Power, editors

Toronto and Oxford
Dundurn Press
1991

Editing: Curtis Fahey
Cover desing: JAQ
Page design and Production: GSN Consulting
Printing and Binding: Gagné Printing Ltd., Louiseville, Quebec, Canada

The writing of this manuscript and the publication of this book were made possible by support from several sources. The publisher wishes to acknowledge the generous assistance and ongoing support of **The Canada Council, The Book Publishing Industry Development Programme** of the **Department of Communications,** and **The Ontario Arts Council.**

Care has been taken to trace the ownership of copyright material used in the text (including the illustrations). Credit for each quotation is given at the end of the selection. The editors and publisher welcome any information enabling them to rectify any reference or credit in subsequent editions.

J. Kirk Howard, Publisher

Canadian Cataloguing in Publication Data

Main entry under title:
The Capital Years: Niagara-on-the-Lake, 1792-1796

Co-published by the Niagara Historical Society.
Includes bibliographical references and index.
ISBN 1-55002-149-4

1. Niagara-on-the-Lake (Ont.) - History.
I. Merritt, Richard. II. Butler, Nancy. III. Power, Michael . IV. Niagara Historical Society.

FC3099.N5C36 1991   971.3'38   C91-095604-9
F1059.5.N5C36 1991

Dundurn Press Limited
2181 Queen Street East, suite 301
Toronto, Ontario
Canada
M4E 1E5

Dundurn Distribution
73 Lime Walk
Headington, Oxford
England
OX3 7AD

THE CAPITAL YEARS
Niagara-on-the-Lake, 1792-1796

Richard Merritt,
Nancy Butler, and
Michael Power, editors

Published with
the assistance of the
Ontario Ministry of
Culture and Communications
and
the Niagara Foundation

CONTENTS

PREFACE

In 1987 the Niagara Historical Society received a letter from Dr Peter Moogk of the University of British Columbia suggesting a collection of articles on the early history of Niagara as a way of commemorating the bicentennial of the opening of the first parliament of Upper Canada in 1792 at Niagara-on-the-Lake, which Lieutenant Governor Simcoe had just christened Newark. We were intrigued by the idea.

A publications committee consisting of Richard Merritt, Nancy Butler, and Michael Power was formed to give editorial direction to the project, and nine authors, known for their expertise on different aspects of Niagara's past, were asked to contribute essays. To our delight, these writers very generously responded by donating their time and talents to our cause. Later, Curtis Fahey was recruited as project editor, Professor J.M.S. Careless agreed to prepare a foreword, and Dundurn Press expressed interest in publishing the volume. The Niagara Foundation kindly contributed funds in memory of Harold Usher, and the Ontario Ministry of Culture and Communications offered generous and enthusiastic support. Without the assistance of all of the above, this project would not have been realized. The Niagara Historical Society is in their debt.

The Publications Committee of the Niagara Historical Society also wishes to thank the following: Una Abrahamson, Ian Butler, Maria Carvacho, Barbara Challis, Meredith Chiltern, Laura McFadden, Carolin Muise, William Severin, Glenn Smith, and Faye Whitfield.

Finally, an editorial explanation concerning Niagara's many names is in order. In its early years, the small community on the west bank of the Niagara River opposite Fort Niagara was known as Butlersburg, New Niagara, West Niagara (to distinguish it from Fort Niagara), or simply Niagara. To add to the confusion, government officials in Quebec recommended the name Lenox. In 1792 Lieutenant Governor Simcoe proclaimed that the first capital of Upper Canada was to be called Newark, but most of the local inhabitants preferred and continued to use the earlier Indian name, Niagara. After Simcoe returned to England, the name Niagara was officially adopted by an act of the legislature in 1798. At the beginning of the twentieth century, the post office, to avoid confusion with Niagara Falls, named the town Niagara-on-the-Lake.

For the sake of editorial consistency and historical accuracy, in each of the essays in this volume, the pre-1792 community is identified as "Niagara (Niagara-on-the-Lake)" on first mention and merely as "Niagara" thereaf-

7

ter. The town of the capital years is called "Newark (Niagara-on-the-Lake)" on first mention and "Newark" subsequently. "Niagara," with no parenthetical identification, is used to refer to the general area.

FOREWORD

J.M.S. CARELESS

There is the Niagara of the giant Falls, hydroelectric power, modern industry, and constant traffic across the Canadian-American border. But farther down the Niagara River where it flows into Lake Ontario, there is another storied Niagara of early Canadian beginnings: of Indian trade and French or British forts, of loyalists battling against the American revolution who remained to settle in the area in the 1780s. And in this place, too, emerged the little town of Newark, later Niagara-on-the-Lake, which became capital of the new British province of Upper Canada — the future Ontario, set up in 1791 in response to the spread of loyalist settlement along the upper St Lawrence and Great Lakes shores. It is that community which now concerns us, masterfully portrayed in the illuminating studies that follow. Representative democracy in inland Canada effectively began in Newark, the first home of Ontario provincial parliaments from 1792 to 1796. Moreover, it was in Newark that provision was made for the gradual abolition of black slavery, some forty years before it was legislated to an end in the rest of Britain's empire, and seventy years before that evil was removed by force from the "free" republican United States. In sum, the capital years of early Niagara-on-the-Lake provide a fascinating record in themselves.

In 1796 the Upper Canada legislature left Newark for York (Toronto), more safely distant from the border with a still decidedly unfriendly United States. The government seat was to stay at York-Toronto, right on to the present. Yet, while Newark-Niagara lost its political importance, it did not experience uninterrupted tranquillity after 1796; far from it. During the War of 1812 with the United States — just across the Niagara River — the town went through invasion and devastation; and long afterward, its military ramparts still formed a bastion against threats of new border attacks. Nonetheless, at least by the later nineteenth century, the town of Niagara had settled comfortably into being the focus of rich surrounding farmlands, a place of gracious heritage homes and proud historical memories — as it yet remains today. In more recent years, of course, the admired Shaw Festival of drama, held annually there, the elegance of well-preserved old buildings, public and private, and the garden-beauty of this favoured southern Ontario river-area have all drawn large numbers of visitors to Niagara-on-the-Lake, in a combined and successful mixture of theatre-going and tourism. Consequently, old Newark, historic Upper Canadian capital and still a capital of the heart, stays glowingly alive in fine old houses set on handsome, shady streets which are thronged each summer but which best regain their serenity each autumn, as the golden leaves drift quietly down.

The patterns of life in Newark-Niagara are graphically and substantially set out in the pages of this book. The first essay, Joy Ormsby's "Building a Town," investigates the plans, surveys, and general layout of the urban centre which developed from 1779 onward to 1796. Then comes "Patronage and Power," by Bruce Wilson, a piece that focuses on sharp public realities: how the officeholders and interest-groups, the dominant merchants such as Robert Hamilton, the loyalist officers, the assembly representatives, and others, dealt with making Upper Canada work (in their own direction) within the small political cockpit that was Newark then. Next comes "Military Life" — fundamental to Niagara — by Brian Dunnigan, and Michael Power's "Religion and Community," a subject of crucial importance to the beliefs, culture, and society of the Niagara residents of the time. This is followed by "Muslin Gowns and Moccasins," by Elizabeth Severin, which examines the dress and costume that came to Niagara with Upper Canada's first lieutenant governor, John Graves Simcoe (who chose it as capital and named it Newark), and his keenly observant wife, Elizabeth, not to forget the other leading lights in the rising local community.

We are then introduced, in Dorothy Duncan's "Victuals and Viands in the New Province," to the foods and cooking that nourished Upper Canada's early inhabitants. The next piece, Peter Moogk's "At Home in Early Niagara Township," deals evocatively with the domestic buildings and furnishings of this warm and living community. Following on this essay is Richard Merritt's "Early Inns and Taverns," a detailed picture of the functions performed by public hostelries in the Niagara area — institutions that were central to the existence of a pioneer community. Finally, to remind us of how meals, dress, plans, or politics are all subject to sterner natural forces, we have "Health, Disease, and Treatment in Early Upper Canada" by Charles Roland. It makes clear that the most highly regarded soldier, shining social leader, or sharpest politician had to live with "puking and purging," amid epidemics, broken bones, fierce surgery, and childbirth deaths, in a harsh Upper Canadian reality from which we have mercifully escaped to a large extent. The grand old times were not consistently glorious, as this instructive piece warns us very plainly.

In any event, this book is a splendid series of well-researched chapters, vividly describing what early Newark-Niagara in truth was like. Yet, at the end, one might attempt here to add just a little bit more — as to how the Niagara area began, well before the town community depicted in these pages had made its appearance late in the eighteenth century. Never forgetting that the native peoples had known Niagara in pre-historic centuries before any European newcomers had reached the area, we still may note that the Niagara River appeared on the historical record in a map published with Champlain's *Travels* in France in 1632. Niagara Falls along that waterway was examined in 1678 by the French, who in 1676 had set up a trading post at the Lake Ontario entry to the Niagara River. That post became a major, stone-built French fort and key to a vast continental interior: southwest to the Mississippi and the Gulf of Mexico, northwest to the upper Great Lakes and the great plains beyond. Finally, however, the fort was taken by British forces and Iroquois allies in 1759; and thereafter Fort Niagara in turn became a British trade and military key to the interior. It certainly filled that role during the American revolution that burst forth in the 1770s. The fort then served as the strategic base for British, loyalist, and Iroquois operations in a bitter conflict across up-state New York. And after the recognition of American independence in 1783, it still formed a protective shelter for the loyalist families who had flocked there, some to settle on the "Canadian" side of the Niagara River, others to move further into Upper Canada to-be.

Fort Niagara was located on the United States shore of the river, and was finally given up to American occupation in 1796. It was, in fact, now replaced on the Canadian shore by Fort George. Just outside this new fortification, the town-site where Simcoe had fixed his capital was steadily filled in, as soldiers, merchants, workers, and loyalist farmers together built up a flourishing community. Butler's Barracks stood there, the headquarters for the loyalist unit known as Butler's Rangers which had fought across New York; so did Navy Hall, as base for British naval forces on Lake Ontario. Simcoe, indeed, made Navy Hall his official residence. In short, even by the time this energetic soldier-governor had arrived at Niagara in the summer of 1792, the formation of a town was already well advanced on the Canadian shore — so that Newark, the capital, blossomed very fast.

But behind Newark, or Niagara-on-the-Lake, there stretched the long past of the fur trade, its batteaux and canoe brigades that had gathered at Niagara, the military garrisons, the Indians, the powerful fur merchants and army contractors. Accordingly, when we turn to the world of Upper Canada's founding capital in the 1790s, we might well remember that the weight it possessed during its brief but highly memorable period of ruling power in Ontario had substantially older underpinnings.

This book is dedicated
to the memory of
John Field,
teacher and historian

"Lt. General Simcoe," oil by Jean Laurent Mosiner, c. 1791 (Metropolitan Toronto Library, T30592).

John Graves Simcoe (1752–1806) was educated at Oxford and first came to North America in 1771. Eventually commanding the First American Regiment, the original Queen's Rangers, from 1777 to 1781, Simcoe was appointed the first lieutenant governor of Upper Canada in 1791 after the passage of the Constitutional Act. It was Simcoe who chose the tiny community at the mouth of the Niagara River opposite Fort Niagara as the first, but temporary, capital of Upper Canada. He arrived at his capital (which he had named Newark) on 26 July 1792 with his wife and two of his six children. The actual opening of the first parliament at Newark was delayed because Simcoe had suffered a concussion after standing too close to a cannon firing a salute upon the arrival of Prince Edward, Duke of Kent, the future father of Queen Victoria. Simcoe presided over the five sessions of the first parliament at Newark, 1792–1796, until his return to England in 1796 owing to ill health. On the orders of his superior, Governor-in-Chief Lord Dorchester, he began construction of a new capital at York (Toronto) in 1793 but it was Peter Russell, administrator in Simcoe's absence, who reluctantly supervised the government's move to York in 1797. Mrs Simcoe, née Elizabeth Posthuma Gwillim (d. 1850), through her letters, diaries, and sketches, portrayed many aspects of daily life in Niagara and Upper Canada during the 1790s.

CHAPTER ONE

BUILDING A TOWN

Plans, Surveys, and the Early Years of
Niagara-on-the-Lake

Joy Ormsby

As the principal inhabitants of Niagara waited, on 26 July 1792, for the *Onondaga* carrying John Graves Simcoe, first lieutenant governor of the new province of Upper Canada, to dock near Navy Hall, the group of four buildings erected in 1765 for the use of the Provincial Marine, many of them were no doubt pleased that, no longer part of Quebec, they would henceforth use English customs and law. At the same time, however, they were likely apprehensive about the effects the new administration might have on their possessions and their status in the community.

Chief among these early inhabitants were Lieutenant-Colonel John Butler, deputy agent of Indian affairs and former commander of Butler's Rangers, the loyalist corps whose disbanded members formed the nucleus of the Niagara farming community, and Robert Hamilton, a prominent merchant. Butler, who had begun the settlement in 1780 under the aegis of Governor Frederick Haldimand and had shaped its development, retained at age sixty-seven the role of elder statesman. Hamilton, a newcomer by comparison but a rising star in Niagara, was Butler's colleague in the Court of Common Pleas, Court of Quarter Sessions, and land board, a local body responsible for issuing certificates for land. Both men were uneasy about whether they would retain these appointments — made by the governor general in Quebec before the establishment of Upper Canada in November 1791 — under the new administration. Surveyor Augustus Jones, who had completed a survey of the town plot only a month earlier, and Walter Butler

Sheehan, John Butler's nephew, who had been appointed sheriff in August 1791, also had concerns about retaining their positions. Other members of the community included farmers such as Adam and Isaac Vrooman, Peter and David Secord, John P. and Joseph Clement, Jacob Servos, and Jacob, George, and Joseph Ball. Merchants George Forsyth, Archibald Cunningham, William Dickson (cousin of Robert Hamilton), Joseph Edwards, John McEwen, and Daniel Servos also waited, as did Robert Kerr, surgeon to the Indian Department in Niagara, and James Muirhead, former surgeon's mate.

These men with thirty others from the Niagara district, had, the previous February, signed a statement prepared by Butler and Hamilton which under the guise of a welcome address to Simcoe set forth the major concerns of the entire community. Their settlement, they noted, had made rapid progress and had emerged from indigence and obscurity; their possessions had at last become valuable; and their latest crops were abundant. Yet they lacked deeds to confirm ownership of their land. Reasons for the long delay in issuing these vital proofs of ownership are made clear by plans, surveys, and associated documents which illustrate the state of flux in the early years of the settlement on the west bank of the Niagara River from its beginning in 1779 as a government-sponsored farming community to its capital period from the autumn of 1792 to 1796.

In its first stage from 1779 to 1783, the settlement was officially a temporary arrangement, designed to provide food for Fort Niagara, which during the War of Independence had become a staging ground for Butler's Rangers. From this base the Rangers and their Indian allies made raids against American posts in the border area, ravaging the country in order to destroy their enemy's food supply and eating most of the captured cattle. Some refugees had followed the Rangers to Fort Niagara. More came as a result of the Rangers' scorched-earth policy, and finally, as American troops advanced north, dispossessed loyalists and Indians made for the fort seeking refuge. They put such an enormous strain on the resources of the fort, whose provisions had to be shipped from England via Montreal "at great expense and difficulty," that Lieutenant-Colonel Mason Bolton, commanding officer at Niagara, wondered at one point whether maintaining the post was not costing "old England" more than it was worth. In order to reduce the expense, Governor Frederick Haldimand suggested to Bolton in October 1778 that he encourage and assist some capable people to cultivate the land "about the fort in order to supply entirely the post with bread."[1] After consulting "several gentlemen" Bolton advised Haldimand in March 1779 that "both from the soil and situation, the West side of the river" was

16

"by far preferable to the East."[2] At that time, the gentleman most familiar with soil conditions on the west bank was Major John Butler, who, in order to alleviate overcrowding at Fort Niagara, had moved his Rangers' headquarters across the river and had built barracks in the fall and winter of 1778 and additional log houses and a hospital in the spring of 1779 at the considerable cost of more than £2,500. Butler's input no doubt influenced Bolton's recommendation, a recommendation that resulted in Haldimand's approving, without waiting for authorization from Britain, the sending of three or four refugee families to farm the west bank.[3]

This very small-scale initiative was expanded after Haldimand had received approval from Britain in March 1780 and had consulted, in June, with John Butler, by then promoted to lieutenant-colonel, about the mechanics of establishing and operating a settlement. Haldimand's plan, outlined in a letter to Colonel Bolton in July 1780, called for the reclamation of a strip of land formerly "granted by the Mississaugas to Sir William Johnson ... opposite the Fort"[4] and the distribution of that land to loyalist refugees willing to farm it until they could be restored to their former homes in the American states. The land (some of which had already been cleared by Butler's Rangers by the summer of 1780) remained the property of the crown and crops could be sold only to the garrison, whose commanding officer set their prices. In essence, then, the first loyalist settlers were squatters occupying land under military direction.

The Haldimand project was put in charge of Lieutenant-Colonel Butler. Before the end of 1780, Butler reported that he had established four or five families who had built themselves houses. The head of one of these, Peter Secord, a former Ranger, was later allowed an extra grant of 100 acres for having been the first to have settled his family on the west bank in 1779.[5] Another, John Secord, in 1780 was host to Elizabeth Gilbert, one of a family of fifteen captured by Indians who brought her with them to Butlersburg to get provisions. Other heads of families who claimed to have reached Butler's barracks by 1780 included Mary De Peu (petition of 21 April 1797), Catherine Clement (petition of 27 July 1797), and James Secord (petition of his sons of 3 August 1795). In May 1781 the purchase of the strip of land from the Mississaugas was completed at a cost of "300 suits of cloathing."[6] By mid-summer 1782, sixteen farmers, whose names were recorded by Butler in the settlement's first census, had settled their families and cleared 236 acres. All were producing food. Peter Secord, for example, produced 200 bushels of corn, 15 of wheat, 70 of potatoes, and 4 of oats on 24 acres of land cleared at the foot of the escarpment near the present St Davids. John Depue grew 200 bushels of corn and 50 of potatoes on 16 acres cleared near

Queenston, and Michael Showers produced 40 bushels of corn, 6 of oats, and 15 of potatoes on 12 acres cleared along the river a few miles south of Navy Hall. In addition, the Rangers had prepared a block of land known as the Government's Farm in order to plant Indian corn[7] and several of them had "got their families from the frontiers" and had shown interest in settling after discharge.[8]

During 1783 the temporary status of the young community ended as a result of the signing, on 30 November 1782, by Great Britain and the United States of a treaty of peace which established the Niagara River as an international boundary. The Treaty of Paris also recommended an amnesty for the loyalists and the restitution of their property, but left implementation of that recommendation to the legislatures of the individual states, many of which preferred confiscation to restitution and execution to amnesty. By the spring of 1783 it was clear that land would soon have to be found on the Canadian side of the boundary for those unable to regain their former homes.

For Lieutenant-Colonel Butler's settlers, tenure of the land now became a pressing issue. Their spokesmen, Isaac Dolson, Elijah Phelps, Thomas McMicking, and Donald Bee, all of whom but Bee had been included in Butler's first census, asked for "leases or some other security"[9] so that their farms could not be taken by the commanding officer at Fort Niagara for the benefit of potential new settlers. Butler and eight of his officers who were also farming shared this interest in establishing tenure or, at the very least, obtaining some documented proof of occupation prior to 1783. Perhaps to supply this evidence, Butler employed Allan Macdonell to survey the settlement without waiting for official approval.[10] This first survey, completed before 3 May 1783, drew a mixed response from Governor Haldimand, who, though pleased that Butler had made a beginning, charged that he had exceeded his authority by marking out "seventy lots of land, thirty of which were nominated for different persons."[11] "Nominated," meaning the endorsement by the surveyor in the name of a specific settler, suggested tenure, which was not part of the Haldimand plan of settlement.

In the Haldimand papers there is an undated, unsigned plan of the "New Settlement, Niagara" which marks out lots on the west side of the river, thirty of which are nominated mostly in the names of Rangers and former Rangers. This may be the Macdonell survey. It shows the extent of the "temporary" settlement and its concentration along the river bank and in a block of smaller lots north of the Due West Line — now called the East-West Line — on land that would be reserved for the crown in 1784. The latter group, with the Rangers' barracks nearby, probably constituted the village

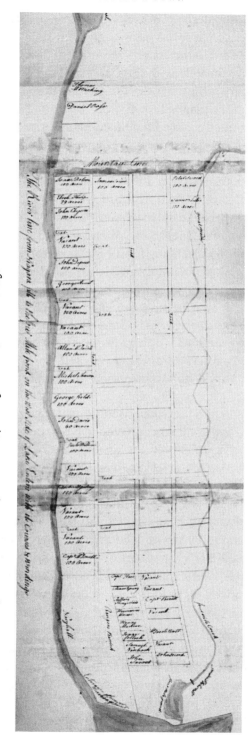

"The New Settlement Niagara," Haldimand Papers 85, 71-2, probably c. 1783. (British Library)

of Butlersburg. Although the plan is not to scale — in particular the Four Mile Pond is located too close to Mississauga Point and the path of the Four Mile Creek is not correct — the eastern boundary of the block of smaller lots does coincide approximately with the Garrison Line, which later became the western boundary of the town, dividing it from Butler's land and cutting off a large corner of the planned town plot.

When Haldimand dismissed the Macdonell-Butler plan as unauthorized, he promised to send a surveyor to Niagara to make an official survey that would be in accord with instructions from the British government, which had by then acknowledged that the settlement had entered a new permanent stage of development. These instructions encompassed several new rules. Land was to be laid out in seigneuries, as befitted an area that was still part of the province of Quebec, on which loyal subjects would be settled according to a set formula, ranging from 1,000 acres for a field officer to 100 acres for a private or head of family and 50 acres for each family member. Settlement of officers and privates was to be contiguous and, therefore, 100-acre lots were to be drawn for randomly; and, in each seigneury, between 300 and 500 acres were to be reserved for the clergy. In the spring of 1784 two further directives were issued. The high ground from Navy Hall to the Four Mile Creek was to be reserved for the crown and, on 24 June, major troop reductions (which would lead to increased demand for land) were to be implemented.

A week or two before the troop disbandment, Lieutenant Tinling, the surveyor promised by Haldimand, arrived in Niagara with orders to mark off the crown reserve, to survey the area of the Niagara seigneury, to conduct a draw for its 100-acre lots, and to enter names of individual drawers on certificates.

Tinling, an assistant engineer at Cataraqui (Kingston), had problems, especially with the early settlers, who had already cleared land and naturally wanted to keep it. By the time he arrived, there were, according to Lieutenant-Colonel Butler's list of May 1784, forty-six farmers in the area, including a few on the land about to be reserved for the crown. Among these were four or five officers of the Rangers and Butler himself (though he was not included in the list of forty-six) who had already declared that, "having cultivated and built good farm houses" on the land between Navy Hall and Four Mile Creek, they intended to stay there.[12] These were men that the surveyor could not challenge with impunity. In addition, Tinling had difficulties with the influx of newly disbanded Rangers, about eighty of whom had grabbed land preferably with water frontage and had begun to clear it before the process of drawing for lots began. Moreover, neither the surveyor's parcel of certificates of possession nor all his required tools arrived in Niagara.

Indeed, Tinling's problems were such that Philip Frey, who superseded him as surveyor in December 1785, suggested, in a letter to Deputy Surveyor General John Collins, that Tinling never completed a survey and that plans he submitted were possibly spurious: "The person who had been employed in the surveying business previous to me had made few and very erroneous surveys, having only laid out a few lots for particular people, many plans may have been transmitted, which may not have been effectively executed."[13] Augustus Jones, Frey's successor as surveyor at Niagara, was also critical of Tinling's expertise, though he charitably attributed disparities in his "lines" to "an instrument very imperfect called a plane table."[14]

Whether Tinling's work or not, several similar plans survived from his relatively short and frustrating period of duty at Niagara. One of these, included in the papers of Shubbal Walton, who farmed in Niagara Township near the present village of Virgil, and dated "1784 or earlier," generally observed the government's instructions of 1783-84. It showed a township laid out in 100-acre lots, with part of the river frontage of some lots in the first tier severed in order to make all the lots uniform and to leave the river bank a crown reserve; five lots were set aside for the clergy; and the ground north of the Due West Line between the river and Four Mile Creek was reserved for the crown. Within the latter area, blocks were nominated for Lieutenant-Colonel Butler, John Secord, and F. (Francis) Pilkington. Not fortunate or influential enough to be named on the plan was William Pickard, a private in the Rangers, who complained in a petition of 10 October 1796 that, though he "was one of the first settlers on the Four Mile Creek when the land was all vacant about him," he had been deprived of this acreage east of the creek after 1784 because he lacked acceptable proof. A rectangle marked the location of the "village" shown on the 1783 survey but the Rangers' barracks were located much nearer to Navy Hall than in the earlier plan, so much nearer that one wonders if they had been moved.[15] Most lots south of the Due West Line were nominated; some of them were also annotated "ticket given," signifying authorized occupation; some were labelled D (Disputed?); and some had already had more than one occupant. Very few undisputed lots were still vacant. A few of the nominees were not on the list of existing settlers, disbanded Rangers, Joseph Brant's volunteers, and loyalists which was submitted to Governor Haldimand in July 1784 by Lieutenant-Colonel A.S. DePeyster, commanding officer at Fort Niagara since November 1783, and may have been post-1784 additions to the plan. Nevertheless, the plan is evidence of substantial development in Township no.1 in 1784. Many of the settlers already held land in blocks of 300 or 400 acres that were obviously not acquired by random draw. They included Peter, Stephen, and David Secord, Adam Chrysler, Samson Lutes, John, Joseph, and James Clement, Christian Warner, Walter Butler Sheehan, and Cornelius Lambert, as well as Samuel Street, whose store at the fort across the river was prospering. Robert Hamilton, who also had a store at the fort, had at this point only one lot but it was in a prime location on the river at the Landing (Queenston).

Plan of Niagara, c. 1784, hand-copied from the Shubbal Walton Papers in the National Archives on 22 January 1909 by J. Simpson. Mr Walton's farm was at the corner of Four Mile Creek and the Due West Line on township lot 111. (Niagara Historical Society Museum, 986.003)

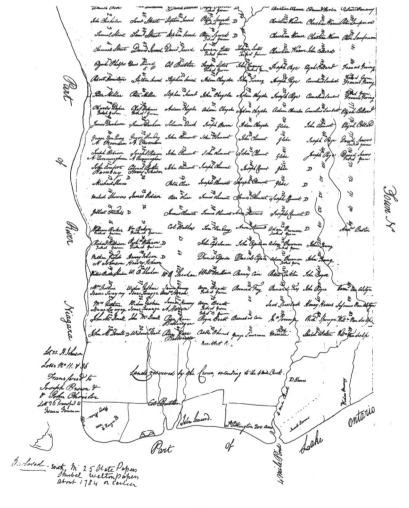

An eyewitness account of the settlement during Tinling's Niagara period confirms that the community had made considerable progress in the first few years after the revolution. In a letter to his son, St John de Crevecoeur wrote that, having dined at Ellsworth's house (at the Falls), "we mounted our horses and after riding some miles in the woods we came to a fine cultivated country interspersed with good farms ... After a ride of eighteen miles we arrived at Butlersburg, so called from Colonel Butler who had barracks for his Corps of Loyalists and another for the Savages. There are several good buildings here and an appearance of civilization."[16]

De Crevecoeur's "savages," the Indians, were one of the sources of John Butler's power. As acting superintendent of the Six Nations Indians from May 1782 to his death in 1796 — except for a short period when he was absent in England—the lieutenant-colonel was in charge of negotiations for the purchase of Indian land as well as the distribution of "presents" of food, clothing, and rum provided by the British government for the Indians in order to retain their loyalty. Later Lieutenant Governor Simcoe, jealous of Butler's control over the Indians, tried to divest him of these distribution rights, believing them to be the main source of his influence.

The growth and prosperity of the settlement made an accurate survey essential and so, in the summer of 1786, the government in Quebec commissioned Philip Frey to make a new survey of the whole Niagara settlement to correct "the irregularity allowed of amongst the first settlers upon Government lands."[17]

Like his predecessor, Frey found the task frustrating. A man not given to diplomacy, he responded to criticism by his superiors with complaints of his own, especially about settlers changing property so often that he had to alter his book of locations three or four times a week and about the shortage and expense of paper. Perhaps to emphasize his point about the paper shortage, he wrote many of his "tickets" of possession on the back of playing cards which he gave to the settlers merely to provide them with the satisfaction of knowing the numbers of their lots. The plan of Township no. 1 that he belatedly submitted to Deputy Surveyor John Collins on 18 September 1787 was not appreciably different from the 1784 Shubbal Walton document except in the layout of the first-tier lots along the river. Here Frey followed the original lines made by Allan Macdonell, leaving land on the east side of the road to Queenston to the widows Field and Van Every and to Michael Showers, Charles Depeu, and Peter Millar,[18] and changing the boundaries of Elijah Phelp's lot to the advantage of the more influential Robert Hamilton. Possession of these desirable river-front lots remained contentious for several years. The original lines as made by Allan Macdonell in 1783 were confirmed in 1790 in order not to "derange the whole settlers" [19] and reconfirmed by a partial survey in 1792. [20] Yet Lieutenant Governor Simcoe was able to challenge Samuel Street's claim to part of a front lot at Queenston in November 1792, a lot Street argued he had possessed since early 1784 and in which he had invested more than £2,000. [21]

In 1787 and 1788 Lord Dorchester, who had succeeded Haldimand as governor in April 1786, instituted several new directives in order to reduce the complaints of the farmers wanting, among other things, more control of

Section from an 1892 copy of the official plan of 1788–89, showing the proposed location of the town site at the centre of the township's waterfront and reservations for the crown (A), public squares (C,G), public buildings (H), church, parsonage, and schoolhouse (B,C), and markets (F). This plan was not followed in Niagara. (Niagara Historical Society Museum, 987.017.2)

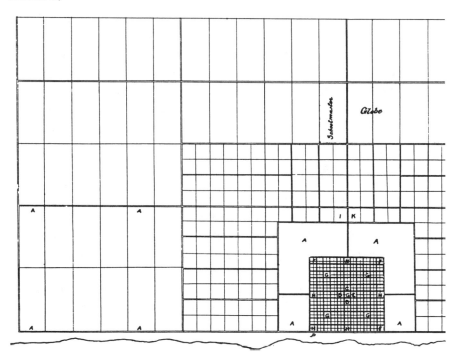

the interior management of their settlement, speedier confirmation of their rights to specific lots, and above all, a change in the system of tenure from French seignorial to English freehold.[22] Thus Niagara became part of the District of Nassau (one of seven new administrative divisions in the province of Quebec), a local land board was appointed to oversee the issuing of lots (superseding a committee of the Executive Council in "distant" Quebec), and lands were granted in "free and common soccage," as in the English tradition.[23] In addition, to allay the jealousy of former officers of Butler's Rangers, the size of their grants was increased to match those allowed to former officers of the 84th Regiment.[24]

A new stage in the development of the community began when Dorchester decided that it was time to foster the establishment of towns in order to provide local administrative centres for the agricultural settlements. In August 1788 he sent to Frey a plan of a town and township approved by the governor in council and ordered him to use it in future. This plan, with the town site at the centre of the waterfront lots, would not, however, be followed exactly in Niagara, because its approval had come far too late. The relevant lots in Township no.1 had already been settled, one of them for six years, the others for at least four. Besides, as Frey reported on 2 May 1789, the settlers at Niagara wanted a say in the process: "Our community is as yet divided in opinion with respect of the place most fit for the town and Public buildings, it seems to be the general opinion it had better be voted for."[25] Before the matter of the town site could be settled, Frey grew tired of petty criticism from John Collins (whom Simcoe later described as a man of "neither strength nor intellect") and departed, despite having been refused permission, to visit his family in the United States. He never returned, and so the problem of the site was left to the land board and the diplomatic Augustus Jones, his successor as surveyor at Niagara.

The Niagara land board, composed of the commanding officer of Fort Niagara, Lieutenant-Colonel Butler, Robert Hamilton, Peter Tenbroek, Nathaniel Petit, and Benjamin Pawling, held its first regular meeting in January 1789, but did not deal specifically with the issue of the town site until March 1790. Then, at the last of a series of meetings held at Walter Butler Sheehan's house in the Rangers' barracks, it was decided "that the centre of this township on the bank of the Niagara River is the proper place for a town and other Public Buildings and that the lots No. 15, 16, 17 and 18 in the centre of this township are at present in the possession of Gilbert Fields, Wm. Baker, Richard Wilkinson and Nathaniel Fields which the Board will endeavour to obtain from these proprietors for that purpose."[26]

In June, the combined power of Butler, Hamilton *et al.* having failed to convince the occupants to give up their land, the board adopted Frey's suggestion that the site should be voted for at meetings of the militia. They offered the choice of: first, the crown lands near Captain McDonnell's farm; second, the centre of Township no.1 on the banks of the Niagara River; third, the rise of Mount Dorchester above the Landing; fourth, the glebe lands on Mount Dorchester.[27]

Government approval for the chosen option, the crown lands near Captain McDonnell's, situated on the river at the Due West Line, came in February 1791, when instructions from the surveyor general's office in Quebec ordered Augustus Jones to "engage ten chain bearers and axe men" at a rate "not exceeding one shilling and sixpence per day each man, with an allowance of one shilling and three pence per day to yourself and party for provisions ... And immediately proceed with all diligence to survey and mark a town plot for a county town of the district to be called Lenox on the west side of the Niagara River at such place and according to such plans and dimensions as the Land Board ... may direct."[28]

Progress was not exactly smooth. Three months elapsed before the board (by then enlarged to please the local populace who had entertained "great jealousy of the prevailing majority" of the previous board[29]) instructed Jones to proceed in laying out the town according to the plan issued by Surveyor General Samuel Holland. There was, however, a further problem with the site because Holland had miscalculated. After the reservation needed for the high ground behind Navy Hall had been accounted for, the front left for a town was not three-quarters of a mile plus 140 feet as he had projected, but a mere 800 yards. To remedy the error, the board directed that each front lot be divided into two to "leave as many lots as were originally intended."[30] Four days later, on 24 June 1791, the board changed its mind in favour of a second option offered by the surveyor general, that the town site be located to the northwest of Navy Hall. Again there were difficulties. Part of this site was already occupied by people who had settled there before 1784 by agreement with the commanding officer of Fort Niagara and had built houses and planted crops. Peter Tenbroek, for example, had been there since 1782 on land near the corner of present-day Front and Victoria streets, assigned to him by General H. Watson Powell, commanding officer of Fort Niagara from October 1780 to September 1782.[31] He was not alone; a plan of part of the military reserve in 1790 clearly shows several other buildings on the chosen site. The land board, therefore, ordered that persons inclined to build on town lots were to pay to present possessors two pounds ten shillings New York currency for each improved acre and that present occupants were to be permitted to retain the lot on which their house stood.

In addition, the board ordered that a public house "be built on the corner lot at the east end of Town adjoining the River and a Mason's Lodge on the next to it."[32] Forgotten for the moment were the priorities suggested by the government's plan such as a church, a school, and a market-place.

After the survey of the town officially called Lenox had finally begun in November 1791, yet another variation from the government plan emerged. Augustus Jones explained this final change to John Collins on 15 June 1792: "The plan of the town of Lenox ... does not extend so far back as our former one proposed owing to Colonel Butler and some others who live in rear of and refuse giving up their possessions in consequence of which the Land Board directed me (for the Present) to extend the survey only one mile back from the river bank."[33] This exclusion from the town of land occupied mainly by Butler reduced the government-approved square plot of eleven-

Part of a 1790 plan of the military reserve, hand-copied in 1909 by J. Simpson from an original in the National Archives, (Niagara Historical Society Museum, 986.004)

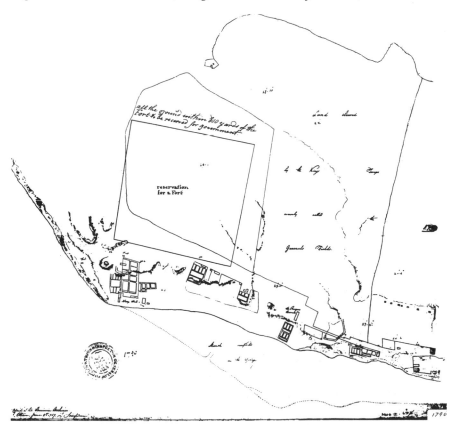

by-eleven four-acre blocks with 484 one-acre lots to an irregular plot with 412 lots minus a corner of approximately sixty-two acres.

Thus Butler and a few early farmers who had settled in Niagara several years before the first large influx of loyalists were instrumental in determining the location, the "shape," and the extent of the town.

Although the 1791 survey became the basis of subsequent plans of the town, it had little immediate impact on its development. The first lots — numbers 1 to 84 — were drawn for in December 1791, but their owners initially invested little in new buildings (except perhaps for Francis Crooks, who built the public house on lot 1). In 1792, despite its public house, its Free Mason's Lodge, and its gaol, the town was variously described as "a poor, wretched straggling village with a few scattered cottages erected here and there as chance, convenience, and caprice dictated"[34] and "a spot on the globe that appears... as if it had been deserted in consequence of a plague."[35] The best buildings were not in town. They included Robert Hamilton's large stone house with covered gallery, built at the Landing in 1791, which he offered to rent in 1792 for £100 per year, an exorbitant sum that no one was willing to pay, Lieutenant-Colonel Butler's frame house south of the town and west of the Garrison Line, Daniel Servos's house near the Four Mile Creek, and Squire McNab's on the lakeshore.

The impetus needed to provoke substantial building in the town was provided by John Graves Simcoe, lieutenant governor of the new Province of Upper Canada. Simcoe's influence on the development of the town was not exactly intentional. He expected to "visit Toronto and the Head of the La Tranche to pass down that River to Detroit, to return and assemble the Legislature in the Autumn at Niagara, to winter at Cataraqui and early in the ensuing Spring to occupy such a central position as shall be previously chosen for the capital."[36]

Consequently, when he arrived in Lenox/Niagara on 26 July 1792, no preparations — other than the repair of one of the Navy Hall buildings — had been made for an extended stay for his entourage. Indeed, the Simcoes, Lieutenant Thomas Grey, who had accompanied them to Canada, Thomas Talbot, the lieutenant governor's private secretary and later founder of the Talbot settlement, Attorney General John White, and Chief Justice William Osgoode began life in Niagara under canvas. Other government officials who sought more substantial accommodations had great difficulty finding any.

The sorry state of the town and the shortage of housing were topics that featured prominently in the correspondence of these eighteenth-century house hunters. Provincial Secretary William Jarvis grumbled that he had searched for ten days in both country and town for "a hut to place his wife and lambs in without success."[37] Receiver General Peter Russell complained that there were only three "habitable" houses north of Navy Hall, Robert Kerr's, William Dickson's, and Robert Addison's.[38] Of these, the house of merchant William Dickson was not in the town *per se,* but very close to it on the crown reserve opposite Fort Niagara on land that had been "improved and occupied under the express permission of several commandants since 1783."[39] Dickson, a canny businessman, had bought the property from Samuel Street probably soon after his arrival in Niagara in 1787 and had spent £600 on improvements because he had guessed that it might be on the site of a future county town. Russell tried but failed to prevail upon him to rent part of the building for three to four months.[40] Dr Kerr apparently had two houses in or close to Lenox, the "habitable" one on the north side of Prideaux Street (lot 27) and a "skeleton" near the Navy Hall complex. A lease for the Prideaux Street house was sought in November 1793 by Angus Macdonell, amateur chemist, inventor of processes for making glass and soap, and discoverer of two valuable salt springs at Fifteen Mile Creek and manager of their operation.[41] The following month

Portrait of William Dickson, (1769-1846), merchant, lawyer, member of the Legislative Council, and founder of the town of Galt, from a watercolour by Hoppner Meyer. (Metropolitan Toronto Library, John Ross Robertson Collection, 1248)

the property was mortgaged to William Wallace.[42] The "skeleton" was repaired for Chief Justice Osgoode and was ready for his occupancy just before Christmas 1792.[43] It became a favourite venue for bridge players in Colonel Simcoe's entourage. The third of Russell's "habitable" houses, that of the Reverend Robert Addison, Anglican minister in Niagara, was located on town lot 8 near the corner of Front and Victoria streets. This was the house that had been built by Peter Tenbroek *circa* 1783 at a cost of over £600.[44] (By the end of the decade, Addison had moved to a new house, Lake Lodge on the Lakeshore Road.) Apart from these few, Russell complained, the only structures were "cabins, skeletons and ruins."[45]

The fact that the 1790 plan of the crown reserve shows several buildings on the land that became the town plot does not negate the views of Jarvis and Russell. Shanties and log huts, early types of buildings that were to surveyors of sufficient importance to be marked on plans, were, to gentlemen with

Lands south of the original town of Niagara as patented from the crown, hand-copied from a scaled drawing by Horton W. Byrne, deputy registrar for Lincoln County, in the Abstract Index for Niagara Township, Books 1 and 2.

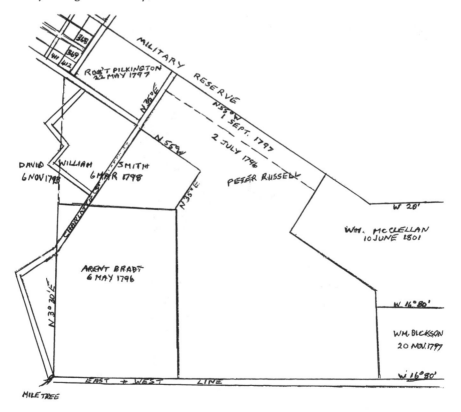

upper-class pretensions, insignificant hovels.[46] Jarvis and Russell, lacking other options, bought two such "hovels" for prices that they considered exorbitant. Jarvis paid £140 for a log hut on lot 3 with three small rooms, two of which he described as very indifferent. Russell's cabin (location unspecified) cost £60 and had only two rooms.

Within a year of the lieutenant governor's arrival, the town's prospects had changed. Dorchester and Simcoe, both stubborn men, could not agree on the site for a capital, Dorchester favouring York (Toronto), and Simcoe, London, and so it became evident that the legislature would meet in Niagara, by then renamed Newark (Niagara-on-the-Lake), for several years rather than for a single session.

Thus the town's first building boom began. In November 1793 Elizabeth Russell, Peter's half-sister, noted in a letter to her aunt and uncle that already about twenty good new houses had been built, giving the town "the appearance of a well inhabited place"; and, in 1794, Simcoe bragged to his superiors that the town that had contained only one or two dwellings on his arrival now "by the temporary residence of the Government" contained "upwards of fifty houses."[47]

Simcoe, who in fact spent very little time in Newark, did not himself contribute directly to this boom. Indeed, the lieutenant governor acknowledged that he was merely "fitting up an old hovel that would look exactly like a carrier's ale house in England when properly decorated and ornamented,"[48] and his intrepid wife continued to prefer the "canvas house" which, fitted with a partition and stove, she found cosier than her husband's drafty alternative. Other construction with which Simcoe was involved was equally utilitarian. For example, he made repairs and additions to Butler's barracks "for the meeting of the Legislature and public offices" in such a manner that when no longer needed for civil purposes (that is when the site of the capital was fixed elsewhere) they could be adapted for military use.[49]

It was government officials and army personnel who initiated the building of fine houses in Newark, many of them superior to those in Kingston.[50] Most of these were at the upper end of the town. Some faced the King Street boundary of the crown reserve. Others may have been outside the confines of the town proper, on reserve land south of John Street that was generously granted by Simcoe to potential Canadian "aristocrats": Peter Russell, David William Smith, Arent Bradt, and Robert Pilkington, aide to Simcoe and a favorite of Mrs Simcoe because he shared her interest in sketching. This land would be added to the town in 1816.

The most renowned of Newark's superior houses was built by David

William Smith in 1793-94 on a four-acre block bounded by King, Johnson, Regent, and Queen streets. Smith was the son of Major John Smith, commander of Fort Niagara (1792-95) and the husband of, to quote Mrs Simcoe, "a beautiful Irish woman," Anne O'Reilly, in whose honour a piece of land south of John Street was named Anneville. He had decided very soon after his appointment as deputy surveyor general of Upper Canada that the legislature would meet at Newark for at least four years[51] and he accordingly built a two-storey, eighty-by-forty foot Georgian house that the visiting Duc de la Rochefoucauld described in 1795 as elegant and distinguished, with a courtyard and gardens surrounded by railings in the best English style. In February 1794, Smith claimed that he had already spent £1,000 and would add at least £500 more before completing the house.[52] When the property was offered for sale in 1798, its estimated value was £3,000.[53]

Other fine houses, whose location is somewhat less certain, were built by Peter Russell, Robert Pilkington, and Alexander McDonnell. McDonnell, a former lieutenant in Butler's Rangers who was appointed first sheriff of the Home District by Simcoe, is perhaps best known for his role as second to John Small, clerk of the Executive Council, in his duel with Attorney General John White in York in January 1800. Russell's Springfield, a two-storey residence, seventy-by-forty feet with four fireplaces, a long front porch, and formal garden, was documented on a plan drawn by Robert Pilkington, dated 17 October 1797. Augustus Jones recorded its location as 34 chains 34 links S61 degrees W from the northwest corner of the block house at Navy Hall. Here Elizabeth Russell displayed her pressed flowers, served her homemade cherry preserves, entertained John White, the town's ladies' man, and fretted about her brother's welfare. And here the Honourable Peter staged literary evenings where he could showcase his sonorous voice and indulge his taste for fine wines. Robert Pilkington owned a one-acre lot in town facing the reserve on King Street (lot 237) as well as twenty-three acres next to Russell. His house, built by September 1793,[54] appears to have been sold to John Elmsley, Osgoode's successor as chief justice. Alexander McDonnell, whose family owned a four-acre block south of D.W. Smith's town property, brought his own carpenter, Pierre Ochu, from Quebec to build his house because carpenters in Newark were in short supply and considered expensive at $1 to $1.50 per day.[55] The men whose duel McDonnell would later witness also built homes in Newark, John Small probably on lot 195 (at the corner of Regent and Centre streets) and John White in a location still unknown.

Unlike most of his fellow officials, William Jarvis, American and unpretentious, remained in the area close to the water where the lots were half an acre and the houses less elaborate. This section of town north of Queen Street became the commercial area as merchants moved in to cater

D.W. Smith's house drawn by Robert Pilkington in 1798 when the four-acre property was offered for sale. (National Archives of Canada, NMC6244)

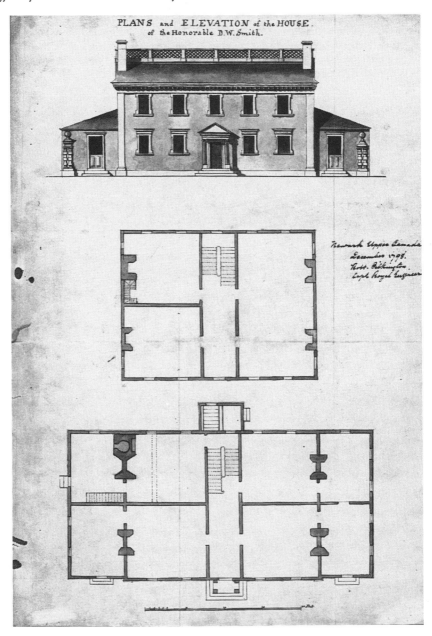

to the needs of officials and troops who followed Simcoe. It contained, as well as the gaol (lot 32), the Free Mason's Hall (lot 33), and the leased hotel (lot 1), the establishments of Alexander Gardiner, a stone mason (lot 29), John Flack, a shoemaker (lot 24), blacksmith Barnabus Cain (lot 39), butcher Samuel Cassady (lot 54), and the enterprises of general merchants, Andrew Heron (lot 34), Andrew Templeton (lot 56), James Farquharson (lot 58),

A 1797 plan of Peter Russell's estate, copied in 1915 from the original drawing by Robert Pilkington. Advertised for sale in October 1796, the house was described as a commodious dwelling with coach-house, stable, and other offices, all built within three years. (Niagara Historical Society Museum, 986.006)

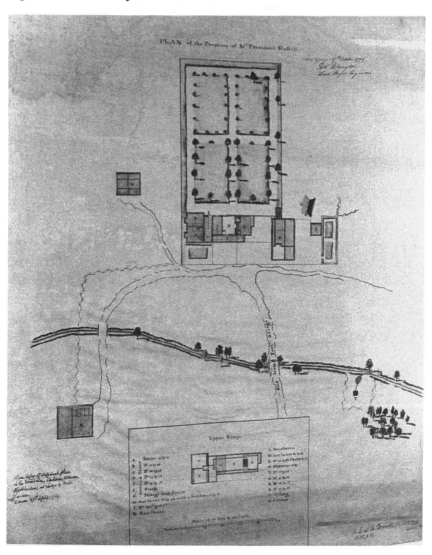

Brick house built by William Dickson, c. 1794, probably on his town lot on King Street, for his bride, Charlotte Adlam. The print is from a watercolour submitted by Dickson with his war-losses claim in 1815. (National Archives of Canada, NMC126553)

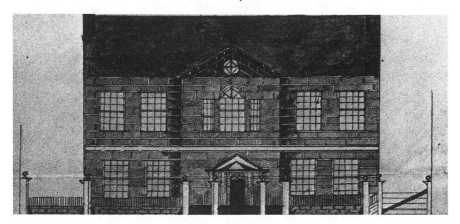

James Fitzgerald (lot 59), Archibald Cunningham (lot 60), George Forsyth (lot 31), and William and Francis Crooks (lot 1). After 1795, Forsyth and the Crooks expanded their establishments in Newark, but before that date they maintained their main stores across the river near the fort, keeping only small subsidiaries on the Canadian side.[56] In 1794 the better houses in this area included the Jarvis house on lot 3, its original three rooms having been enlarged by the addition of a kitchen and two garret rooms to make it "the snuggest and warmest cottage in the province,"[57] the earlier Kerr and Addison houses, and William Dickson's brick house. The latter, the first brick house in the province, was probably built on his town lot on King Street (lot 64) *circa* 1794, after his request to retain his former property on the military reserve had been refused.

Toward the end of 1794, surveyor William Chewitt and Deputy Surveyor General D.W. Smith produced a town plan based partly on the Augustus Jones survey of 1791, and partly on the government's model plan of 1788-89. This new plan responded to some of the developments that had already occurred since 1791 by providing clearly defined streets and market lots, needed after Simcoe had granted the town rights to a market. Perhaps it also attempted to pre-empt future problems by locating the town centre out of range of the guns of Fort Niagara which was due to be handed over to the Americans. This plan also showed very clearly the boundary of lands claimed by Lieutenant-Colonel Butler.

The plan, unlike its 1790 predecessor, did not show buildings or, with a very few exceptions, names of lot holders as the plans of 1783, 1784, and 1787 did. The omission is perhaps an indication of the state of flux in the community in 1794. Rumours of a potential war with the United States, of the removal of government offices to York, of the evacuation of the fort across the river, and of the building of a new fort on the high ground above Navy Hall created prospects of greater volatility in a real-estate market where lots already changed hands extremely frequently. Robert Hamilton observed in 1795 that he doubted that ten of the oldest settlers could "be found on the Spott that they originally occupied."[58] Matters were further complicated by the fact that the government had not yet fulfilled its promise to grant a deed in fee simple to any original occupant who had a certificate of possession and who had complied with its terms. (In Newark, this usually meant building a house within a year.) Most transfers of property had been endorsed on the original certificate by the land board; but the abolition of the land boards became official on 6 November 1794, leaving questions and doubts about legal ownership of land that were still not settled in July 1795 when Simcoe issued his "Memorandum Respecting the General State of Landed Property in Upper Canada." For example, when shoemaker John Flack wanted to sell lot 24 and premises to Thomas Hind, a tavern keeper, in October 1795 he had to swear before notary Thomas

A 1794 plan of the town of Newark, by William Chewitt, surveyor, and D.W. Smith, acting surveyor general. (National Archives of Canada, NMC19073)

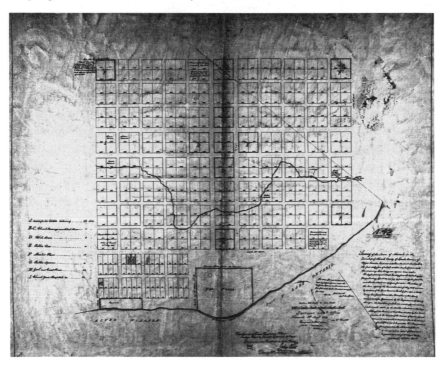

A notice of grants of land in Niagara Township, published in the Upper Canada Gazette, *10 December 1794. Occupants of town lots had to wait at least two more years for their town grants. (Ontario Legislative Library, Toronto)*

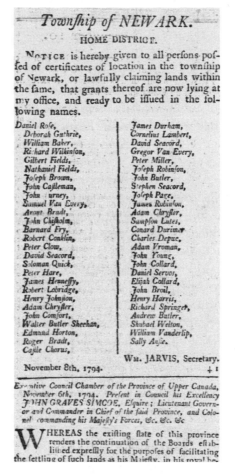

Ridout that he would give his door key and certificate of assignment to Hind pending arrival of the title deed.[59] Clearly, in 1794 it would have been almost impossible for a surveyor to be definitive about ownership of a particular town lot.

The plan as a whole displayed several notable features, including three four-acre blocks of market space, at the three corners of the town plot, a four-acre public square close to the town's geographic centre and out of range of Fort Niagara, and, next to it, blocks for a workhouse and, at last, a church, a parsonage, and a school. The streets abutting the public square were a very generous one and one-half chains wide as was the other main street, now Queen. Here, facing Mississauga Point, another four-acre block was reserved for a court-house. It was, in short, a fine, orderly plan suitable for a town that was expected to continue to be the interim capital of the province for a brief, unspecified period and then to remain the county seat, the hub of a thriving agricultural community and an important commercial and military centre.

In the autumn of 1796, traveller Isaac Weld provided a snapshot of the town. It contained, he wrote, nearly seventy dwellings, nearly all less than five years old and built of wood. Those next to the lake were rather poor, but at the upper end of town, where a few of the principal officers of the government remained in residence, the houses were "very excellent." The town had a court-house, a gaol, and, on the heights above Navy Hall, a new block house, nine feet higher than Fort Niagara, was under construction.

Weld had chosen an eventful year for his visit to the town. In February, government officials, under orders from Simcoe, slowly and very reluctantly prepared to move from their comfortable homes in Newark to "muddy" York, which, in 1795, contained only twelve houses. In May, Lieutenant-Colonel Butler died. In June, the legislature sat for the last time in the town and the ailing Simcoe, granted leave to return to England, sailed from Navy Hall. In August, British troops at last vacated Fort Niagara. Perhaps most important for the majority of settlers, the Executive Council, during the summer, approved the issuing of deeds to vast numbers of property holders, including a great number in Newark, settling at last doubts about the ownership of land.

Though the brief periods of excitement generated by the parliamentary sessions ended in 1796, there were no dramatic changes in Newark. The "very excellent" houses built by officials remained, and so for a while did some of the officials themselves — Peter Russell, Simcoe's successor in fact if not in title, lived in Newark until November 1797, and William Jarvis, despite having lost part of his house in a fire in December 1796, stayed in Newark until 1798, renting Alexander McDonnell's house. Without fanfare, merchants took over the leadership of the community. Some of them forged ties with the farmers and grew prosperous shipping out local produce, flour, butter, cheese, salt pork fatted on Indian corn and nuts, and potash. They benefitted, too, from the need for construction materials in York, selling boards from local sawmills and lime and brick from John McFarland's brickworks on the river road to government officers building houses in the new capital. Some of them eventually bought the Niagara properties of these officials. George Forsyth, for example, bought Jarvis's land and salvaged buildings on Front Street and William Dickson bought Russell's 160 acres on John Street. However, they passed over the two most opulent houses, Russell's Springfield, which was eventually purchased by the Indian Department for the use of visiting officials, and D.W. Smith's home, which, after being turned down by the grammar-school board, was bought by the government and apparently used as a government house. When Robert Hamilton, now the richest and most influential trader of them all, submitted to the lieutenant governor a list of nominees for appointment as magistrates—the most powerful local officials—all but James Muirhead were merchants.[60] These merchant-magistrates maintained the focus of the town close to the waterfront, ignoring D.W. Smith's plan for a public square in the Mary, William, Mississauga, and Butler block, and a new court-house at Mississauga and Queen. They completed the court-house and jail on lot 32 at a cost of £300, providing suitable but not showy facilities for the county seat. Moreover, since most merchants and prominent farmers were Presbyterian, they ensured that the first church built in town would not be Anglican, as Simcoe would have wished. This first church, located not on the church block of the 1794 plan but on a nearby four acres still occupied by St Andrews, rented pews to the highest bidder in March 1796, with the merchant Andrew Heron taking pew one for £10.

Silhouette of Ralfe Clench (1762-1828), artist unknown. Ralfe Clench, elected town clerk at the first meeting of electors of Newark in August 1793, was also elected member of the House of Assembly in 1800, 1804, and 1812. In addition, he served as a judge, registrar of the surrogate court, and lieutenant-colonel of the Lincoln militia. (Metropolitan Toronto Library, John Ross Robertson Collection, T30366)

The military influence also remained strong in Newark. The local militia drilled at Butler's barracks under Major (later Lieutenant-Colonel) Ralfe Clench, a talented man, who also served as clerk for the town and township—then as now a single unit for purposes of local government—and who could speak several Indian languages and even entertain on the hand organ. Regular troops from the vacated Fort Niagara occupied temporary quarters in the Navy Hall buildings, pending completion of the blockhouse at the new Fort George. Their presence ensured a steady clientele for local storekeepers. In addition, the garrison officers continued to provide "colour" in the town, especially at the racetrack laid out on the Fort George military reserve and at the fortnightly subscription dances held at the inn on lot 1.

The reserve, reduced in size by the fort and also by the building of the Indian council house, was, as it had been before 1796, still unofficially appropriated by the townsfolk for use as a common to graze cattle. Already considered too small for a true common as a result of Simcoe's generous grants to prominent settlers, this remnant of the original crown reserve of 1784 had to be defended in 1797 when twenty-seven leaders of the town, fearing that parts of it were about to be granted to William Dickson and John McFarland, petitioned the government to refuse "further grants of the common or lands now used as such."

These petitioners of 1797 extended a tradition of outspoken independence that began in the spring of 1783 with the requests for secure tenure by John Butler's early settlers, and continued in 1788 with farmers' demands for control of local matters and in 1790 with their insistence on participation in the choice of a townsite. Perhaps this tradition is as much a part of the legacy of the builders of Niagara-on-the-Lake as its unrivalled location, its commons, its wide main streets, its square four-acre blocks with original lot numbers, its integrated agricultural area, and its strangely shaped, not quite square, old town plot.

NOTES

1   Haldimand to Bolton, 7 October 1778, E.A. Cruikshank, ed., "Records of Niagara 1778-1783: A Collection of Documents Relating to the First Settlement," Publication of the *Niagara Historical Society*, 38 (1927), 8.

2   Ibid., Bolton to Haldimand, 4 March 1779, 10.

3   Ibid., Haldimand to Bolton, 7 June 1779, 12.

4   Ibid., Haldimand to Bolton, 7 July 1780, 18-19.

5   "Petitions for Grants of Land," *Ontario Historical Society Papers and Records (OHSPR)*, 24 (1927), 119-20.

6   Guy Johnson to Haldimand, 9 May 1781, Cruikshank, "Records of Niagara 1778-1783," 29.

7   Ibid., Watson Powell to Haldimand, 14 April 1782, 37.

8   Ibid., Butler to Robert Matthews, 12 June 1782, 39.

9   Ibid., "Memorial of Farmers," n.d., 50-1.

10   Ibid., Butler to Matthews, 31 March 1783 and 3 May 1783, 49, 51.

11   Ibid., Haldimand to Maclean, 11 September 1783, 65.

12   Butler to Matthews, 8 May 1774, E.A. Cruikshank, ed., "Records of Niagara 1784-7," Niagara Historical Society pamphlet no.39 (1927), 19-20.

13   District of Nassau Letter Book, no.2, Cruikshank,"Records of Niagara 1784-7," 130-1.

14   Niagara Historical Society Museum Collection, memo of Augustus Jones, 26 August 1790, acc. no.X990.5.229, box 105. (Tinling's crooked Due West Line caused problems until 1828, when Jones finally planted "stone monuments marked I.W." on the correct line.)

15   The exact location of the barracks is difficult to determine. It was chosen for the availability of logs; it was not "opposite to the Garrison" at Fort Niagara in 1780. National Archives of Canada (NAC), Haldimand Papers, B 100, Powell to Haldimand, 18 November 1780, 488-92.

16   St John de Crevecoeur, "A Visit to Niagara, July 1785," *Magazine of American History*, October 1878.

17   A. Campbell to Philip Frey, Cruikshank, "Records of Niagara 1784-7," 4 July 1786, 90-1.

18   Niagara Historical Society Museum Collection, memo probably of Augustus Jones, 11 June 1787, acc. no.X990.5.288, box 105.

19   Proceedings of a land board meeting held at Navy Hall, 23 August 1790, E.A. Cruikshank, ed., "Records of Niagara 1790-92," Niagara Historical Society pamphlet no.41 (1930), 58-9.

20   Ibid., plan opposite 32.

21   Ibid., "The Memorial of Samuel Street," 29. See also Simcoe to Dundas, 4 November 1792, E.A. Cruikshank, ed., *The Correspondence of Lieut. Governor John Graves Simcoe* ... (5v., Toronto: Ontario Historical Society, 1923-31), 1:247.

22   Journals of the Privy Council, 24 April 1787, and Journal of Major Matthews, 31 May 1787, Cruikshank, "Records of Niagara 1784-7," 111-12.

23   Ibid., Order in Council 1787, 129. See also Dorchester to Sydney, 10 July 1788, and Quebec Land Book, 29 December 1788, E.A. Cruikshank, ed., "Records of Niagara 1784-9," Niagara Historical Society pamphlet no.40(1929), 43-4, 61-2.

24   Ibid., Quebec Land Book, 22 October 1788, 54.

25   Philip Frey to John Collins, 2 May 1789, District of Nassau Letter Book, 5:23, Cruikshank, "Records of Niagara 1790-92."

26   Proceedings of the land board, Nassau, 31 March 1790, Cruikshank, "Records of Niagara 1790-92," 22

27   Ibid., Proceedings of the land board, 21 June 1790, 53.

28   Ibid., Instructions from the surveyor general's office, Quebec, 22 February 1791, 85.

29   Ibid., Sir John Johnson to Lord Dorchester, 13 September 1789, and Quebec Land Book, 8 June 1791, 77, 113.

30   Ibid., Proceedings of the land board, Niagara, 20 June 1791, 117.

31   "Petition of Peter Tenbroek" *OHSPR*, 24 (1927), 138-9.

32   Proceedings of the land board, Niagara, 24 June 1791, Cruikshank, "Records of Niagara 1790-92," 118.

33   Ibid., Jones to Collins, 15 June 1792, District of Nassau Letter Book, 5:65.

34   Anonymous, *Canadian Letters, A Description of a Tour through the Provinces of Lower and Upper Canada in the Years 1792-93* (Montreal: M.A. Marchand, 1912), 43.

35   NAC, MG 23 H1, 2 (Jarvis Family Papers), William Jarvis to the Reverend Doctor Peters, August 1792.

36   Simcoe to Lord Dundas, 7 December 1791, Cruikshank, *Simcoe Correspondence*, 1:91. See also 67-8, 143, 199.

37   NAC, MG 23 H1, 2, Jarvis to Peters, August 1792.

38   NAC, MG 23 H1 (Russell Family Papers), Peter Russell to Elizabeth Russell, 6 August 1792.

39   "Petition of William Dickson 31 July 1792," *OHSPR*, 24 (1927), 54.

40   NAC, MG 23 H1 Peter Russell to Elizabeth Russell, 6 August 1792.

41   Cruikshank, *Simcoe Correspondence*, 2:105n.

42   Lincoln County Registry, Town of Niagara-on-the-Lake Abstract Book 1, entries for lot 27.

43   NAC, MG 23 G5, Shepherd White Papers, Diary of John White, 22 December 1792.

44   *OHSPR*, 24 (1927), 138-9.

45   NAC, MG 23 H1, Peter Russell to Elizabeth Russell, 6 August 1792.

46   The Wilson plan of 1817, for example, also marks many structures that would have been primitive.

47   Simcoe to the Duke of Portland, 23 October 1794, Cruikshank, *Simcoe Correspondence*, 3:142.

48   Simcoe to James Bland Burgess, 21 August 1792, Cruikshank, *Simcoe Correspondence*, 1:205.

49   Ibid., Simcoe to Alured Clarke, 4 June 1793, 347-8.

50   Duc de la Rochefoucauld-Liancourt, *Travels through the United States of North America, the Country of the Iroquois, and Upper Canada in the Years 1795, 1796, and 1797 ...*(2v., London: 1797), 1.

51   D.W. Smith to John Askin, 13 November 1792, Cruikshank, *Simcoe Correspondence*, 1:261.

52   Petition of D.W. Smith, *OHSPR*, 24 (1927), 128-9.

53   Proceedings of Board of Survey, 11 December 1798, E.A. Cruikshank and A.F. Hunter, eds., *The Correspondence of the Honourable Peter Russell ...* (3v., Toronto: Ontario Historical Society, 1932-36), 3:30-1.

54   NAC, MG 23 G5, Diary of John White, 16 September 1793.

55 Niagara Historical Society Collection, Contract between Pierre Ochu and Alex McDonnell, 1 May 1793, acc no.987.5.135.

56 William Crooks to E.B. Littlehales, 10 September 1794, and Littlehales to John Smith, 10 November 1794, Cruikshank, *Simcoe Correspondence,* 3:70-2, 174.

57 NAC, MG 23 H1, 2, Jarvis to Peters, 3 December 1793.

58 Robert Hamilton to Littlehales, November 1795, Cruikshank, *Simcoe Correspondence,* 4:151.

59 Niagara Historical Society Collection, Agreement between John Flack and Thomas Hind, 29 October 1795, acc. no.987.033.

60 Hamilton to Littlehales, 15 June 1796, Cruikshank, *Simcoe Correspondence,* 4:299.

CHAPTER TWO

PATRONAGE AND POWER

The Early Political Culture
of the Niagara Peninsula

Bruce G. Wilson

Fort Niagara, which sits near the mouth of the Niagara River, was the staging area for a long series of British raids on the rebellious New York and Pennsylvanian frontiers. As a result, it was, by the height of the revolution, bursting at its seams with loyalist soldiers, native allies, and refugees. In

Fort Niagara from the Canadian side, c. 1783, watercolour by James Peachey. (National Archives of Canada, C2035)

order to feed all these mouths, the British military by at least 1780, and perhaps earlier, fostered the development of a small farming community on what is now the Canadian side of the Niagara River.

Such a settlement, which sprang almost literally from nothing, faced a variety of problems. One of its most pressing was its governance and leadership. Niagara was far from the established centres of Quebec on the St Lawrence and distant even from the other emerging loyalist communities. Immediately at first settlement, Niagara would have to develop local leadership and quickly. Who should provide such leadership? Who should assume local office? Obviously, the individuals or groups who did so would be in a prime position to influence future social and economic development in their own interests.

Other settlements that were formed in what is now Ontario (mostly in eastern Ontario) immediately after the revolutionary war were dominated by groups of loyalist officers who had commanded regiments during that conflict. They exercised control often in combination with the more prominent of the later-arriving English immigrants. The major political issues in such communities pitted these groups against the American sentiments of other settlers. The issues were ideological and involved national and religious tensions. The Niagara region proved an exception. Its most powerful figures were merchants, mostly Scots, who had not even fought in the revolution. By far the most prominent of these, and the one on whom this piece will focus, was Robert Hamilton. Under the influence of Hamilton and his fellow merchants, national and religious conflicts at Niagara would be subordinated to the politics of commerce and the local reaction to it.

The answer to the question "Who should lead?" may at first seem an obvious one. The reasons for establishing the new communities at Niagara and elsewhere were ideological: they were created as a refuge for those from the old colonies who had fought for the king. Their natural leaders in peacetime would logically seem to be those who had led them in war: at Niagara, the officers of Butler's Rangers and the Indian Department. The major government officials who held the responsibility for the development of the loyalist settlements in the early years, Sir Frederick Haldimand, Lord Dorchester, and John Graves Simcoe, all proclaimed that the new society should be founded on a loyalist military hierarchy: the lands of the rank-and-file soldiers would be grouped around the holdings of their former officers and the men would defer to their officers as their natural leaders.

In 1789 there were forty-six officers settled at Niagara, all but four from Butler's Rangers or the Indian Department. A list of half-pay officers in 1806, two decades after initial settlement, showed that twenty-nine, or 63 per cent, of these officers were still residing in the Niagara District. The numbers were certainly large enough to constitute a leadership group in that small society.[1]

If the officers were well represented in the Niagara settlements, so were the rank-and-file soldiers who were supposed to defer to them. At its disbandment, Butler's Rangers had a strength of 470 men, while the Indian Department had 60, a total of 530. Almost exactly half of these, 264, settled in the peninsula. They brought with them 304 dependants.[2] With disbanded troops from the regular army and other loyalist corps, settlement of soldiers and their dependants would have been in the range of 850. The total population of the peninsula in 1789 was estimated by contemporaries at 3,100. Ten years later, it was approaching 6,000. While certainly nothing near a majority, the military settlers in the peninsula constituted a significant nucleus.

Moreover, a pattern of settlement did emerge at Niagara which could have aided loyalist officers in exercising a continuing control over their old units. As a result of local topography, early settlement at Niagara was concentrated rather than scattered. Officers were fairly evenly distributed among the rank and file and well situated, geographically, at least, to exercise an influence over the men.

There were, then, good reasons to expect that the officers of the loyalist

Mrs Tice's (loyalist) house. Sketch by Elizabeth Simcoe. (National Archives of Canada, C13922)

units would emerge as the leaders and the main officeholders of the Niagara peninsula. There were a significant number of them, geography favoured their influence, and the British officials who organized the settlements saw them in a leadership role.

If at Niagara a general leadership group was easy to identify, then so was its foremost member. The most obvious candidate for social and political leadership at Niagara was Lieutenant-Colonel John Butler, who had commanded both Butler's Rangers and, for a time, the Indian Department at Fort Niagara. Butler was a politically astute and ambitious man. Throughout the revolution, he had been well aware that his actions during the conflict would greatly affect his social standing and political power at its end. Even before the war was over, Butler assumed responsibility for the management of the tiny settlement across the river from Fort Niagara.

In fact, however, no coherent loyalist officer élite rose to control the Niagara peninsula. In part, the reasons for the failure of a military leadership group to coalesce went back to Butler's selection of officers. The

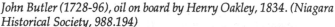

John Butler (1728-96), oil on board by Henry Oakley, 1834. (Niagara Historical Society, 988.194)

number of prominent, well-established families on the New York frontier had been small; those who remained loyal and from which Butler could choose his officers were even more minuscule. Despite his own preference, Butler, in most cases, had to choose small farmers as officers for his Rangers, many of whom were recent immigrants not much distinguished from their neighbours. Such men neither had, nor would quickly acquire, prominence in the new society that could work to their political and social advantage.

The officers of the Indian Department at Niagara were certainly a more respectable group than those of the Rangers. Unfortunately for Butler, they were less under his influence than the Ranger officers were. During the revolutionary war, there had been a vicious struggle for control of the Indian Department at Niagara between Butler and the Johnson family, heirs of Sir William Johnson, the first superintendent of the northern Indians. Butler had signal successes in influencing the Indians, especially during the early years of the war. The Johnsons were jealous of Butler's influence and feared that he might even emerge as the head of the Indian Department. By the midway point in the revolution, the Johnsons had managed to place one of their own number, Guy Johnson, in charge of the Indian Department at Niagara. Butler was reduced to leadership of his Rangers only.

The rivalries between Butler and the Johnson family did not lessen in the post-war period. Sir John Johnson, Sir William's son and successor as Indian superintendent, had not forgotten the threat Butler had posed to the power of the Johnson family in the revolutionary period, and he exerted himself to prevent Butler or those who had been closely associated with him from gaining a significant amount of power in the new society.

As important a consideration in the formation of an officer élite at Niagara as the questions of the prior status and internal coherence of the officer group was the relationship of the officers to the men they had nominally commanded. The loyalist corps which had operated from Niagara had not been traditional military units with an instilled sense of hierarchy. The Rangers and the Indian Department forces had in fact been an informal agglomeration of guerilla units whose major functions had been to conduct small raids on the isolated communities of western New York and Pennsylvania. The Niagara loyalist corps tended to serve in small parties mixed with Indians, other loyalist and Indian Department units, numerous white volunteers loosely under the command of Joseph Brant, and regular army forces. Such promiscuous mixing inhibited the development of a clear chain of command, a sense of subordination to officers, and an *esprit de corps*.

Whatever the weaknesses of his officer corps, and they were serious, it was even more germane to Butler's specific interests that the revolutionary war had left no large residue of respect or affection for him among those whom he had commanded. During the revolution, Butler had concentrated his efforts with a passion on forwarding the influence of himself and his family, often at the expense of his subordinates. Many of his officers and men must have remembered with bitterness his bullying attempts to monopolize loyalist trade for the merchant firms with which he was associated. Others would have hotly resented his biased choice of officers, particularly of his own sons.

The lack of coherence in the loyalist units which settled at Niagara and their personal lack of established status meant that the loyalist officers could not expect to elicit automatic deference from the local society; the old resentments of the war period in turn meant that Butler had little prestige with either his officers or his men.

The most powerful figure in the post-revolutionary Niagara peninsula was not to be John Butler, but Robert Hamilton. Hamilton, together with his Scots relatives, quickly rose to dominate the politics and the patronage as well as the merchandising, credit, milling, and land speculation of the early peninsula. Just as the seeds of the loyalist officers' failure lay in the revolutionary period, so did the roots of Robert Hamilton's success.

Robert Hamilton (1763-1808), miniature, artist unknown. (Metropolitan Toronto Library, John Ross Robertson Collection, T-17077)

Demand for goods at Niagara and the posts above during the war years was virtually insatiable. The real El Dorado was the provisioning of the Indian Department. Delighted merchants had watched this market grow from nothing at the beginning of the war to a point at the end of 1779 when 5,000 Indians had fled to Niagara. The provisions and presents necessary to retain their active support was staggering.

Not surprisingly, a struggle for position and patronage emerged at Fort Niagara during the war and the army, as the purchasers of supplies for the Indians, was the final arbiter in the contest. The conflict ultimately had few victors. The merchant firms which sought wealth by associating with one or the other side in the Butler-Johnson dispute were toppled by the vagaries of the struggle and the vicissitudes of trade. Yet one firm, composed of Robert Hamilton and Richard Cartwright, was able to navigate the stormy waters of the factional struggle, forge strong links with the military, and begin to build an influence that would be felt long after the clash of the revolution had died away.

Robert Hamilton had begun business quietly at Niagara in 1780. From Bolton in East Lothian, Scotland, Hamilton was the son of a Presbyterian clergyman. Like many middle-class Scots of the late eighteenth century, he came to British North America through connections with the fur trade. In March 1778 he signed a three-year contract with the Ellice brothers, lowland Scots who had long been prominent in the fur trade. By July 1779 Hamilton was in the province of Quebec, where he served an apprenticeship as a clerk at Montreal and Carleton Island, New York, while building up a small trade at the upper posts on his own account. In May 1780 he left the Ellices to form a partnership with the New York loyalist Richard Cartwright at Fort Niagara, an arrangement supported by a supply agreement with Todd and McGill, one of the earliest and most substantial of the Montreal fur-trade supply houses. Todd and McGill in turn arranged a copartnership for Hamilton and Cartwright with a major firm involved at Detroit in the southwest fur trade. Such trade links would be important after the revolution not only economically but also politically for garnering patronage and exercising influence.

After a series of increasingly sordid scandals in the supply of the Indian Department, the well-bred officers of British military, disdainful of commerce at the best of times, were thoroughly disgusted by the crass traders at the Great Lakes posts. They longed to discover men in trade who would demonstrate more responsibility and patriotism. Both Hamilton and Cartwright came from genteel backgrounds. Before 1780 neither had had direct experience in the Indian trade and neither was tainted with its reputation for sharp practice. Both shared the language and assumptions of the educated officer élite of the regular army and the officers felt comfortable in dealing with them. Although they had entered trade too late to make much immediate profit from the war, the impression they had made on the military would stand them in good stead after the conflict ended. Indeed, the fur trade and the British military would be among the most important influences in determining the distribution of political power in post-war Niagara.[3]

The deciding authority in the first assignment of office in the Niagara peninsula was external to the local society. All initial offices in the new society — justices of peace, judgeships on the Court of Common Pleas, and positions on the land board — were appointed; and they were assigned by the government in Quebec City. These appointments proved to be extremely important because administrative power in early Niagara society was cumulative. Those who received positions in the first years of settlement were often chosen for subsequent appointments or, equally important, were consulted on such appointments.

The problems the government of Quebec faced in making the first local appointments in the upper country were essentially ones of communication. The central government in Quebec had little direct knowledge of the new citizenry at distant Niagara. It therefore turned for advice to the three organizations which had been closely connected with the upper country and which had knowledge of the new settlements: the army, the Indian Department, and, to some extent, the fur-trading community. The involvement of all three of these groups with provisioning and supply meant that their most direct contacts in settlements such as Niagara had been with the local merchants who had participated in Great Lakes trade. Not unnaturally, they showed a predilection for merchants in their recommendations for office at Niagara.

When asked in 1787 by the Quebec government for general recommendations of persons deserving of civil trusts, John Butler named six former members of the Indian Department and the Rangers and two merchants, Robert Hamilton and Samuel Street, who had been suppliers of the department. Captain Watson, the commandant at Niagara, however, showed a strong preference for the mercantile element. His list of six recommendations included four merchants, Hamilton among them, and only one loyalist, Butler, who had seen military service in the war. In the event, by 1789 the judges of the Court of Common Pleas (a court with all civil and criminal jurisdiction saving only in murder cases) and the justices of the peace (who, in the absence of any elected township government, regulated all local civil matters) for the settlements at Niagara consisted of four merchants and seven loyalists, only four of whom had actually seen military service with Butler. Considering their limited numbers, the representation of the merchants among the local officeholders was remarkable.[4]

Hamilton fared well in this initial distribution of office: he became both a justice of the peace and a judge. His power was further augmented in 1788 by his placement on the land board (which assigned land grants to incoming settlers) for his district. The recommendation came from Sir John Johnson — who would have known Hamilton both as a supplier of the Indian Department and a partner of Johnson's client, Richard Cartwright.[5]

Even more significant in institutionalizing Hamilton's influence were recommendations for appointed provincial office, especially for the seats on the Legislative and Executive councils to be filled in 1791 for the new province of Upper Canada. The lists of recommendations for these posts submitted to London were composed by Sir John Johnson. Johnson was well placed to exercise an influence on appointments in the upper country; he held a powerful position as a member of the Executive Council of Quebec and was a trusted advisor of Dorchester on all matters relating to the loyalists.

In 1788 Johnson had personally recommended the men who had composed the first land board at Niagara. Three of the six had not served with Butler. Johnson sought to reinforce this tendency in 1790 when recommending additional appointments to the land board: his recommendations were two merchants, a member of his own loyalist regiment, a loyalist who had served under Butler in the Indian Department but who had been personally associated with Johnson before the revolution, and a loyalist officer who had served under Simcoe. The two merchants and the loyalist who served in Johnson's corps were actually appointed.[6]

Johnson excluded Butler from his list of recommendations for seats in the Executive and Legislative councils, positions Butler must have expected to hold. Indeed, Johnson excluded all members of Butler's Rangers from consideration, although he did recommend five officers who had served directly under his command in the King's Royal Regiment of New York. Johnson did recommend Hamilton as well as Cartwright for both the Legislative and Executive councils. Only two of his other nominees were from Niagara, one for the Legislative Council, Nathaniel Pettit, who had seen no military service, and one for the Executive Council, Robert Kerr, who had served with Johnson's own corps rather than at Niagara. Johnson had ranked his lists and Pettit and Kerr were both at the bottom. Neither was appointed while both Hamilton and Cartwright were selected to serve on the Legislative Council.[7]

Johnson's influence was not the only factor in the final choice of members for the councils. William Robertson, a relative of Hamilton and an important figure in the southwest fur trade who resided in London, recommended Hamilton to Simcoe, the newly appointed lieutenant governor of Upper Canada. Isaac Todd while in London had performed the same service for Richard Cartwright by recommending him to Simcoe. He probably recommended Hamilton as well. Indeed, when the lists of members for the councils were first published, Sir John Johnson was shocked at how few of the loyalist officers he had recommended were included. By their influential contacts, the fur-trade community had secured the most significant offices for merchants such as Hamilton and Cartwright.[8]

In contrast to the merchants with their web of connections and patrons, the loyalist officers at Niagara had no influential allies at the centres of power. As a result, their share of the initial offices in the peninsula and in the province was meagre. Nor did the loyalist officers prove capable of improving their patronage position over time by impressing their abilities and their prior claims upon the colonial government.

Butler's officers represented an almost static minority within the largest group of appointed officeholders, the justices of the peace. In 1789 they constituted four of eleven, in 1808 seven of twenty-eight, and in 1812 six of twenty-seven. None of the rank and file served as magistrates. No individuals bearing the family names of the officers became justices of the peace, suggesting that whatever prerogative the officers did enjoy did not extend to their offspring. Three of the five members of the Court of Common Pleas in 1789, and four of the eleven members of the land board in 1794, were former Rangers and Indian Department officers. Again, none of the rank and file were represented.[9]

Butler himself fared better in gaining public position than did his officers. To central government officials it was probably unthinkable that the commander of the loyalist forces at Niagara should be entirely excluded from the management of the new settlement. By 1788 Butler had been appointed a justice of the peace, a judge of the Court of Common Pleas, and a member of the land board. Although he never attained provincial office, Butler was by 1792 lieutenant of the county, the most significant local office. Such offices, however, availed Butler but little, since he appears to have been unable to establish a loyal faction through which he could exercise power. A clear indication of Butler's limited influence was that in his lifetime none of his three sons held a post more elevated than that of captain in the local militia.

Butler's most important office was his position in the Indian Department as deputy superintendent of the Six Nations. Although his attempts to exploit that position for substantial personal gain after the revolution through use of department supplies and land speculation were foiled, it is undeniable that Butler owed what post-war prominence he did enjoy to his position in the Indian Department. He played a large part in the purchase of much of southwestern Ontario from the Mississauga Indians and was significant in the diplomatic manoeuvring with the Americans and the Indians in the years before the evacuation of the border posts in 1796. The Johnson faction, however, was vigilant to prevent Butler from turning his prestige to his own advancement. As early as 1782 Sir John Johnson made an attempt to remove Butler from his post and to replace him with his own nephew; when that failed, Johnson blocked payment of Butler's personal accounts and also stepped up his family's barrage of innuendo in official circles against Butler. When he died in 1796, Butler's successor was William Claus, the son of Butler's most vociferous opponent in the Johnson faction, Daniel Claus. The Butler influence within the Indian Department was decisively terminated.

Hamilton's use of his commercial contacts and of local office were not the only sources of his rise to power and influence at Niagara. Shortly after the revolution, Hamilton began to further consolidate his influence by utilizing another system of linkages, the ties of marriage and consanguity among a group of Scots entrepreneurs at Niagara and Detroit. He married into the family of John Askin, the chief trader at Detroit and in the southwest, who was also Hamilton's former partner. The marriage linked Hamilton into a small group of three Detroit families, the Askins, the Grants, and the Robertsons, who were important in forwarding his interests. Hamilton's construction of a network of family alliances was quite deliberate. Before 1791, he brought some of his own relations from Scotland — Robert, William and Thomas Dickson, and Thomas Clarke — and arranged for their training in Upper Canadian enterprise. He then organized their establishment in businesses at Niagara which were offshoots of his own. Other relations and acquaintances arrived over time. Each continued to cooperate closely with his fellows, with Hamilton, and with other contacts Hamilton provided. Such a network, a form of economic patronage in itself, greatly extended the political influence of its Scots members.[10]

For up-country merchants such as Hamilton, trade provided not only the matter of politics but the means to influence it. The network that joined traders along the St Lawrence and the Great Lakes could be used not only for trade but also for communication and political lobbying. Information and opinion as well as goods and furs moved up and down the system. In the pioneer communities along the lakes, those who had knowledge of events beyond their own locales, who were privy to the direction of central-government policy, and who had the ability to make their opinions known at the centres of power possessed a significant influence denied to the rest of their society. Indeed, the rest of the civilian society in the new loyalist settlements appears to have availed itself on occasion of the merchants and their contacts in its communications with the central government.

Hamilton and Cartwright found their trade connections to be their chief source of information on government policy and their prime means of influencing that policy. Through Todd and McGill, for instance, the two up-country partners first heard rumours of the establishment of a new province for the loyalist settlements. When Hamilton and Cartwright had complaints of the harsh terms imposed by the Quebec government for the building of mills or the shifting of port functions from Cataraqui (Kingston) to Carleton Island, it was through Todd and McGill rather than directly through government channels that they registered their complaints. The loyalists themselves quickly learned that the most efficacious means of communication with Quebec City was through the merchants of the Laurentian trading system. At the behest of others, Hamilton and Cartwright took general social concerns — for example, the necessity of travelling to Halifax in order to make claims for loyalist losses — to Todd and McGill in order that they and the rest of the Montreal fur-trade community might use their influence with government to effect a change.[11]

Merchants had done well in gaining a large proportion of the initial administrative positions in the Niagara peninsula. But the winning of office was one matter; the exercise of the powers of office and of general political influence might have been quite another. In fact, by the vigorous use of their offices, merchants magnified their impact upon the settlements at Niagara.

The new civilian society at post-war Niagara posed important problems for its merchants. Pioneer farmers were notorious for their ability to build up commercial debts and even more notorious for their reluctance to pay them. Resentment of the merchant system of payment for product in bons (notes redeemable for his merchandise by the merchant who issued them) ran high and merchants found it useful to have judicial sanction to enforce both debts and their commercial system. For merchants, the most effective way to influence the decisions of the courts was to serve upon them. Likewise, the granting and transfer of land was of increasing significance in the post-war society and merchants quickly became immersed in matters of land speculation. The pattern of road development and the location of towns were also a prime commercial concern. Hamilton found a means to be informed of, and to exercise an influence over, all these matters through the Court of Common Pleas and the district land board. He maintained a near-perfect record of attendance at the sessions of both the court and the board, being far more assiduous than the loyalist appointees. The loyalist officers had less incentive than a merchant such as Hamilton to attend the court or the land board. They all lived at some distance from Niagara, where sessions were held; they found the journey to attend them onerous at a time when they were absorbed in the creation of new farms; and they did not find the weight of their responsibilities offset by any immediate benefit to themselves.

Through the court, Hamilton was able to establish community policy on such vital economic matters as the sale of liquor, the exchange of land, and the verification of wills. The major business of both the court and the land board — debt and land — was important to a merchant. The enforcement of debts was the prime concern of the court; in its six years of existence, 75 per cent of its cases involved the payment of debt. Many merchants placed a substantial reliance on the court in the conduct of their business. Certainly, there was a strain of popular resentment against the court's strict interpretation of the law relating to debts. The first attorney general of Upper Canada, John White, when resident at Niagara, reported that he had been told that those who controlled the courts "have lorded it with a rod of iron."[12]

The district land board was the only effective local authority for the granting of land, the selection of town sites, the laying out of new roads, and the improvement of primitive ones. Such functions made it the single most significant administrative institution in the colony, and its decisions were of great interest to the communities it regulated. One of the thorniest matters the board at Niagara had to resolve early in its life was the selection of a site for the district town. As the administrative centre, the town would draw business for shops in or near it; to farmers in its vicinity, it would be a convenience and would ultimately increase the value of their property. Controversy over the location of the town probably pre-dated the land board. After its inception, the board declared its preference for a town site in the middle of Niagara Township on the banks of the Niagara River. The site was within two miles of Queenston and so located on major roads that settlers coming from most parts of the peninsula would pass by Hamilton's shop on their way to and from it.

The proposal stimulated opposition; alternative proposals for sites above the escarpment nearer to the centre of Niagara and Stamford townships were put forward. Such locations would have been more attractive to the loyalist settlers clustered in that area, but less favourable to Hamilton's commerce. In the end, Hamilton's interests were favoured. The land board, almost certainly with Hamilton's active participation, submitted a petition to the government at Quebec asking for a grant of land near Navy Hall on which to erect government buildings. The petition was accepted. This, the present location of Niagara-on-the-Lake, was in the same geographical relationship to Hamilton's store as the site originally proposed by the board.

By 1793 complaints against the operations and decisions of the court and the land board at Niagara were becoming frequent. Such complaints often identified the source of discontent as merchant control of those institutions. The complaints were largely justified. Impelled by the needs of their commerce and aided by the infrastructure and alliances provided by their system of commercial supply, merchants had edged aside their rivals and assumed control of the administration of the Niagara peninsula.[13]

As suggested earlier, it was this issue of economic and political power, rather than matters relating to ideology, that dominated the politics of the Niagara peninsula. Of course, Hamilton and his relations were influenced by political ideology. As befitted an established and respectable merchant, Hamilton accepted the dominant tory philosophy of his time and place. He was a confirmed monarchist and loyal constitutionalist who harboured no doubts about the correctness of a hierarchical society. Hamilton and his relations accepted the conventional tory wisdom that the mass of men were

Hamilton house at the Queenston end of the portage (house nearest the river), artist unknown. (National Archives of Canada, C3354)

base and ignorant, moved, as one of them wrote, by "Low cunning & flattery"[14] in political affairs. Human passions, they believed, had to be restrained by the bonds of social deference. It followed naturally to the Scots that political leadership should be the prerogative of the responsible and respectable elements of society — elements they tended to equate with themselves.

In his private affairs, Hamilton adopted to the full the lifestyle of a tory gentleman. In 1791, when others in the peninsula might be considering the construction of their first permanent homes, Hamilton began to build an impressive Georgian mansion. Perched on a cliff high above the Niagara River at Queenston, the house with its two-storey greystone façade, side wings, and covered galleries rose incongruously above its modest wooden neighbours and the pioneer clearings. Hamilton entertained lavishly at his home and his guests included Prince Edward Augustus, who in 1792 stopped there for refreshment on his way to the Falls. Elizabeth Posthuma Simcoe, the wife of the lieutenant governor, was a constant companion of Mrs Hamilton. Around his home, Hamilton kept a fairly extensive farm, a practice that reinforced his public image as a man of the landed gentry. He and his children showed a marked respect for books and learning. To indicate his own status and to prepare his offspring for their future social roles, Hamilton was assiduous in their education; all received their higher education in Scotland.

Yet, in some important respects, Hamilton differed from conservatives in other parts of the colony. Many Upper Canadian spokesmen who shared Hamilton's conservative ideology firmly believed that American settlement should be excluded from Upper Canada in favour of British immigration; they also tended to associate themselves with the Church of England in its opposition to religious sects, which were seen as American and subversive. Hamilton, on the other hand, when speaking on the subject of American settlement, stressed the home truths of the North American economy: Americans adapted to local conditions more rapidly than Europeans and made better farmers. Such a view fitted with Hamilton's economic interests. He clearly perceived that only with American settlement could he fill his lands and retail his goods. Hamilton emphasized the ties of British subjects and Americans rather than their differences. He distinguished sharply between the two republican states, France and the United States, emphasizing the Anglo-Saxon bond of American Englishman rather than America's republican unity with France.[15]

Hamilton's pro-Americanism also expressed the general sentiment of the Niagara peninsula. With its proximity to the American border and its function as the prime route of American migration into Upper Canada, the region had closer and more extensive contacts with America than did any other area of Upper Canada. Heavy post-loyalist settlement from the United States necessitated, in the minds of the early settlers of the peninsula, a moderate toleration of Americans. This was early expressed in the resistance of the area's representatives to legislation, passed in 1800, establishing a seven-year residence requirement for the franchise. The representatives of the peninsula opposed the bill; in fact, with two exceptions a recorded vote on the issue was a split of the east against the west of the province in favour of the qualification. In 1804 an attempt to repeal the limitations on American voters was solidly opposed by the representatives of the loyalist strongholds along the St Lawrence and supported by the rest of the province, including the three voting members from the peninsula.[16]

The tolerant attitude of the peninsula towards Americans also found expression in the area's attitude to religion. Many sects which had emigrated from the American states were heavily represented in the Niagara peninsula and its politicians were sympathetic to their desires. From the first meeting of the legislature in 1792 to 1812, the region's representatives introduced and consistently supported legislation for the extension of religious privileges. They moved or seconded bills in aid of Methodists, Quakers, Mennonites, and Tunkers. Hamilton himself in the Legislative Council supported liberalization of the marriage laws and seconded legislation "to afford relief to the religious society of people called Methodists."

Attitudes to Americans and to religious sects, then, tended to be points of consensus rather than division in the Niagara peninsula. The same could not be said of the economic and political power concentrated in the hands of Robert Hamilton and his Scots relations. Using his substantial wealth, Hamilton had created an extensive network of merchandising and land speculation which touched the lives of the inhabitants of the Niagara peninsula more directly and intimately than any governmental or social institution of their time. What credit or income the settlers realized in the first years of development came to a large extent through Hamilton. He was the major wholesaler of their grain, the principal holder of their mortgages, their supplier of goods, and the chief purchaser of their lands. Indeed, the total known amount of land in which Hamilton held an interest by purchase, grant, or mortgage was 130,170 acres. If contiguous, his lands would have stretched one township deep from the Niagara River almost to Burlington Bay (Hamilton Harbour). Although he invested heavily in land, much of it undoubtedly came to him as payment for outstanding debts. Only 11 per cent of his total holdings came as direct grants from the crown.

A man of such wealth and power was, not unnaturally, resented.

In politics as in commerce, Robert Hamilton had in general laboured hard and well to establish his influence. Through his position as justice of the peace, judge of the Court of Common Pleas, and member of the land board, he worked in the eight years between the end of the revolution and the inception of Upper Canada to guarantee the continuance of that degree of social order essential to the functioning of his commerce. He also used the court and the land board with notable success to facilitate his control of the new commerce generated by the loyalist settlements at Niagara. Hamilton was successful in creating for himself the political equivalent of his commercial primacy in his community. The petitions and early politics of the community in turn reacted against his creation and control of a commercial authority structure.

Windsor Chair. This chair, donated by a local loyalist family, is made of native wood and is reputed to be one of the chairs used in the first legislature of Upper Canada. (Servos collection, Canadian Parks Service, FA.69.3.236)

The community's resentment of the mercantile element found expression in the first election for the new legislative assembly of Upper Canada in 1792. Little is known of the contest for that election, but its results were clear: all four candidates elected for seats in the peninsula were former loyalist officers and farmers; none were merchants. The one merchant who is known to have run, Samuel Street Sr in Second Lincoln, was soundly defeated by his opponent Benjamin Pawling, 148 to 48. The election was only a prelude to the stormy first parliament of Upper Canada where the agrarian element sharply and consistently opposed its interest to that of the merchants.[17]

A prime issue with the assembly, for which it had the support of Lieutenant Governor John Graves Simcoe, was the influence of merchants in the Courts of Common Pleas. Hamilton and Cartwright in the Legislative Council were the chief opponents of change, but they received no support in the assembly or the council. The Courts of Common Pleas were abolished in 1794. Likewise, the district land boards, another local institution that had been of value to the merchants, were terminated by Simcoe through a minute of the Executive Council. Simcoe also moved to abolish an exclusive contract for the provisioning of Niagara's garrisons which Todd and McGill had won for Hamilton and Cartwright.

If one sees these in part as victories of local Niagara society over the power of its merchants, their actual impact is hard to assess. Both the court and the land board had served Hamilton well in the period of initial settlement. It is difficult, however, to imagine such institutions having a continuing impact of such magnitude in later years, and their major use to the merchants may have been accomplished by the time they were abolished. Certainly, the merchant interest was sufficiently entrenched by the time of their abolition that it would find other means to protect and forward itself. Established status and economic power proved more important than structures of administration. When Hamilton brought his claims for land, based upon the transfer of settlers' certificates to him, before the Heir and Devisee Committee of the Executive Council, the committee passed his claims without controversy. Likewise, the courts continued to be used by merchants to sue for debt and there is no evidence that merchants found them unduly lenient. The abolition of the provisioning contract did little to affect the actual supply of the garrisons or the dominance of the major merchants in the local economy.[18]

If the merchants emerged from the first legislature relatively unscathed, then the election of 1796 in fact showed a marked increase in their power. None of those elected in 1792 were returned. Whereas those in the first assembly had been loyalist officers and farmers, three of the four in the second had entrepreneurial backgrounds. Included among the representatives were Richard Beasley, himself a merchant as well as Richard Cartwright's cousin, Samuel Street Sr, whose entrepreneurial activities in the peninsula stretched back into the revolutionary period, and Benjamin Hardison, a miller and major store owner at Fort Erie. The most interesting new representative, D.W. Smith, sat for Hamilton's home riding, Third Lincoln. Smith, although a British officer and a government official rather than a merchant, undoubtedly came well recommended to Hamilton by his attempts in the first assembly to serve the interests of Hamilton's western relatives, the Askins.

The tone of the second assembly changed markedly from that of the first. As the sheriff of the Niagara District wrote to Simcoe: "The lower house is composed of more respectable men than formerly; only two of the old members were returned at the last Election .... No opposition in either house, Several useful statutes have been created ...." Much of the legislation, such as acts for the better regulation of coinage, for the registration of deeds of bargain and sale, and for the regulation of trade between the United States and Upper Canada, worked to the advantage of merchants such as Hamilton. In future provincial elections, the peninsula would swing back to opposition to the merchant interest, but would never substantially weaken it.

In 1796 one other highly significant local office came to Robert Hamilton and it can be seen as the capstone of the merchants' power and influence in the Niagara peninsula. Lieutenant Governor Simcoe was concerned about the regulation of local government from the centre. "The distance that the seat of Government, wherever placed, must be from many parts of the Province," he asserted, "seem to me to require a gradation of Officers as absolutely necessary for its internal and subordinate regulation."[19] Simcoe in fact concentrated upon one local office of his own creation, lieutenant of the county. This office was to be the focus of power within each region of Upper Canada and the linchpin between the regions and the central government. Its holders were to be at the head of local government and were to control virtually all significant local offices; to the lieutenants of the counties would be given the first place in the Courts of Quarter Sessions and the recommendation of its constituent justices of the peace. The lieutenants would be the commanding officers of the militia with the right to nominate their subordinate officers. In practice, they would be consulted on most local appointments made from the centre, and because of the lack of other sources of information, their recommendations would almost always be accepted. Simcoe concentrated much power within one office for political

and administrative reasons: it would guarantee the creation of an acceptable and loyal social hierarchy in Upper Canada. The office of lieutenant of
the county, with its power and prerogatives, would stimulate the development of a nucleus of privileged families around which local aristocracies
would develop.

Because Simcoe had initially seen the power of merchants such as
Hamilton as a negative influence, he deliberately chose the first lieutenants
of the counties from loyalist officers. His choice for Lincoln County was a
natural one: Lieutenant-Colonel John Butler. Much, however, occurred
between Butler's appointment in 1792 and his death in 1796, and Simcoe's
choice of a successor indicated a change in his attitudes. The new lieutenant
was not a military man at all, but Robert Hamilton.

Nor was the choice of Hamilton a single deviation in favour of the
merchant interest. When called upon to recommend individuals for the
most important offices subordinate to himself, justices of the peace, Hamilton submitted a list of names for the Home District; all were merchants and
he mentioned three other individuals "equally entitled with those recommended." Hamilton did not, however, push their claims because, he asserted with some understatement, "they are all merchants and I feared that
such addition might, to His Excellency, have the appearance of professional
preference."[20]

He need not have worried. Simcoe accepted the list as submitted and
instructed that two of the three other merchants mentioned be added to the
list. Likewise, in the militia, Simcoe approved the creation of a prestigious
artillery company officered, at Hamilton's recommendation, by merchants,
many of them his relatives.[21]

Although he had initially opposed them, Simcoe had come to recognize
the power of merchants within the society. The only effective source of
power within the Niagara peninsula had proved to be commerce. If one
wished, as Simcoe did, to centralize power, one had to rely on those who had
effective local knowledge and control. Through commercial operations
merchants had the only effective network of local contact and local influence. In the end, Simcoe decided to attempt to harness it to governmental
purposes.

As early as 1796, then, merchants at Niagara had established their local
control. Their impact on Niagara and beyond was destined to be a long-term one.

Yet the continuing influence of Robert Hamilton and especially of his
family was not to be as extensive as one might have expected. Hamilton died
in 1809 and his enterprises survived him by only three years. The pillars of
his commercial edifice, provisioning and portaging, had been cracking in

the last decade of his life. A heavy investment in land and a wide extension of credit to his customers in his retail operations made it difficult for Hamilton to offset his declining profits in portaging and provisioning. The situation was complicated by the ineptitude of his heirs, the coming of the War of 1812, and a complex will that virtually froze the assets of his estate until 1823. Although several of his sons rose in time to become successful entrepreneurs, officeholders, and public figures in the higher echelons of Upper Canadian society, none succeeded to the social and political predominance of Robert Hamilton.

Robert Hamilton and his associates, however, did stand at the head of a tradition of "commercial toryism," an association of business with politics whose leadership would later be assumed by such men as William Hamilton Merritt and Allan McNab, both, by no accident, connected with the Niagara peninsula. That tradition would ultimately be the dominant strand in the conservatism of the nation-building era of John A. Macdonald. The political culture of early Niagara would have a long currency.

NOTES

The author thanks Carleton University Press for permission to use material originally published in his book *The Enterprises of Robert Hamilton: A Study of Wealth and Influence in Early Upper Canada, 1776-1812* (Ottawa: Carleton University Press, 1983).

1   National Archives of Canada (NAC), RG 1 L4 (Upper Canada State Papers, Land Board Records), 5, Return of Officers and Rank and File, 27 April 1789, 26-7; NAC, MG 21 (Haldimand Transcripts), 115, List of Indian Department Officers, 4 December 1783, 194-5; NAC, MG 11 (Colonial Office 42 Transcripts), 306, List of Half-Pay Officers and Military Pensioners in Upper Canada, 1 June 1806, 306.

2   NAC *Annual Report*, 1891, 2-5; NAC, RG 1 L4, 5: 26-7.

3   On events at Fort Niagara during the war period, see: Bruce G. Wilson, "The Struggle for Wealth and Status at Fort Niagara, 1775-1783," *Ontario History*, 68, no.3 (September 1976), 137-54; Wilson, *The Enterprises of Robert Hamilton*, chap. 1.

4   "Names of Persons Recommended for Civil Office ... August 18, 1787," E.A. Cruikshank, "Records of Niagara: 1784-89," Publication of the *Niagara Historical Society*, 39 (1928), 60; NAC, MG 11, 37, Minutes of Council, 14 May 1788, 182; *Quebec Almanac* (Quebec, 1789), 19-20.

5   "Extract from Quebec Land Book, December 27, 1788," Cruikshank, "Records of Niagara: 1784-89," 61-2; NAC, MG 23 H I 1(Simcoe Papers), series 3:1, Hunter to Farquharson, 12 February 1789, 260.

6   "Extract from Quebec Land Book, December 29, 1788," Cruikshank, "Records of Niagara: 1784-89," 61-2; NAC, MG 21, 46, Johnson to Dorchester, 13 September 1790, 77; Cruikshank, "Records of Niagara: 1789-93." Publication of the *Niagara Historical Society*, 41 (1930), 96.

7   Dorchester to Grenville, 15 March 1790, E.A. Cruikshank, ed., *The Correspondence of Lieut. Governor John Graves Simcoe ...* (Toronto: Ontario Historical Society, 1923-31), 1:10.

8   University of Western Ontario, William Robertson Collection, Hamilton to Robertson,

20 October 1791, 52; Archives of Ontario (AO), Cartwright Transcripts, Letterbooks, Cartwright to Todd, 21 October 1792, 21; NAC, MG 11, 278, Sir John Johnson to Simcoe, 24 November 1791, 32-3.

9   *Quebec Almanac*, various years.

10 See Wilson, *The Enterprises of Robert Hamilton*, chap. 5.

11 AO, Cartwright Transcripts, Letterbooks, Cartwright and Hamilton to Todd and McGill, 3 February 1786, 21; Cartwright to Todd and McGill, 6 March 1786, 206-7; Cartwright and Hamilton to Todd and McGill, 28 April 1786, 212; Cartwright to Todd and McGill, 13 February 1786, 205.

12 NAC, MG 23 H I 5 (John White Papers), White to Sir Samuel Shepherd, 25 February 1793, 5-6.

13 On the court and land board, see Wilson, *The Enterprises of Robert Hamilton*, 52-7.

14 Detroit Public Library, Askin Papers, John Askin to Nichol, 28 August 1800.

15 AO, Russell Papers, Hamilton to Russell, 1 November 1798; Askin Papers, Hamilton to John Askin, 17 March 1798.

16 Statutes of Upper Canada, 40 Geo. III, c. 3, Journal of the Legislative Assembly, 23 June 1800, AO *Report*, 1909; ibid., 22 February 1804, 443.

17 "Diary of Francis Goring," Publication of the *Niagara Historical Society*, 36 (1924), 63.

18 See Wilson, *The Enterprises of Robert Hamilton*, 105-21.

19 Simcoe to Portland, 30 October 1795, Cruikshank, *Simcoe Correspondence*, 4:115-18.

20 Ibid., Hamilton to Littlehales, 15 June 1796, 299.

21 Ibid., Littlehales to Hamilton, 12 July 1796, 329; NAC, RG 9 1B1 (Upper Canada: Militia Adjutant General's Office, Correspondence), 1:89.

CHAPTER THREE

MILITARY LIFE AT NIAGARA,
1792–1796

Brian Leigh Dunnigan

Garrison Orders, May 30, 1793
*A Subns. Guard of the 5 Regt. to mount tomorrow
at half past 12 o Clock, at the council Chamber
(late Butlers Barr[ack]s) opposite the Garrison ...*[1]

THE MILITARY SITUATION

Each time the legislature of Upper Canada met between 1792 and 1796 in the young and recently renamed village of Newark (Niagara-on-the-Lake), it did so under the protection of a military guard of honour. The soldiers came from the garrison of Fort Niagara, and the protection they offered was more than just symbolic. They provided Lieutenant Governor John Graves Simcoe with the military force necessary to protect his province from both external and internal threats during a period of tension in North America and Europe.

The political situation that influenced military activities in the Niagara region from 1792 to 1796 could be symbolized by the fact that the chief protection for the capital of Newark came from a British garrison stationed within United States territory. Fort Niagara had commanded the mouth of the Niagara River from the east bank for nearly seventy years. During the American Revolutionary War of 1775-83, it had been the bulwark of British defence of the Great Lakes. Although Fort Niagara was never taken or even attacked, British negotiators relinquished the post and much of the vast territory it protected in the peace of 1783.[2]

67

Niagara's situation was reflected throughout the Great Lakes where a string of posts, unconquered during the war, were given up. These included Oswegatchie (Ogdensburg, New York), Carleton Island and Oswego (both in New York), Detroit, and Michilimackinac. The boundary between the United States and British Canada was drawn through the lakes, so the Iroquois country of western New York and the vast wilderness north and west of the Ohio River fell to the Americans. Only Fort Erie remained in British territory.

Although gained by treaty, these posts and lands remained beyond United States control. By the autumn of 1784, American non-compliance with certain treaty terms had provided justification for the British to retain the forts. The United States was unable to take them by force. A further barrier was presented by the native American tribes of the region. Most had been hostile to the United States during the revolution. Their resistance continued after the war as American settlers flooded into the Ohio valley. When a small federal army was organized in 1784 from the remnants of continental forces, its focus soon became protection of the Ohio settlements and active campaigning against the Indians of the northwest.[3]

Initial American forays into the Indian country were not auspicious. Colonel Josiah Harmar was defeated at the headwaters of the Maumee River in October 1790. A far greater disaster overtook Governor Arthur St Clair's expedition the following year. His force, which included most of the federal army, was virtually annihilated on 4 November 1791 on the upper Wabash.[4] Native successes intensified the American belief that the British were supplying and encouraging them through the Great Lakes posts.

Although the Indians had triumphed in the first encounters, growing American military strength was alarming to Canada. The colony's military forces were prepared to act. Early in 1791, in the wake of Harmar's incursion, the commandant of Fort Niagara was ordered to prepare for both defensive and offensive action should "armed parties" again move into the Indian country. He was to reinforce Detroit, the post most threatened by the Americans, and call out the militia to supplement his garrisons. Similar warnings were conveyed to Niagara following the defeat of St Clair.[5]

Into this highly charged atmosphere were born both Upper Canada and the administration of Lieutenant Governor John Graves Simcoe. When the orders in council of 12 August 1791 divided the province of Quebec into Upper and Lower Canada, Simcoe, a veteran leader of provincial troops during the 1775-83 war, was appointed to the upper province. He was given command of a new corps of infantry to assist in its protection and undertake public works. Control of the regulars stationed at the military posts of Upper Canada, however, remained with Governor Dorchester at Quebec.[6]

Simcoe arrived at Niagara on 26 July 1792 and took up his duties in his new capital.[7] For the next four years the lieutenant governor would devote much energy to planning and executing schemes for the defence of Upper Canada. Simcoe's papers outline the external threats he most feared. In the west, American military activity menaced the Indian tribes and Detroit. Nearer at hand, American troops from Pittsburgh were establishing posts on the upper Allegheny River and moving toward Presque Isle on Lake Erie. On Lake Ontario, American settlers were encroaching on Fort Ontario and the mouth of the Genesee River. Simcoe's concerns resulted in a variety of plans, and his fear of the increasing proximity of American forces led him, in 1793, to establish a new naval and military post at Toronto.[8] Simcoe's task was complicated when, in 1793, Great Britain joined a European coalition opposing revolutionary France. Although the French posed no immediate threat in North America, the war drained British military resources and allowed fewer troops for the defence of Canada.[9]

The real military crisis occurred during 1794. It had taken American forces several years to recover from St Clair's 1791 disaster, but the job was accomplished by a far more capable commander, Major-General Anthony Wayne. The results were decisive. Wayne led his army north from the Ohio River during the summer of 1794. On 20 August he defeated the Indians at the Battle of Fallen Timbers on the Maumee River, a few miles above its junction with Lake Erie. Wayne's actions caused a confrontation that nearly sparked war between the United States and Britain. A short distance from the battlefield stood a British post, Fort Miami, which had been erected earlier in the year. Although its commandant barred the retreating Indians from the fort and did nothing to assist them, Wayne demanded that the British abandon a post which had been erected since 1783. The British officer refused, and stalemate ensued, neither side willing to fire the first shot. Wayne's army withdrew soon after.[10]

The campaign stimulated much military activity at Niagara. Simcoe called out the militia, ordered regulars from Fort Niagara to reinforce Fort Miami, and strengthened the old post.[11] War did not come, however, and even as the crisis reached its climax a resolution to the conflict was being achieved. The distraction of war with France made for a cooperative climate when American envoy John Jay reached London in June 1794. His treaty, signed in November, addressed the disagreements between the two countries. Most significant for Upper Canada — and the Niagara region in particular — the treaty set a timetable for the surrender of the Great Lakes posts to the United States. The boundary provisions of the 1784 treaty were to be met by 1 June 1796.[12]

NIAGARA'S FORTIFICATIONS

Military life at Niagara between 1792 and 1796 revolved around the fortifications, the central link in a chain of posts from which the British controlled
the Great Lakes. Niagara had been the keystone and headquarters of British
defences in the region since 1760. The establishment of the capital of Upper
Canada at Newark only increased its significance.

The administrative post of "Niagara" consisted of more than just Fort
Niagara, the fortification at the mouth of the river. "Niagara" was a series
of outposts guarding the important portage around Niagara Falls. Subsidi-
ary to Fort Niagara were tiny establishments at each end of the portage and
on the shore of Lake Erie. There was also a naval station across the river from
Fort Niagara.

The bulwark of the post of Niagara was the main fortification, usually
referred to as "Niagara Fort" or, simply, "the Fort." Fort Niagara was, by
1792, the product of seven decades of evolution. It had begun as a defensible
stone house constructed by the French in 1726. A stockade was erected
around the building, but the need to make the position tenable against
artillery caused the French to convert it from a modest frontier post to a
large, "regular" fortification in the style of Vauban. Following the British
capture of Fort Niagara in 1759, its earthworks had been allowed to
deteriorate as security against Indians became paramount, and stockades
again provided the main defence. The American war of 1775-83 reversed
this process. The earthworks were restored, and, by the end of the conflict,
Fort Niagara was the most sophisticated fortification west of Quebec.[13]

The cession of the post to the United States did not bode well for the
preservation of Fort Niagara. On 20 July 1784 post commandant Lieutenant-
Colonel Arent S. DePeyster acknowledged orders that, hereafter, "no works

*Niagara Fort, shown in a rare view from the east or United States side of the Niagara River.
Watercolour of the 1780s, possibly executed by James Peachey. (Royal Ontario Museum,
Toronto, 956.129)*

whatever shall be undertaken on this side of the water."[14] For the next twelve years the fort would receive only that attention required for the security of its garrison. Worse, Lake Ontario was eroding the ground on which the fort stood. With eventual surrender to the Americans assured, there was little sense in spending large sums to improve the defences against either human or natural enemies.[15]

Few British officers were pleased with the location or the design of Fort Niagara. Simcoe believed that the "fortress of Niagara is not defensible with its present fortifications or Garrison, or if reinforced to double its numbers against the formidable attack which may be combined [*sic*]." The problem lay in the fort itself; he considered it to be "a badly constructed field work" which would "require all the Forces in this Country to garrison it in case of a siege."[16] The position was cramped, and its deficiencies could not be corrected, wrote engineer Gother Mann, "without breaking new ground and going into the labour and expense of a new system."[17]

The form of Fort Niagara was described by Lieutenant Thomas Hughes in 1786 as "a regular hornwork, dry ditch and ravelin, with stone block houses in the bastions." Hughes referred to the main defensive works on the land side — the front from which attack was most likely. "The fort towards the landing is stoccaded," he continued, "it being in no danger from the water."[18] The land-side walls were constructed of earth, faced with sod to

Mouth of the Niagara River, sketched from His Majesty's Armed Vessel Mississauga *by Elizabeth Simcoe, 13 September 1794. She identified, left to right, Niagara Fort, Navy Hall, and the village of Newark. (Archives of Ontario, Simcoe Sketch #90e)*

prevent erosion. This was an impermanent if inexpensive way of construct-
ing defences against cannon. Because frost and rain were potent natural
enemies, however, sod works had to be repaired frequently. They had other
foes as well. In 1794 post orders noted that: "His Excellency Colol. Simcoe
having observed how much the sod work of the Fort has been damaged by
the Sheep and Poultry which run about the Yard; it is the Comm[andan]ts.
orders that those to whom they belong take the necessary steps to prevent
their getting loose in future ..."[19]

Repairs made to the fortifications during 1794 included an attempt to
reduce chronic erosion of the earthworks. The solution was "a revetment of
boards" laid against the exterior "scarp" or face of the wall, a treatment
similar to that seen today on the bastions of Fort George. Alas, the plank
revetment was no cure, and one of Fort Niagara's first American commandants suggested, in 1799, that "good works of Solid clay well sodded"
(ironically, the pre-1794 treatment) would have provided a more durable
fortification.[20]

The interior was crowded with buildings. Most prominent was the
large stone house, known today as the "Castle," which served as officers'
quarters. A square stone redoubt, enclosed by pickets to make it more
defensible, stood in each of the land-side bastions. Three other masonry
structures, a bakehouse, powder magazine, and provisions storehouse,
were supplemented by twenty wooden officers' quarters, barracks, store-

*Niagara Fort, shown in a more conventional view from the west or Canadian shore by
Elizabeth Simcoe. Navy Hall is shown in the left foreground. This sketch was probably made
about 27 June 1793. (Archives of Ontario, Simcoe Sketch #57)*

houses, and a forge.[21] These buildings, like the fortifications protecting them, had been neglected since 1784, causing Elizabeth Simcoe to comment that "tho the buildings look so well from the other side, I found the quarters very indifferent."[22] Indifferent or not, they sheltered the main body of troops responsible for the defence of Niagara.

"Navy Hall" was the dependent post nearest Fort Niagara. It was situated on the opposite shore and provided a wharf, storehouses, and quarters for the vessels and men of the Provincial Marine. Navy Hall, a two-storey gambrel-roofed barracks, had been constructed in 1765. The building provided a residence for the Simcoes once it had been rehabilitated.[23] On the hill above Navy Hall stood a group of wooden barracks that had housed Butler's Rangers during the war of 1775-83. At least one of these was converted for use as the council chamber for the legislature.[24]

The next of Niagara's military posts marked the beginning of the portage. In order to move goods to Lake Erie, it was necessary to carry them overland from the mouth of the Niagara Gorge to a point above the cataracts where small boats could safely navigate. From the earliest French explorers in 1679, the portage had been maintained on the east shore. This practice was continued by the British, and storehouses, fortifications, and machines to lift goods up the bank were constructed at a place known as the "Lower Landing" (Lewiston, New York).[25]

Simcoe and his government arrived soon after important changes had taken place on the Niagara portage. The facilities of the Lower Landing were in poor condition by the late 1780s. Rather than maintain them, Governor Dorchester ordered, early in 1790, that the portage be shifted to the west side of the river. Thereafter, the Lower, "West," or "New" Landing would be at the village of Queenston, and the "carry" would be on the Canadian shore.

Elizabeth Simcoe's sketch of Navy Hall, 3 June 1794. (Archives of Ontario, Simcoe Sketch #90d)

Queenston was not fortified, although twenty-eight log barracks were constructed there to house the Queen's Rangers during the winter of 1792-93. A small military detachment was stationed at Queenston thereafter.[26] The old storehouse on the east bank was so quickly forgotten that, when Lieutenant Governor Simcoe crossed the river in 1792, he went to see what he assumed were "the remains of the french Fort." Only a ferry house remained on the New York side by 1793.[27]

The next stop on the portage was its "Upper Landing." This, too, had been located on the American side of the river. The fort at the Upper Landing, which had never been anything more than "an inconsiderable stockade intended merely for the protection of stores & merchandize" and a small garrison, had been known as Fort Schlosser since 1763.[28] Although the usefulness of Fort Schlosser ended with the relocation of the portage after 1790-91, its buildings were valuable enough that a detachment from Fort Niagara was stationed there at least as late as the autumn of 1793.[29] By 1794 Fort Schlosser was no longer in use.

Fort Schlosser's replacement was an equally inconsiderable stockade established two hundred yards up Chippawa Creek in 1791. Like its predecessor on the opposite shore, it was occupied by a subaltern's detach-

When Surgeon Edward Walsh painted this view of Fort Erie in April 1804 the post was little more than a poorly defended cluster of buildings graced by a Union flag. The appearance of the place had changed little in the decade since 1794. (Royal Ontario Museum, Toronto, 952.218)

ment from the main garrison at Fort Niagara. Fort Chippawa provided a defensible storehouse where goods could be transferred to boats in the sheltered creek. The post also guarded the river crossing of the portage road which continued on to Lake Erie. Fort Chippawa was not an impressive structure. In 1796 Isaac Weld noted that it occupied about a square rod of ground and consisted of "a small block house, inclosed by a stockade of cedar posts about twelve feet high, which is merely sufficient to defend the garrison against musket shot."[30]

Fort Erie, situated on the shore of its namesake, was the southern terminus of the portage and the last of Niagara's posts. Established in 1764, Fort Erie was a collection of barracks and storehouses surrounded, in its original form, by "four small Bastions, two of bad mason[ry] work washed by the Lake, and two on the land side stockaded." From the time of its construction, however, Fort Erie had suffered from being "very improperly placed ... [and] exposed to injury from the Lake in Southerly and Westerly winds" which, with storm-driven ice, badly damaged the post on several occasions. By 1790 Fort Erie was "quite in ruin."[31] It became ever more dilapidated and difficult to maintain. During 1792-96 the place was hardly recognizable as a fort, more resembling a poor collection of buildings with the water-side fortifications scoured away by the lake. Fort Erie was relocated to higher ground after 1805.[32]

NIAGARA'S GARRISONS

Niagara's motley collection of fortifications was guarded by regular soldiers of the British army. At the heart of the garrison, throughout most of the capital period, were the men of the 5th Regiment of Foot and a small detachment of the Royal Regiment of Artillery. They were reinforced, soon after Simcoe's arrival, by the Queen's Rangers, a regiment raised especially for service in Upper Canada. The Queen's Rangers, either complete or in detachments, spent extended periods of time at Newark and Queenston, but the corps was also detached for other duties including its best-known service of establishing the garrison at York in 1793. The regulars of the 5th Regiment, Royal Artillery, and Queen's Rangers were supported by the sailors of the Provincial Marine and supplemented, in times of crisis, by the Upper Canada militia. Also of considerable importance to the security of the colony was the military potential of native American warriors (in the Niagara region principally from the Six Nations of the Iroquois). Niagara's garrison included a small group of officers of the British Indian Department to provide liaison with the Iroquois.

The 5th Regiment of Foot

Regular soldiers had always formed the backbone of the defence of Canada. Prior to the American revolution, it had been common practice to station a single ten-company regiment of foot (infantry) at the Great Lakes posts. This body of fewer than five hundred men (at full strength) was distributed in the five main posts between Oswegatchie and Michilimackinac. The threats posed by the American war of 1775-83, however, required augmented forces. By 1783 the better part of five regular and provincial regiments were defending the Oswegatchie-Michilimackinac line. Three regiments were usually assigned to the Great Lakes after 1786. One watched the west from Detroit and Michilimackinac. Another was concentrated at Niagara. The third garrisoned Oswego, Kingston, and posts along the upper St Lawrence. Regiments were usually rotated every two years.[33]

At the beginning of the capital period, Niagara was garrisoned by the 26th Regiment of Foot. The 26th had arrived at Niagara in August 1790 with eight and one-half of its companies assigned to Fort Niagara and detachments at forts Schlosser and Erie. The 26th was due for rotation in 1792. Relief came in June when the 5th Regiment of Foot, which had been at Detroit and Michilimackinac since 1790, was replaced by the 24th and moved to Niagara. The 5th would remain at Niagara for four years rather than the usual two. Although the regiment was to have been relieved and transferred to the Richelieu valley in 1794, the unsettled situation made the move inopportune. The 5th would thus defend Simcoe's centre while the 24th covered the exposed Detroit front. Detachments of the 2nd Battalion, 60th or Royal American Regiment held Oswego and the eastern posts.[34]

Major John Smith's regulars of the 5th, although highly professional, provided a thin shield for the Niagara settlements. In September 1793, for example, the 5th numbered only 17 officers and 265 enlisted men in Fort Niagara. A further 4 officers and 81 men were at forts Erie, Schlosser, and Chippawa, for a total of 21 officers and 346 men, roughly three-quarters of the regiment's authorized strength. These numbers were typical throughout the period.[35]

The ten companies of the 5th Regiment were divided between eight "battalion" or "centre" companies and two "flank" companies, the grenadiers and light infantry. Each was led by three officers, usually a captain, lieutenant, and ensign, with a complement of non-commissioned officers and a single drummer to provide the necessary signals in garrison or on the battlefield.

The dress of the 5th Regiment of Foot was typical of regiments of the British army. The men received uniform clothing each year, the cost of which was withheld from their pay. Regimental distinctions, such as the colour of the facings (collars, lapels, and cuffs) of the red coats, had been specified by a royal warrant in 1768. The facing colour of the 5th Regiment was "gosling" green. Buttonholes were trimmed with a white regimental lace containing two red stripes applied in "bastion" shape. Pewter buttons of the enlisted men excavated at Fort Niagara bear an Arabic "5" within a broken or "French" circle. This was a new pattern; buttons found at Fort Michilimackinac, where the regiment was stationed in 1790-92, are of a different design, incorporating a Roman "V" within a laurel wreath. White woolen small clothes (waistcoats and breeches) and knee-length black woolen gaiters completed the clothing. Battalion company men wore the felt "cocked" hat while light infantrymen had leather caps and grenadiers

Officer (left) and private soldier of a battalion company of the 5th Regiment of Foot from paintings done by Edward Dayes in 1789. Both men sport the white feather commemorating a victory over the French in 1778, and the officer wears the unlaced coat common until at least 1793. His rank is otherwise indicated by the epaulette on his right shoulder, the gorget at his throat, a sash, and a sword. (Metropolitan Toronto Library, John Ross Robertson Collection, T17117))

and drummers sported distinctive bearskins.[36] The latter apparently also had cocked hats since the grenadiers and drummers who stood guard at the Upper Canada council chamber in May 1794 were specifically ordered to wear their caps.[37] Headgear was trimmed with a white feather commemorating a 1778 victory over the French on the West Indian island of St Lucia.[38]

Drawings of officers and men of the 5th made about 1789 before their departure for Canada give a good sense of their appearance.[39] Major Smith's regimental orderly book provides further information about alterations made for Niagara's variable climate. Each June, the men were allowed to don linen waistcoats with linen trousers and short gaiters in place of the woolen breeches and long gaiters worn during cooler weather.[40] Warmer dress was provided for the Canadian winter. By 1 December each year the men were to wear their long black woolen leggings, and blanket coats were permitted for the guard. Fur caps were worn, except on parade, and the felt hats would not reappear for regular duty until spring.[41] Comfortable red woolen jackets were made for the men from old coats for wear in the barracks, on fatigues, aboard the naval vessels, or at artillery practice in order to "save their Coats."[42]

Officers dressed in similar though finer fashion. Scarlet fabric for coats and silver-plated rather than pewter buttons were among the many visual

Private soldier of a battalion company of the 5th Regiment of Foot, c. 1792. Drawing by Joe Lee. (Old Fort Niagara Association)

distinctions that marked the difference in rank between officers and men. Officers' "appointments" of either gold or silver were specified for each regiment, with the latter colour assigned to the 5th. This meant that buttons,

Buttons of the 5th Regiment of Foot as drawn by H.G. Parkyn for Shoulder Belt Plates and Buttons. Both styles have been excavated at Old Fort Niagara. The design incorporating a Roman numeral is associated with officers' buttons, while the Arabic number within a broken circle or "French scroll" is found only on the pewter buttons of enlisted men.

hat and coat lace, gorgets, belt plates, and sword hilts were of that metal.[43] Officers' buttons excavated at Fort Niagara are silver-plated copper. Interestingly, all bear the older style Roman "V" and laurel-wreath pattern.

If the design of the officers' buttons did not change, the manner of treating the buttonholes did rather drastically while the regiment was at Niagara. As early as 1768, officers of the 5th Regiment had worn unlaced

Officer, 5th Regiment of Foot, 1793, in the properly laced coat ordered to be worn for all occasions in 1793. Painting by J.C.H. Forster. (Toronto Historical Board)

coats, that is, the buttonholes were left plain rather than being trimmed with silver lace. In November 1793, however, Major Smith conveyed to his officers an order from King George III that they were to wear only laced coats. There was clearly some reluctance to make the change, probably because of regimental tradition, for the order was repeated in December and all officers were to be properly dressed by 23 April 1794.[44]

The 5th Regiment was also entitled to a number of special distinctions. As one of the "Six Old Corps," it was allowed to display certain "Devices and Badges" on drums, colours, and other parts of the uniform. The centre of the king's colour and three corners of the gosling green regimental colour, both of which were carried at Niagara, were emblazoned with a representation of "St. George killing the dragon." The same device was painted on the drums and the bells of arms (small tents to shelter muskets) and included, along with the king's crest, on the grenadier caps.[45] The caps of the light infantry company were almost certainly treated in similar fashion.

The Royal Regiment of Artillery

The second and much smaller component of the regular Niagara garrison was a detachment of the Royal Regiment of Artillery. These men were the specialists of the army, responsible for the ammunition and for maintaining and serving the garrison artillery. The number of cannon provided for Fort Niagara was substantial. As a regular fortification, it might be expected to face enemy guns during a siege. In such a case, a successful defence would rest on the quality of the artillery. Fort Niagara was well armed with thirty-six guns, one howitzer, and five mortars in 1794. These ranged in calibre from eighteen-pounders down to light brass three-pounders for use in the field.[46]

With more than forty cannon in Fort Niagara, the number of men required to serve them effectively would be considerable. Niagara's artillery detachment of the early 1790s was large, at least by the standards of the 1760s and 1770s. In September 1792 it numbered one drummer and thirty enlisted men under Captain Seward's command. One year later his detachment had been augmented by three gunners.[47] This was still insufficient to man properly the artillery or provide detachments for field service, so it was common practice at Niagara as elsewhere for the gunners to train infantry to assist them. Soldiers of the 5th Regiment and picked men of the militia were so instructed during the turbulent year of 1794.[48]

The specialized enlisted men of the Royal Regiment of Artillery were distinctively dressed in blue coats. These were faced in red and trimmed with yellow lace around the buttonholes. Their brass buttons, bearing three

Officer and soldier of the Royal Regiment of Artillery, from contemporary paintings of c.1789. (National Army Museum, London)

Gunner of the Royal Regiment of Artillery, 1793. Brass buttons, such as that shown on the left, have been excavated at Old Fort Niagara. Painting by J.C.H. Forster. (Toronto Historical Board)

cannon and three cannonballs within a shield, have been recovered at Fort Niagara and other military sites on the Great Lakes. White small clothes, tall black gaiters, and black cocked hats completed the uniform. Like his counterparts in the 5th Regiment, Captain Seward was more opulently dressed in a finer uniform of the same colours with gold buttons, lace, epaulettes, and sword.[49]

The Queen's Rangers

The Niagara garrison was substantially augmented in 1792 by a new and specialized military unit intended to assist in both the defence and the development of Upper Canada. This corps, known as the "Queen's Rangers," was the creation of Lieutenant Governor Simcoe and recalled his distinguished service at the head of a unit of the same name during the 1775-83 war.

The Queen's Rangers was raised during 1791 with authorization for its formation coming soon after Simcoe's appointment to the lieutenant governorship. The Rangers, in addition to their military duties, were to assist in

Captain David Shank of the Queen's Rangers (d. 1831), oil by Thomas Beach, painted about 1800 when he was lieutenant-colonel of the regiment. The Queen's Rangers were disbanded in 1802. (Royal Ontario Museum, Toronto, 948.197.4)

the creation of an infrastructure for Upper Canada. The corps was to assist in "the making of Roads of communication between the different Parts of the Province, in building of Bridges, erecting of Barracks, clearing of Lands, navigating of Craft, and in short, on any Military or Civil Service which may occur." Enlistments were encouraged by the promise of land at the end of each man's service, and the eventual settling of these trained soldiers in Upper Canada was expected to improve the quality of the miltia.[50]

The size and composition of this unique military unit differed greatly from that of the regular regiments of the British line. The Queen's Rangers was organized into two large companies, each of six officers, twelve non-commissioned officers, one drummer, and 194 privates. The addition of six staff gave an authorized strength of 432 officers and men.[51] When the Queen's Rangers reported a total of 368 officers and men at York (Toronto) in September 1793, it was, by North American standards, a strong unit in a land where it was always difficult to keep a corps at full strength.[52]

Although the Queen's Rangers was raised in England, many of its officers had served in the Thirten Colonies with Simcoe's former provincial corps.[53] The first elements reached Quebec late in May 1792 and immediately moved to Niagara. Upon Simcoe's arrival there on 26 July, he found the Rangers encamped on the west side of the river, about one-half mile behind Navy Hall.[54] The Queen's Rangers would not be quartered in Fort Niagara, but would usually be kept for duty on the Canadian side of the river. The men constructed huts at the Lower Landing, by this time known as Queenston, and spent the winter of 1792-93 in that cantonment.[55]

Simcoe's plan to establish a more secure military and naval base on Lake Ontario resulted in the transfer of the Queen's Rangers from Niagara during 1793. They occupied Toronto, renaming it York, where the unit spent the following winter.[56] However, the crisis of 1794 caused part of the corps to be recalled to Niagara where, by early June, one hundred men were repairing Navy Hall and Fort Niagara. The detachment was ordered back to York at the beginning of August. Two weeks later, the impending crisis created by Wayne's march into the Indian country caused Simcoe to order Ranger Captain David Shank to return "without delay to Niagara Fort with every man and officer you can muster, leaving Quarter Master and your convalescents or disabled men to take care of the Barracks, Stores and Baggage."[57]

Detachments of the Queen's Rangers would serve at Fort Miami and Detroit during 1794-95. Although the corps was useful in complementing the red-coated regulars of the 5th and 24th Foot, Simcoe did not consider it to be on a proper war establishment since it lacked the number and proportion of officers necessary to perform well as a military unit. He

William Jarvis (1756-1817),painted in the distinctive uniform of the Queen's Rangers. Jarvis's son, Samuel, is dressed in imitation of his father. (Royal Ontario Museum, Toronto, 981.791)

Watercolouar by Capt. Murray of a light infantryman and hussar of the Queen's Rangers, 1780. When the new Queen's Rangers were authorized in 1791, the men were to dress in a uniform similar to that of the earlier corps. The new regiment was composed only of foot soldiers. (Metropolitan Toronto Library, John Ross Robertson Collection, T30757)

pointed out that the intent of the original organization of the Rangers had been "obtaining an efficient Number of private Soldiers," and he suggested an augmentation of officers to make it more effective as a fighting force. This was not done.[58]

The designation of Simcoe's 1791 regiment as the Queen's Rangers suggested a connection, at least of tradition, with his distinguished provincial regiment. In keeping with this fact, and suggestive of the designation "Rangers," the corps was provided with uniforms of green rather than the red of regular infantry. The king authorized the men to be "clothed in green, with a blue cuff, and collar, bordered with white lace." Uniform orders noted that it

Officer of the Queen's Rangers, 1793. The officers' pattern swordbelt plate is shown at upper left. The coat, however, is not shown laced in the peculiar "tear drop" style seen in contemporary officers' portraits. Painting by J.C.H. Forster. (Toronto Historical Board)

should also be "of the same pattern as was worn by the late Corps of Queens Rangers which Colonel Simcoe commanded during the last war." Headgear for the men, and perhaps officers when in the field, was a brimless cap, decorated with the crescent badge used by the earlier corps during the American revolution.[59] Portraits and artifacts confirm that officers' appointments were silver and that they wore cocked hats for dress occasions.[60]

The Provincial Marine

Lieutenant Governor Simcoe had one more "regular" military unit, and it greatly facilitated his efforts to protect Upper Canada. The southern boundary of the province was formed by lakes Ontario and Erie, and respectable squadrons of armed naval vessels cruised both bodies of water. In addition to giving absolute naval command of the lakes, they provided convenient and rapid transportation for British troops, artillery, and supplies. Simcoe and his officers had the advantage of interior lines of communication (by water) if the Americans should make an attempt on Upper Canada. Reinforcements were moved speedily from Niagara to Detroit during the summer of 1794. A similar shifting of troops by the Americans would have meant fatiguing overland marches that would have taken an entire season to accomplish.

Simcoe's sailors were not men of the Royal Navy, although in their dress and equipment they would have been practically indistinguishable from salt-water sailors. The "Provincial Marine" had grown out of the former "Naval Department" which the British had maintained on the American lakes since the close of the Seven Years' War. The Naval Department was under the control of the commander-in-chief in North America until 1775 and, thereafter, the governor of Canada. Ships and men were provided out of army commissariat expenses although, during wartime, there was nominal supervision by the Royal Navy through the admiral assigned to the Quebec station. Officers and men were hired by the department. The former were either half-pay army officers or merchant captains while the latter were engaged for service at Quebec and other seaports. In time of war, "marines" were drawn from the military garrisons and assigned to the vessels, a duty that was well known to the men of the 5th

Seaman, Provincial Marine. Sailor dress of the late eighteenth century was almost universal in appearance, regardless of whether the man served aboard a vessel of the Provincial Marine, Royal Navy, or merchant marine. Drawing by Joe Lee. (Old Fort Niagara Association)

Regiment of Foot. The change to the term "Provincial Marine" seems to have occurred about the time of the establishment of the provinces of Upper and Lower Canada.[61]

Upper Canada was actually defended by two squadrons physically separated by the great falls of Niagara. The upper lakes (Erie, Huron, and Michigan) were commanded by "Commodore" Alexander Grant, a former Highland officer of the Seven Years' War who would hold his post well into the coming century. From his headquarters at Detroit, Grant had responsibility for the well-armed snows *Chippewa* and *Ottawa*, the old schooner *Dunmore*, the sloop *Felicity*, and several small gunboats. His squadron was augmented by the sloop *Francis* and the schooner *Maria* in 1794-95.[62] Grant's vessels shuttled between Fort Erie and Detroit and would have been the first line of naval defence had Wayne pushed on to Lake Erie in 1794.

Although Grant's vessels called frequently at the upper end of the Niagara portage, it was "Commodore" David Betton (or Beaton) who was most familiar to the officers and men of Fort Niagara. He commanded the Lake Ontario vessels, the snow *Onondaga*, the sloops *Caldwell* and *Mississauga*, and several small gunboats. Betton's bases were at Kingston and Navy Hall, and the security of his vessels was one justification for the establishment of the new garrison of York in 1793.[63]

Betton's warships would not have been impressive on salt water. In size, sailing rig, and appearance, they were much like the small merchant vessels and privateer warships familiar to the Atlantic seaboard. The largest were of no more than one hundred tons and of less than one hundred feet in length. "Snows" were two-masted square-riggers, similar in appearance to brigs, while the two-masted schooners and single-masted sloops were popular fore-and-aft rigs. The largest of the vessels carried only six pounder guns, usually no more than six to a side. The gunboats were armed with a single heavy cannon of twelve or eighteen-pound calibre, but they were useful only in confined waters.[64] Many of the vessels were creaky veterans of the American revolution — *Caldwell*, for example, had been launched in 1775.[65]

Nor did Betton's sailors impress Mrs Simcoe. On her way from Kingston to Niagara in 1792 aboard the commodore's flagship, *Onondaga*, she noted that the "men who navigate the Ships on this Lake have little nautical knowledge & never keep a log book."[66] Perhaps her judgment was coloured by the fact that the vessel nearly ran aground, a hazard common to lake navigation. All other sources indicate that the vessels and men of the Provincial Marine functioned well enough to be a major asset to Lieutenant Governor Simcoe's military force.

The Militia

The last body of conventional troops available for the defence of Niagara was composed of the inhabitants themselves. The tradition of militia service was strong in North America. Many of Niagara's first settlers had been enrolled in the militia of the former Thirteen Colonies. They later joined loyalist military units, particularly Butler's Rangers which was disbanded at Niagara in 1784. These men were given lands in the Niagara peninsula.

Legal military responsibilities continued after the area had been incorporated into the District of Nassau. All able-bodied men between the ages of eighteen and sixty were enrolled for service. In May 1791, on the eve of the formation of Upper Canada, the Nassau militia was organized into three battalions with a strength of 779 men and 56 officers. Lieutenant-Colonel John Butler noted, however, that only 155 could be turned out for service without neglecting agriculture.[67]

This organization was carried over when Nassau became the county of Lincoln in the province of Upper Canada. The number of men enrolled for duty had not changed significantly when the three Lincoln County battalions were counted in June 1793. Like the earlier Nassau report, this included men up to the age of sixty.[68] A general return of militia in the enlarged Home District (with Lincoln as its sole county), taken during the summer of 1794, recorded a force of more than nine hundred men, all of them fifty years of age or younger, enrolled into four battalions.[69]

The Upper Canada militia was called upon by Lieutenant Governor Simcoe during August 1794. Major Ralfe Clench, a veteran officer of both the 8th (King's) Regiment of Foot and Butler's Rangers, commanded ten officers and 210 men called out of the Home District. They were quartered in the old barracks of Butler's Rangers and issued arms, accoutrements, and ammunition from Fort Niagara. Two three-pounder cannon were sent across the river to the militia detachment in September, and a gunner of the Royal Regiment of Artillery was assigned to drill the men daily. The detachment remained on duty until dismissed and ordered to return its small arms and cannon on 20 October.[70]

Simcoe's call for a significant proportion of the Upper Canada militia was in response to Wayne's movement against the Indians. At the conclusion of the crisis (and near harvest time), the lieutenant governor dismissed the men who had answered his call.[71] How effective they would have been had the province exploded into war? Simcoe reported at the end of 1794 that the "British Militia to a Man, on the first appearance of Hostilities have avowed the most determined Loyalty." He noted, however, that they were best suited for offensive warfare and would have been "impotent" in the fortifications. Simcoe's recommendations for mobile use of the militia was reminiscent of the earlier role of Butler's Rangers, and, indeed, many of his militia were veterans of that unit.[72] Although he did not suffer under the same apprehensions of disloyalty that would plague Isaac Brock nearly two decades later, Simcoe never considered the militia an effective substitute for regular troops in the defence of the province, noting that: "The Militia, unless exercised and in part called out, cannot be reckoned upon as an efficient strength. There is an universal appearance of loyalty among the British inhabitants, but it does not become me to place any military reliance on such assistance unless it shall actually be proved; nor would it be wise to make this probation, but under the assemblage of a competent body of Troops."[73] For Lieutenant Governor Simcoe, the best way of defending Upper Canada was to have an adequate number of regulars at his disposal.

The militia were not provided with uniforms. They were expected, instead, to appear for duty in their own clothing and, as at Niagara in 1794, receive arms and accoutrements from government stores. With many veterans of former loyalist corps in the Lincoln militia, it seems likely that some uniforms of those regiments were in evidence. Although officers of the Nassau militia probably had uniforms before 1791 (a copper button inscribed "NASSAU * BRITISH * MILITIA" has been recovered at Old Fort Niagara), no uniform was established for the militia of Upper Canada until the summer of 1794. In July, responding to requests of militia officers for distinctive dress, Simcoe prescribed "a scarlet coat, plain gilt metal buttons, with blue facings, a white waistcoat, with trousers, linen or woolen, or breeches and leggins." Officers on half pay were allowed to wear the uniforms of "their respective Corps, which were so honorably distinguished during the course of the late War."[74]

The Indian Department

The British and Canadian troops at Niagara possessed one last and most helpful advantage over their potential adversaries. Since the time of the American revolution, the British had been able to rely on the support of the native American peoples of the Great Lakes. Indeed, it was the continuing war between the United States and the Ohio tribes that almost dragged the new province into war. Detroit was, however, the main post of communication with the Indian nations of the west. The native people resorting to Niagara were of the Six Nations of the Iroquois who, although not then at war, were distinctly hostile to the Americans. The Iroquois had demonstrated their prowess during the 1775-83 conflict, and after it ended they continued to provide a reserve of well-trained frontier fighters. Fort Niagara had been the most important point of contact between British officials and the Six Nations since 1759. The post was a depot from which Britain's Indian allies could be supplied with both guns and domestic goods, a role that expanded greatly during the American revolution. That conflict, however, also resulted in tremendous population displacement for the Iroquois. Driven westward by American pressure, they clustered near the posts at Niagara and established a number of new villages in the area, the largest on Buffalo Creek (Buffalo) and near the old Lower Landing. With the end of the war the Six Nations found their traditional homelands ceded by British negotiators of the 1783 peace treaty. During the 1790s many moved to lands provided by the crown in Upper Canada, largely along the Grand River, while others made their peace with the Americans and settled on reserves in western New York.[75]

Assigned to the Niagara garrison throughout the British occupation were a small number of officers of the Indian Department. Their duties were to deal with the Iroquois, distribute presents and supplies, encourage their allegiance to Britain, and advise the military commandant in his contacts with them as King George's official representative. Indian Department officers had been commissioned since the 1750s, and they played an important role in the frontier

An Indian conference at Sandusky, Ohio, in 1793. Those held at Fort Niagara and Buffalo Creek would have presented similar scenes. The group includes two British officers (extreme left and centre). Behind the second British officer is a Queen's Ranger in the regiment's distinctive cap with crescent badge. Watercolour by Lewis Foy. (Montreal Museum of Fine Arts)

military fighting of the American revolution. The officers from Niagara and Detroit did much to keep the Six Nations in the field and in the loyal service of King George.[76]

The activities of Niagara's Indian Department officers were centred in a cluster of storehouses, residences, and a council house situated on the low land between Fort Niagara and the river. Responsible for the Indian Department post from 1792 until his death on 14 May 1796 was Colonel John Butler, as experienced a frontier officer as could be found. A veteran of the Seven Years' War and the American revolution, Butler's service had been entirely with the Six Nations or irregular colonial troops, such as his own "Butler's Rangers," which fought alongside them. Butler and his officers regularly distributed presents and supplies and held councils with the Six Nations and other native visitors to Niagara. Many of the meetings were held at the Buffalo Creek village. Another duty of the Indian Department officers was to monitor the activities of United States Indian negotiators who also visited Buffalo Creek on several occasions attempting to resolve the continuing unrest on the western frontier.[77]

Had war come, and had the Iroquois once again joined in a general conflict against the Americans, the officers of the Indian Department would have accompanied them in the field. The issue was decided elsewhere, however. The defeat of the Ohio tribes at Fallen Timbers in 1794 and their conclusion of a treaty of peace with the Americans the following year meant that Niagara's native soldiers would not be called into action.

MILITARY LIFE

The regular soldiers of Niagara's garrisons were men from the British Isles (and Canada) who had decided to adopt the life of a soldier. They came from a variety of backgrounds, and officers and men were separated by a wide gulf of social status. The conditions of service for enlisted men of the time were neatly summarized in a notice that appeared in Newark's *Upper Canada Gazette* during the summer of 1794:

ADVERTISEMENT FOR RECRUITS.

His Majesty's Garrison of Niagara.

TEN GUINEAS BOUNTY Money will be given to all Gentlemen Volunteers, who are willing to enlist themselves in His Majesty's 5th Regiment of Foot now in the Garrison of Niagara on being approved of at the Head Quarters of the Regiment, they will be Clothed, accoutred, victualled and paid agreeable to His Majesty's Regulations.

Active men such as are fit for Service, not less than 5 feet 5 inches high, between 16 & 40 years of age, will receive every encouragement at the Garrison, at Forts Erie and Chippawa, at Queenstown Landing and at the Drum Head.

GOD SAVE THE KING.

An advertisement for the Queen's Rangers gave nearly identical details except that men of one-half inch less stature would be accepted.[78]

The recruit of the 1790s embarked upon a life that, in spite of its harshness, provided the benefits of regular pay, food, clothing, and shelter. This was more than could be said for the urban and rural poor of late-eighteenth-century Britain, the class that provided the bulk of men for the army. Although much of a soldier's pay was withheld for his necessaries, he was otherwise well cared for. Basic rations of salt pork, flour, peas, rice, and butter were plentifully supplemented at Niagara by garden produce and fish. Mrs Simcoe noted that huge quantities of sturgeon and whitefish were netted by soldiers of the 5th Regiment.[79]

The soldiers were housed in wooden barracks in Fort Niagara or blockhouses at the smaller posts. They were provided with furniture, blankets, and other necessities. Their daily routine was unavoidedly monotonous from morning reveille until "tapto," played at 9:00 p.m. in the summer. The time was filled with guard duty, infantry and artillery drills, and fatigues ranging from cutting firewood to working on the fortifications. For the latter duty the men at least received additional pay.[80] There was little time for leisure, although the birthdays of both Queen Charlotte (18 January) and King George III (4 June) were celebrated. The soldiers had access to a canteen, and spirits were available, until 1794, from merchants in "the bottom" below the fort. After that date the soldiers might, with a pass, cross the river to Newark as long as they did not appear "undressed and dirty." All of these diversions involved the consumption of alcohol, and drunkenness was a persistent affliction among the soldiers and a frequent case for punishment.[81]

Brutal discipline was a fact of life. "His Majesty's Regulations" provided a framework within which a man's conduct was judged. Those who strayed were punished severely, usually with the lash. More draconian measures were taken during wartime. On 29 October 1793 (war with France was underway) Private Charles Grisler of the 5th Regiment was marched outside the walls of Fort Niagara. There, in front of the entire garrison, including even the sick from the hospital, he was shot to death for desertion by six of his comrades who had been selected by lot.[82]

Officers came from a very different stratum of society. Often the younger sons of the gentry, most officers still obtained their commissions by purchase.[83] They formed the upper level of society at Niagara, and Mrs Simcoe's diary indicates how frequently she and the lieutenant governor socialized with them. Dinners, levees, teas, official visits, and celebrations, such as that held on 1 September 1794 in honour of Lord Howe's naval victory of the "Glorious 1st of June," enlivened days that were little more varied than those of the men.[84] Most officers were caught in the routine of guard, drill, and the petty administration of companies. A few came close to military action when they were ordered to Fort Miami in 1794. Others drew duties away from the garrison, primarily recruiting. Lieutenant David William Smith of the 5th kept busy as acting deputy surveyor general of Upper Canada. Lieutenant Roger Hale Sheaffe was sent to warn off encroaching American settlers. Others filled their spare time by hunting or, in the case of Lieutenant Henry Darling, gathering and preserving bird specimens.[85]

Women were also a part of Niagara's military society. A number of officers' wives were present during the service of the 5th Regiment. Like their husbands, the wives of Major John Smith, Lieutenant David William Smith, and Lieutenant John M.R.D. Mason formed the upper crust of local society. Dinners, teas, and boating excursions were a regular part of their lives as were more formal occasions such as the christening of the junior Mrs Smith's son on 5 July 1794.[86] Many of the soldiers also had wives at Niagara. Army regulations permitted six wives per company. These wives, who were provided with rations, laundered for the soldiers. Unattached women were strictly regulated, particularly when, as in 1793, it was feared that they might bring any "malignant disorder" into the garrison.[87]

THE MILITARY AND THE COMMUNITY

The relationship between Niagara's military and civilian populations was more than just social, and the army could not exist within a vacuum in a settlement as isolated as the Niagara of 1792-96. The presence of several hundred soldiers and their officers presented economic opportunities as well as occasional civil annoyances for the farmers, merchants, and craftsmen of the developing area.

Prior to the American revolution, the British garrison of Fort Niagara had formed the core of the community. The few civilians at the post were either involved in the Indian trade or were licensed sutlers to the troops. There were no farmers aside from the soldiers themselves, who maintained garden plots to supplement their rations. Staple foods were shipped directly from England.[88] This situation changed dramatically during the American revolution. The difficulties of supplying the posts of the Great Lakes had been apparent since the onset of British occupation, and when the war brought larger garrisons, refugee loyalists, and hordes of Indians — all needing to be fed — the system nearly collapsed.

Finding a solution to the chronic supply problem of the Great Lakes posts was one of the preoccupations of General Frederick Haldimand, governor of Quebec from 1778 until 1784. Haldimand encouraged the military garrisons to grow as much food as possible, but he realized that only a civilian agricultural community could provide the necessary quantities of produce. Detroit was the one settlement capable of producing large amounts of food, and its *Canadien* farmers were unable to generate the necessary surplus. Several years before the conclusion of the war, therefore, Haldimand began encouraging the establishment of farms at Niagara by loyalist refugees and soldiers.

The post-war settlement at Niagara was intended largely to relieve the problems of provisioning the post. With the end of the American revolution and the disbanding of Butler's Rangers came a great increase in the number of farms. Although the settlement was unable to produce a significant amount of food for the soldiers until 1786, from that time until 1800 provisioning of the garrison provided the basis of the local agrarian economy and helped enrich merchants such as Robert Hamilton.[89] In 1795 alone the garrison purchased 283,748 pounds of flour, most of it provided by five Niagara merchants.[90]

Another local business opportunity provided by the garrison was as old as the military use of Niagara. The original reason for the fortifications had been the protection of the portage around Niagara Falls. The relocation of the portage road from the east to the west bank of the river in 1790-91 did

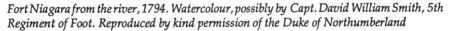

Fort Niagara from the river, 1794. Watercolour, possibly by Capt. David William Smith, 5th Regiment of Foot. Reproduced by kind permission of the Duke of Northumberland

not diminish its importance. Operation of the portage had been in the hands of civilian contractors since the mid-1760s, and the carriage of goods, many of them government property, provided a substantial income for the contractor and jobs for his employees. Much of the actual portaging was done by local farmers with their teams and wagons, a further boost to the local economy.[91]

Soldiers, from time immemorial, have presented yet another traditional business opportunity to the civilian community outside the garrison precincts. The men of the 5th Regiment contributed to the prosperity of a number of taverns, although until the summer of 1794 these were concentrated in the "Bottom" between Fort Niagara and the river. It appears that when the tavern keepers were ordered to evacuate that area in the summer of 1794 they moved to the opposite shore. In 1796 Isaac Weld noted the operation of at least four taverns in the village of Newark.[92] The relocation of these vital establishments soon elicited the first orders regarding the need for passes for the soldiers to cross the river and rules for their appearance and behaviour.[93]

Official sources are relatively silent on any friction between off-duty soldiers and the civilian populace. The orderly book of the 5th Regiment contains no records of courts martial for disruptive conduct by men relaxing in Newark, although it is difficult to believe that such incidents did not occur. Fishing, however, was a source of friction. The rich bounty of the Niagara River was being exploited by more and more people, and in 1795 the soldiers had to be ordered to fish only on Mondays, Wednesdays, and Fridays in order to "avoid clashes with the inhabitants."[94]

For the most part, however, the relationship between the military and civilian communities at Niagara seem to have been more harmonious than most such unions. Perhaps the military experience of many of the settlers and the commonly perceived threat of the Americans provided additional reasons for tolerance.

THE AMERICANS ARRIVE

The men of the 5th Regiment, Royal Artillery, Queen's Rangers, Provincial Marine, Lincoln militia, and Indian Department responded with enthusiasm to the orders of Lieutenant Governor Simcoe during the crisis of 1794. They would likely have given a good account of themselves had war begun. The danger soon passed, however, and Jay's Treaty provided a diplomatic solution. By 1 June 1796, American forces were to be in possession of Niagara and the other posts.

This official confirmation of the 1783 boundary meant that the British garrison of Fort Niagara would soon be in need of a home. Newark was the obvious location since the strategic importance of the Niagara River was not diminished by its new role as an international boundary. Thought had been given to the eventual need for relocated fortifications since the 1780s, and the high ground behind Navy Hall was under consideration as early as 1789. The Simcoes and the Queen's Rangers had camped there in 1792, and the commanding height of that land over Fort Niagara partially compensated for its lack of control of the river's mouth.[95]

Yet it was not until 1795 that the British decided to construct block-houses and storehouses on the west bank to accommodate the regular garrison. Construction was delayed until the end of May 1796, perilously close to the deadline for the surrender of Fort Niagara. The initial phase included the large "central" blockhouse which served as both storehouse and quarters, a stone powder magazine (which still stands), and a number of smaller structures. Sometime during 1796 the new post was named Fort George in honour of the king. Construction of additional blockhouses, officers' quarters, and other buildings would continue for the rest of the decade. The scattered buildings were enclosed by a stockade and earthen bastions in 1799, giving Fort George its familiar extended hexagon form.[96]

Jay's Treaty permitted a drastic reduction in the size of the military force that had been assigned to the posts since 1786. In November 1795 Lord Dorchester informed Simcoe of his intention to recall the 5th, 24th, and 2/60th regiments, leaving only the Queen's Rangers and a detachment of artillery in Upper Canada.[97] Preparations for transferring the forts began that winter. April saw the anticipated orders to send the redcoats to Lower Canada and to assign detachments of the Queen's Rangers to the Detroit and Niagara frontiers.[98] On 1 June the officers commanding "the Forts at Ontario, Niagara, Miamis, Detroit and Michilimackinac" were ordered to evacuate their posts "completely, with all convenient speed, taking care to prevent all disorders." Once the king's stores and artillery had been removed, caretaker detachments were to await the arrival of the Americans. A captain, two subalterns, and twenty men were to watch over Fort Niagara until the new owners arrived.[99]

The deadline came ahead of American troops, however. Two months later, the Union flag still flew above Fort Niagara. Nor had the last of the 5th Regiment departed. One captain, two lieutenants, two sergeants, two drummers, and sixty-six rank and file still guarded the old walls. One artillery officer and eleven men were also present while a small detachment of the Queen's Rangers were stationed in Newark.[100] It was not until 5 August that United States Army Captain James Bruff, accompanied by Senator Henry Glen and fifty soldiers, took passage from Oswego aboard a chartered British merchant vessel. They arrived five days later.[101] The fort had been left in the charge of Captain Roger Hale Sheaffe of the 5th Regiment who had orders to inspect the post with the American officer, sign a duplicate statement certifying its condition, and then withdraw to the opposite shore.[102]

American troops entered Fort Niagara at sunset on 10 August. Sheaffe immediately led his men to their boats, leaving only a sergeant to point out obligingly the sentry posts to his American counterpart. The United States colours were displayed the following morning, and Sheaffe returned soon after to complete the transfer. One American officer noted that the British captain was "very polite and attentive" in his duties. Bruff reported also that Sheaffe, in fulfilling his orders, "was so polite as to walk around the works, and give me every information necessary for a relieving officer."[103]

The 5th Regiment returned to Quebec. In 1797 its private soldiers were drafted to other units in Canada, and the officers and non-commissioned officers sailed for England to rebuild the regiment.[104] During the summer of 1796 the Queen's Rangers were scattered among the several small posts between York and the new fort on St Joseph's Island opposite Michilimackinac. They would provide military protection for the province until the regiment was disbanded in 1802.[105] Simcoe also departed during 1796, leaving a land that had been preserved from war with the United States owing in part to his energetic leadership and a competent military force. Thus ended uncontested British control of the Niagara frontier. Thereafter the waterway would be an international boundary, and American and British soldiers would face each other across the river until military conflict finally came sixteen years later.

NOTES

1   Metropolitan Toronto Library, Baldwin Room (MTLBR), David William Smith Papers, Orderly Book of Maj. John Smith, 1793-95, Garrison Orders, 30 May 1793.

2   For a concise overview of the history of Fort Niagara, consult Brian Leigh Dunnigan, *A History Guide to Old Fort Niagara* (Youngstown, NY: Old Fort Niagara Association, 1985) and *History and Development of Old Fort Niagara* (Youngstown, NY: Old Fort Niagara Association, 1985).

3   Gerald M. Craig, *Upper Canada: The Formative Years, 1784-1841* (Toronto: McClelland and Stewart, 1963), 23; James Ripley Jacobs, *The Beginning of the U.S. Army, 1783-1812* (Princeton, NJ: Princeton University Press, 1947), 13-39.

4   Jacobs, *The Beginning of the U.S. Army*, 53-60, 84-123.

5   Lord Dorchester to Lt. Col. Andrew Gordon, 14 April 1791, E.A. Cruikshank, ed., *The Correspondence of Lieut. Governor John Graves Simcoe...* (5v., Toronto: Ontario Historical Society, 1923-31), 1:22-3; Francis Le Maistre to Gordon, 23 January 1792, Cruikshank, *Simcoe Correspondence*, 5:10.

6   Craig, *Upper Canada*, 22.

7   Mary Quayle Innis, ed., *Mrs. Simcoe's Diary* (Toronto: Macmillan, 1965), 75.

8   Carl Benn, "The Military Context of the Founding of Toronto," *Ontario History*, 71, no.4 (December 1989), 303-22.

9   Henry Dundas to Simcoe, 9 February 1793, Cruikshank, *Simcoe Correspondence*, 5:32-3.

10 Jacobs, *The Beginning of the U.S. Army*, 153-77.

11 Simcoe to Dorchester, 23 July 1794, Cruikshank, *Simcoe Correspondence*, 2:335-7; ibid., E.B. Littlehales to Maj. John Smith, 15 August 1794, 377.

12 Craig, *Upper Canada*, 37.

13 Dunnigan, *History and Development*, 27-8.

14 British Library, Sir Frederick Haldimand Papers, Add MSS 21763, Lt. Col. Arent S. DePeyster to Capt. Robert Mathews, 20 July 1784.

15 Report of Capt. Gother Mann, 29 October 1792, E.A. Cruikshank, "Notes on the History of the District of Niagara, 1791-1793," Publication of the *Niagara Historical Society*, 26 (1914), 33.

16 Simcoe to Dundas, 23 February 1794, Cruikshank, *Simcoe Correspondence*, 2:157-63; ibid., Simcoe to Dorchester, 23 July 1794, 335-7.

17 Report of Capt. Gother Mann, 29 October 1792, Cruikshank, "Notes on the History of the District of Niagara," 33.

18 Thomas Hughes, *A Journal by Thomas Hughes* (Port Washington, NY: Kennikat Press, 1947), 151.

19 MTLBR, Smith Orderly Book, Garrison Orders, 23 March 1794.

20 Library of Congress, Alexander Hamilton Papers, Maj. John J.U. Rivardi to Alexander Hamilton, 3 April 1799.

21 Elizabeth Cometti, *The American Journals of Lt. John Enys* (Syracuse: Syracuse University Press, 1976), 144-6; See also Great Britain, Public Record Office, MPI 211, "Plan of Niagara," n.d. [1795] by Ens. John M. Hamilton.

22 Innis, *Mrs. Simcoe's Diary*, 78.

23 William L. Clements Library, Thomas Gage Papers, 45, Capt. Hugh Arnot to Maj. Gen. Thomas Gage, 20 November 1765; Great Britain, National Army Museum, "A View of Fort Niagara," 1773, by Henry De Berniere; Innis, *Mrs. Simcoe's Diary*, 75.

24 Louis B. Wright and Marion Tinling, eds., *Quebec to Carolina in 1785-1786, Being the Travel Diary and Observations of Robert Hunter, Jr.* ... (San Marino, CA: The Huntington Library, 1943), 95; MTLBR, Smith Orderly Book, Garrison Orders, 30 May 1793 and 17 June 1795.

25 Brian Leigh Dunnigan, "Portaging Niagara," *Inland Seas*, 42, no.3 (Fall 1986), 177-83, 216-23.

26 Report of John Collins, 6 December 1788, E.A. Cruikshank, ed., "Records of Niagara, 1784-89," Publication of the *Niagara Historical Society*, 40 (1929), 58-60; Proceedings of Nassau Land Board, 31 March 1790, E.A. Cruikshank, ed., "Records of Niagara, 1790-92," Publication of the *Niagara Historical Society*, 41 (1930), 21-2; George Seibel, *The Niagara Portage Road: 200 Years, 1790-1990* (Niagara Falls, Ont.: City of Niagara Falls, 1990), 131-5.

27 Innis, *Mrs. Simcoe's Diary*, 78, 99-100.

28   Maj. Robert Mathews to Evan Nepean, 9 July 1790, Cruikshank, "Records of Niagara, 1790-92," 54; Dunnigan, "Portaging Niagara," 216.

29   National Archives of Canada (NAC), RG 8 (British Military Records), Q66:235, State of the Forces in Upper Canada, 1 September 1793.

30   Seibel, *The Niagara Portage Road*, 209-10; Isaac Weld, *Travels Through the States of North America and the Provinces of Upper & Lower Canada During the Years 1795, 1796 & 1797* (New York: Augustus M. Kelley, 1970), 136.

31   Mathews to Nepean, 9 July 1790, Cruikshank, "Records of Niagara, 1790-92," 55.

32   David Owen, *Fort Erie (1764-1823): An Historical Guide* (Stevensville, Ont.: by the author, 1986), 33-41.

33   See Stephen G. Strach, *The British Occupation of the Niagara Frontier, 1759-1796* (Niagara Falls, Ont.: Lundy's Lane Historical Society, 1976).

34   Charles H. Stewart, *The Service of British Regiments in Canada and North America* (Ottawa: Department of National Defence, 1962), 90, 148, 154; NAC, RG 8, Q66:235, State of the Forces in Upper Canada, 1 September 1793; Distribution of Quarters and Cantonments ... for the Year 1794, 27 March 1794, Cruikshank, *Simcoe Correspondence*, 2:197.

35   NAC, RG 8, Q66:235, State of the Forces in Upper Canada, 1 September 1793.

36   Hew Strachan, *British Military Uniforms, 1768-1796* (London: Arms and Armour Press, 1975), 179, 182; Brian Leigh Dunnigan, "Milestones of the Past: Military Buttons and Insignia from Mackinac," *Mackinac History*, 2, no.3 (1975), 4; William L. Calver and Reginald P. Bolton, *History Written With Pick and Shovel* (New York: New York Historical Society, 1950), 100.

37   MTLBR, Smith Orderly Book, After Orders, 30 May 1794.

38   S.R. Lushington, *The Life and Services of General Lord Harris, G.C.B., During his Campaigns in America, the West Indies and India* (London, 1840), 95.

39   These are shown in Cecil C.P. Lawson, *A History of the Uniforms of the British Army*, 3 (London: Norman Military Publications, 1961), 96.

40   MTLBR, Smith Orderly Book, Regimental Orders, 30 May 1793, 31 May 1794, and 3 June 1795.

41   Ibid., Regimental Orders, 29 November 1793, 14 January 1795, and 28 March 1794.

42   Ibid., Regimental Orders, 15 February 1794, 17 April 1794, 1 May 1794, and 1 June 1794.

43   Strachan, *British Military Uniforms*, 172-3, 179.

44   MTLBR, Smith Orderly Book, Regimental Orders, 3 November 1793, 19 December 1793, and 20 April 1794.

45   Strachan, *British Military Uniforms*, 176.

46   NAC, RG 8, C511:57-81, Return of Ordnance, 1 January 1794.

47   NAC, RG 8, C930:3, Return, 25 September 1792; and RG 8 Q66:235, State of the Forces in Upper Canada, 1 September 1793.

48   MTLBR, Smith Orderly Book, Regimental Orders, 1 May 1794; E.B. Littlehales to Smith, 9 September 1794, Cruikshank, *Simcoe Correspondence*, 3:49.

49   Strachan, *British Military Uniforms*, 275-98; J. Duncan Campbell, "Military Buttons: Long Lost Heralds of Fort Mackinac's Past," *Mackinac History*, 2, no.7 (1965), 1; Calver and Bolton, *History Written With Pick and Shovel*, 98.

50   Henry Dundas to Sir George Yonge, 4 September 1791, Cruikshank, *Simcoe Correspond-ence*, 1:59-60.

51   Ibid., Establishment of a Corps of Infantry, 29 August 1791, 57; ibid., Yonge to Col. John Graves Simcoe, 21 September 1791, 71.

52   NAC, RG 8 Q66:235, State of the Forces in Upper Canada, 1 September 1793.

53   List of Officers for a Corps of Foot in Upper Canada, 21 September 1791, Cruikshank, *Simcoe Correspondence*, 1:72.

54   Ibid., Simcoe to Dundas, 28 May 1792, 160; Innis, *Mrs. Simcoe's Diary*, 75.

55   Simcoe to Dundas, 4 November 1792, Cruikshank, *Simcoe Correspondence*, 1:246-9.

56   Strach, *The British Occupation of the Niagara Frontier*, 21. See also Benn, "The Military Context of the Founding of Toronto," 303-22.

57   Simcoe to Dorchester, 2 June 1794, Cruikshank, *Simcoe Correspondence*, 2:256-7; ibid., Littlehales to Maj. Smith, 2 August 1794, 348; ibid., Simcoe to Capt. David Shank, 15 August 1794, 378.

58   Strach, *The British Occupation of the Niagara Frontier*, 21; Simcoe to Dundas, 20 June 1794, Cruikshank,*Simcoe Correspondence*, 2:279-80.

59   This cap is shown on a Queen's Ranger depicted in a painting by Lewis Foy of the 1793 Indian council at Sandusky. The painting, owned by the Montreal Museum of Fine Art, is illustrated in Robert S. Allen, "The British Indian Department and the Frontier in North America, 1755-1830," *Canadian Historic Sites Occasional Papers in Archaeology and History, no.14* (Ottawa: Parks Canada, 1975), 57.

60   Strachan, *British Military Uniforms*, 263; Donald Blake Webster, "The Queen's Rangers (1st American Regiment)," *Military Collector & Historian*, 41, no.2 (Summer 1989), 50-5.

61   See Brian Leigh Dunnigan, "British Naval Vessels on the Upper Great Lakes, 1761-1796," *Telescope*, 31, no.4 (July-August 1982), 92-8.

62   Ibid., 95-8.

63   See Benn, "Military Context."

64   See Dunnigan, "British Naval Vessels."

65   Paul L. Steven, *A King's Colonel at Niagara, 1774-1776: Lt. Col. John Caldwell and the Beginnings of the American Revolution on the New York Frontier* (Youngstown, NY: Old Fort Niagara Asociation, 1987), 38.

66   Innis, *Mrs. Simcoe's Diary*, 74.

67   Return of the 1st, 2nd, 3rd Battalions, Nassau Militia, 2 May 1791, Cruikshank, *Simcoe Correspondence*, 1:24.

68   Ibid., Return of the Three Battalions of Militia, County of Lincoln, 4 June 1793, 348.

69   General Return of the Militia, Province of Upper Canada, 23 June 1794, Cruikshank, *Simcoe Correspondence*, 2:293.

70   Littlehales to Maj. Smith, 27 August 1794, Cruikshank, *Simcoe Correspondence*, 3:6; ibid., Littlehales to Smith, 9 September 1794, 49; ibid., Field Return of a Detachment of Militia, 20 October 1794, 136; ibid., Littlehales to Ralfe Clench, 20 October 1794, 140.

71   Ibid., Simcoe to the Duke of Portland, 24 October 1794, 147-8.

72   Ibid., Simcoe to Portland, 20 December 1794, 230-4.

73   Ibid., Simcoe to Dorchester, 16 August 1794, 382-4.

74   Circular, 26 July 1794, Cruikshank, *Simcoe Correspondence*, 2:342-3; Cecil C.P. Lawson, *A History of the Uniforms of the British Army*, 5 (New York: A.S. Barnes and Company, 1967), 98-100.

75   See Barbara Graymont, *The Iroquois in the American Revolution* (Syracuse: Syracuse University Press, 1972).

76   See ibid. For a history of the Indian Department see Robert S. Allen, "The British Indian Department and the Frontier in North America," 5-125.

77   Ibid., 46-58, 104.

78   Advertisements for recruits from the *Upper Canada Gazette*, July-September 1794, Cruikshank, *Simcoe Correspondence*, 2:302.

79   Dennis Farmer and Carol Farmer, *The King's Bread, 2d Rising: Cooking at Niagara, 1726-1815* (Youngstown, NY: Old Fort Niagara Association, 1989), 54-7; Innis, *Mrs. Simcoe's Diary*, 92; the Smith Orderly Book at MTLBR also includes a number of orders relating to fishing by the garrison, especially Regimental Orders, 27 January 1795.

80   Much information on routine at Fort Niagara from 1793-95 is included in MTLBR, Smith Orderly Book, "Tapto," Regimental Orders, 17 April 1794; Drills, Regimental and Garrison Orders, 1 May 1794; Pay for fatigues, District Orders, 4 June 1794.

81   MTLBR, Smith Orderly Book, Garrison Orders, 17 January and 3 June 1794; Canteen, Garrison Orders, 28 August 1794; Merchants, Garrison Orders, 17 August 1794; Passes to Newark, Regimental Orders, 13 May 1795.

82   Ibid., Garrison Orders, 28 October 1793; Regimental Orders, 28 October 1793.

83   Ibid., Regimental Orders, 5 May 1794 and 19 July 1795.

84   Innis, *Mrs. Simcoe's Diary*, 134.

85   "Smith, Sir David William," *Dictionary of Canadian Biography*, 7 (Toronto: University of Toronto Press, 1988), 811-14; Lt. Roger Hale Sheaffe to Capt. Charles Williamson, [15 August] 1794, Oliver Turner, *Pioneer History of the Holland Purchase* (Buffalo: George H. Derby and Co., 1850), 339-40; Innis, *Mrs. Simcoe's Diary*, 82, 129.

86   Innis, *Mrs. Simcoe's Diary*, 128

87   MTLBR, Smith Orderly Book, Garrison Orders, 31 August 1794.

88   Farmer and Farmer, *The King's Bread, 2d Rising*, 31-2, 54-7.

89   Bruce G. Wilson, *The Enterprises of Robert Hamilton: A Study of Wealth and Influence in Early Upper Canada, 1776-1812* (Ottawa: Carleton University Press, 1983), 76-8.

90   Ibid., 76.

91   Dunnigan, "Portaging Niagara," 177-83, 216-23; Wilson, *The Enterprises of Robert Hamilton*, 69-73.

92   MTLBR, Smith Orderly Book, Garrison Order, 17 August 1794; Weld, *Travels Through the States of North America and the Provinces of Upper & Lower Canada*, 91.

93   MTLBR, Smith Orderly Book, Regimental Order, 13 May 1795.

94   Ibid., Regimental Order, 27 January 1795.

95   Yvon Desloges, *Structural History of Fort George* (Ottawa: Parks Canada, Manuscript Report no.189, 1977), 4.

96   Ibid., 4-46.

Dorchester to Simcoe, 5 November 1795, Cruikshank, *Simcoe Correspondence*, 4:123-4.

Ibid., George Beckwith to Simcoe, 4 April 1796, 231.

99 Ibid., General Order, 1 June 1796, 286.

100 Ibid., State of the Troops in the Province of Upper Canada, 1 August 1796, 344.

101 New York State Historical Association, Henry Glen Papers, Journal of Henry Glen, 5-20 August 1796.

102 General Order, 2 June 1796, Cruikshank, *Simcoe Correspondence*, 4:286.

103 Capt. James Bruff to Secretary of War, 20 August 1796, *Philadelphia Gazette and Universal Daily Advertiser*, 10 September 1796; Letter from an Officer, 19 August 1796, *Columbian Centinel*, 17 September 1796.

104 Stewart, *The Service of British Regiments in Canada and North America*, 90.

105 State of the Troops in the Province of Upper Canada, 1 August 1796, Cruikshank, *Simcoe Correspondence*, 4:344; Strach, *The British Occupation of the Niagara Frontier*, 21.

CHAPTER FOUR

RELIGION AND COMMUNITY

Michael Power

AN OVERVIEW: ANGLICANS, PRESBYTERIANS, ROMAN CATHOLICS, AND DISSENTERS

The subject of this chapter is the stirrings of organized religion in the town of Newark (Niagara-on-the-Lake) during the years when it served as the capital of Upper Canada. Our focus, then, is necessarily limited to approximately four years, 1792-96, and consequently to two denominations only: the Church of England, whose adherents were later called Anglicans, and the Church of Scotland, whose members referred to themselves as Presbyterians. There is a compelling reason for focusing on these two religious groups: the historical evidence for religious activity in this part of Upper Canada is almost entirely dependent upon documents generated by the Reverend Robert Addison, the missionary to the Anglicans of the Niagara peninsula, and by the Reverend John Dun, the man chosen by the Presbyterians of Newark and Stamford to be their minister. Each congregation kept full records of their church-related activities, and providence has preserved these records for our use.

St Mark's register of baptisms, marriages, and burials begins on 9 July 1792. The first entry in the records of the Presbyterian church is dated 30 September 1794. The Presbyterian records are particularly valuable because they specify the contractual terms governing Dun's ministry, detail the size and cost of the congregation's proposed church, and list the names of subscribers and pew holders along with the amounts each household head was willing to contribute. Additional material on Dun and his congregation is located in the minutes of the Albany Presbytery, the papers of Lieutenant

Governor John Graves Simcoe, and the pages of the *Upper Canada Gazette*. For Addison, we are obliged to turn to the journals of the Society for the Propagation of the Gospel in Foreign Parts (SPG). The SPG posted Addison to the Niagara area, and it paid his salary. In return for its sponsorship, he submitted to his superiors semi-annual reports which were then edited and entered into the official record of the SPG. Addison's reports provide a rich source of information not only on the statistical ledger of his missionary labours — the number of people he baptised, married, and buried — but also on his own state of mind, and his unflattering opinions of his far-flung and parsimonious flock. Complementing the journals are numerous and revealing references to Addison in Simcoe's papers. Through them we are offered a glimpse of the secular side to Addison as he petitioned for land, preferments, and economic opportunities. In this respect, he differed only in degree, not in kind, from his Presbyterian counterpart.

Addison and Dun headed congregations that were fairly numerous, well organized, relatively prosperous (they could afford their own resident ministers), and effectively connected to one or more of the sources of power and patronage in Upper Canadian life: Simcoe and his circle, the small but influential civil service, politicians, freemasons, and the all important merchant class. The Anglicans and the Presbyterians formed Newark's religious élite, with the Presbyterians the more ambitious of the two congregations. They constructed Newark's first church, and it remained the town's only Christian house of worship until the Anglicans finally opened theirs in 1809.

In contrast to the rich documentation on Newark's Anglicans and Presbyterians during the years 1792-96, little can be said about the community's Baptists, Roman Catholics, and Methodists. None of these denominations would make their presence felt within the town until well after the close of the capital period.

Baptists arrived in the peninsula prior to 1790. The Overholts, who settled in Clinton, and the Beams, who founded Beamsville on Thirty Mile Creek, are recognized as pioneers. However, an ordained Baptist minister did not appear in the peninsula until the turn of the century, and it was 1807 before the Beamsville Baptist church was built.[1] In none of the primary historical sources do we read of Baptists in or near Newark when Simcoe was lieutenant governor. Only much later is there recorded the presence of a Baptist minister at Fort George. A former soldier, the Reverend John Oakley began to preach in Niagara in 1814. He was responsible for building the town's first Baptist church in 1830. Ironically, the majority of subscribers to the building fund were not Baptists and the congregation was mainly black, the white Baptists preferring to travel to nearby Virgil for Sunday services.[2]

The Roman Catholics were also few in number at this time. Only in 1827 were there enough of them in the town and vicinity to found St Vincent de Paul parish, and only in 1831 did their numbers warrant the circulation of a subscription for a church.[3] Documented references to Catholics in the area, from Simcoe's administration to the close of the eighteenth century, are limited to three Catholic priests, two French laymen, and the Catholic soldiers at Fort George. The Reverend Philippe-Jean-Louis Desjardins and Louis La Corne, his assistant, arrived in Newark in August 1793 to plead for Simcoe's help in settling French royalist refugees in Upper Canada. The next priest to appear at Simcoe's doorstep was Edmund Burke, a native of Ireland and vicar-general of Upper Canada for the diocese of Quebec. He came in October 1794, on his way to the Catholic missions of Rivière-aux-Raisins (Monroe, Michigan). Before he left with Simcoe's best wishes and promises of financial support, Burke visited Antoine Le Dru, a French Dominican priest much disliked by Simcoe, who had put him in jail for his republican agitation among the French-speaking fur traders and liquor merchants at Rivière-aux-Raisins, at that time still an integral part of the province. Burke returned to the capital in July 1796. For his loyalty to the crown and his willingness to serve the government's interests, he was granted for church purposes two parcels of land: one acre in Newark (lot 227, the present corner of Centre and Dorchester streets), and one acre in York (lot 6, the northeast corner of Richmond and George streets). He failed to build a church at either location. He did not settle permanently in town until 1798, and he stayed for only three years. During that time he took care of the largely Catholic Second Battalion, Royal Canadian Volunteer Regiment of Foot, did his best to rein in the Catholic soldiers who drank in the grog shops on Sunday mornings instead of attending church, and acquainted himself with his new neighbour and fellow Catholic, Joseph Geneviève, Comte de Puisaye. Puisaye had purchased a home on the river road, in May 1799, hoping to set up his own store and trading centre. Nothing came of the idea. He left the town in 1801, the same year Burke departed for Quebec and then Nova Scotia.[4]

The Methodists fared slightly better than the Baptists and Catholics, although they too were long delayed in building a church in Niagara (Niagara-on-the-Lake). That took place in 1823 when they erected a meeting-house at the corner of Gage and Gate streets where the cemetery can still be seen. Leading up to this historic event were more than thirty years of organizing and recruiting members in the peninsula. On the creation of the

Niagara circuit in 1795, Darius Dunham of the Upper Canada District (a part of the New York Conference of the Methodist Episcopal Church) became its itinerant preacher. At the inaugural meeting of the circuit, held at Queenston, he was pleasantly surprised to find sixty-five names on the membership rolls.[5] The field had been superbly prepared for him by George Neal and Christian Warner, two former military officers.

Born on 28 February 1751, in Pennsylvania, Neal lived most of his early life in the Carolinas.[6] After two brushes with death on the battlefield, during the American War of Independence, Neal underwent a religious conversion at the hands of a Reverend Hope Hull, who brought him to a full recognition of his long dormant religious faith. Stirred to act, Neal became a preacher, beginning his career at the Pee Dee River in South Carolina, "where many souls were awakened and brought to a knowledge of salvation."[7] On 7 October 1786 he set foot at Queenston.[8] He was soon befriended by Conrad Cope, a Methodist who had settled in Niagara two years earlier than Neal. Encouraged by Cope, acting in much the same capacity as Hull, Neal began a self-appointed and sometimes unorthodox ministry that would last for a half-century. Nowhere was his unorthodox and truly democratic style more in evidence than in his relationship with Christian Warner; nor was it ever again to produce such abundant spiritual dividends.

A former sergeant in Butler's Rangers,[9] Warner moved to the peninsula in either 1783 or 1784 and made his home west of the present village of St Davids. Neal personally converted him in 1788. Two years later they founded a Methodist society in Stamford. Neither man had any authority to do this, but neither man was too worried about the niceties of rules and regulations. The seeds of the faith had to be planted, and they went about their work making sure that the seeds fell on fertile soil. Warner was appointed class leader, a position he was to hold for forty-five years. He opened his home to weekly meetings of the brethren and to all those sincerely professing an interest in Christianity. He preached regularly, taught the rudiments of the faith, and helped to set up other classes. From 1796 to 1823, Warner was the Niagara circuit's general steward. He was known the length and breadth of the Niagara peninsula for his commitment to prayer: "His prayer was noted for both its physical and spiritual energies. He had a place of resort for private prayer over half a mile from his home in a nook in the dense forest near the mountain [Niagara Escarpment]. The back of this nook was a great perpendicular surface of rock, surmounted with a beetling rocky ledge, which proved a most effective sounding board for the prayers of this wrestling Jacob of mighty voice. His neighbours declared they could hear his prayers two miles away."[10] Warner's class grew into Warner's chapel. It was built in 1801 on property near his home. This was the first Methodist church in what is now southwestern Ontario.

Darius Dunham and his immediate successors were to solidify the work of Neal and Warner. According to Methodist historian George Playter, Dunham was "a man of strong mind, zealous, firm in his opinions, and had the greatest bass voice ever heard by the people. He was quite indifferent to the censure of men, and used the greatest faithfulness in preaching to the ungodly."[11] Elsewhere he was described as a man "distinguished for fidelity, and faith, and prayer, as well as wit and sarcasm."[12] He was given the sobriquet *"scolding Dunham."*[13]

He stayed a year and then handed the reins of the circuit over to James Coleman, who visited the homes, classes, and meeting-houses of his fellow Methodists from 1796 to 1799. For two of these years he was assisted by Michael Coate. Membership increased from 65 to 154 people. In 1800 Joseph Sawyer took over, and he reported 204 names.[14] Unfortunately, we do not have any evidence of camp-meetings taking place in the peninsula before June 1830, when one was held on the Beaverdams property of Israel Swayze.[15]

By 1802 there were meeting-houses at Four Mile Creek, Twenty Mile Creek, Fifty Mile Creek, Stoney Creek, Barton, Ancaster, Beverley, Flamborough, and Niagara. Actually, 1802 is the first year Niagara is mentioned in the records of the Niagara circuit. Besides Warner, the names of class leaders include Beeman, Culp, Gage, Cornwall, Sweazey, Hopkins, Talman, Jones, and Smith.[16] These people were either first- or second-generation loyalists. They were strongly attached to the British crown.

Methodism was definitely on the rise throughout the Niagara peninsula during the last decade of the eighteenth century. Its grass-roots organization, its financial independence, and its selection and nurturing of dynamic leaders — all these guaranteed its steady growth and influence. Despite their being loathed by many for their non-conformity, their poverty, and their emotional brand of religion, the followers of Wesley were not people easily discouraged.

THE CHURCH OF ENGLAND

Nothing in Robert Addison's formative years prepared him for the decades he was to spend as the chief clergyman of the Church of England in the Niagara peninsula. Born on 6 June 1754, in Heversham, England,[17] Addison was educated at the village school of Levens, the parish rectory, and the Kindall grammar school.[18] Expressing a desire for holy orders, he enrolled as a divinity student at Trinity College, Cambridge, where he received his

BA in 1781 — the same year he was ordained deacon — and his MA in 1785. The year before completing his bachelor's degree, he married Mary Atkinson. According to one author, "His course at the university had given him a standing. He was not without friends. The road he had chosen was a well-beaten and easily travelled one. There was small prospect of adventure, but there was promise of the satisfaction of the mild ambitions in which the men of his profession indulged themselves."[19] This judgment was rendered many years after Addison's death, but it reflects accurately the opinions of his Cambridge contemporaries and religious superiors, such as the Bishop of Llandoff. Moreover, it mirrors perfectly the kind of individual who was attracted to the ministry of the established church. The young Addison could easily have been one of those parsons portrayed so brilliantly and wittily in Jane Austen's novels.

Circumstances, however, were to conspire against Addison's procession to the summit of clerical success in his native England. He began his ascent in typical fashion, tutoring university students for a fee and taking for a time the curacy at Upwell. But his ambitions were cut short. There was nowhere else for him to go and nothing else for him to do. No living came his way. Sadly, his wife, the victim of some unknown mental malady from which she was never to recover, was the greatest impediment to his career. Addison was prohibited, more by custom than by law, from claiming a parsonage if she were not at his side to act the part of the rector's wife. Mary Addison died probably in or just before 1790, leaving a son and two daughters in her husband's care.[20]

At loose ends, he turned to the London-based SPG, asking "to be taken into the Society's service."[21] At its meeting of 20 May 1791, the SPG board decided to accept Addison's offer and to appoint him missionary to Niagara, on condition of its receiving recommendations from the bishops of Ely and Peterborough. These were duly read and noted in the minutes of the next board meeting held 17 June.[22] Addison was judged a worthy candidate, and he was immediately given his post at a yearly stipend of £50 to be paid by the SPG. He was expected to be at his charge by mid-summer.

The Niagara region was familiar to SPG authorities. The Reverend John Ogilvie, chaplain to the Royal American Regiment, had accompanied Sir William Johnson and Brigadier-General John Prideaux on their expedition to Fort Niagara in 1759.[23] He conducted the first Protestant services at the fort, which had been in French Catholic possession since the 1680s. In January 1783, the Reverend John Doty, an SPG missionary in western Quebec, mentioned Niagara specifically in his report on the state of the church: "The inhabitants are for the most part, English Traders, and pretty numerous. It has likewise been for some time past, a place of general rendezvous for loyal Refugees from the back parts of the Colonies: and especially for the greater part of the Six Nations Indians, who have withdrawn, with their families, to the vicinage of that place, where it is likely they will remain: among the rest are a part of the Iroquois or Mohawk nation."[24]

John Stuart was the third SPG missionary to visit the settlement. He had a fond regard for the Mohawks mentioned in Doty's report. They had been Stuart's parishioners at Fort Hunter, New York, and they were now encamped near a chapel they had built on the east (American) side of the Niagara River.[25] They would soon move to a new location, eighty miles to the west near modern-day Brantford, where they were alloted a reserve which is occupied to this day by their descendants. Stuart initially thought to make Niagara the centre of his ministry; later, he instead chose Kingston, believing its prime location on Lake Ontario would bring prosperity and plenty before either would arrive at Niagara. He visited the Grand River Indians in the summer of 1788.[26] On his return home, escorted by Joseph Brant, Stuart rested at Niagara where, in the course of preparing for the final leg of his journey, he had an interesting conversation with Lieutenant-Colonel John Butler and Robert Hamilton, two of the settlement's most prominent citizens. They informed Stuart of their strong desire to have among them a resident clergyman of the Church of England. Stuart personally had no interest in the offer they were proposing — if indeed they had ever offered it to him — but he directed them to Charles Inglis, the bishop of Nova Scotia, who had regular contact with the SPG. Stuart assured the two men that the bishop would be happy to plead their case to the board.

They took Stuart's advice and wrote Inglis a lengthy letter, in which they claimed that up to half the population of 1,000 men, 700 women, and 1,400 children living in the Niagara district belonged to the Church of England; and that twelve principal inhabitants, including themselves, would be willing to post a bond for £100 per annum for seven years towards the support of whomever the SPG sent to them. In addition to the bond, they promised a glebe and house, and pledged the construction of a church from funds currently being collected by the magistrate in each township for that express purpose.[27] The tone of their letter was forceful and sincere. Their argument, bolstered by its many assurances and the public character of the two men who had sent it, was immediately persuasive. Inglis, true to Stuart's predictions, presented their petition and enclosed the bond in an enthusiastic and detailed memorandum to the board, dated 16 March 1790. Stuart seconded Inglis's approval of the project in his 1790 report to the SPG.

He told the board that "the Inhabitants seemed desirous of having a Clergyman placed among them, and are willing to contribute to his support."[28]

This kind of lobbying, coupled with the fortuitous convergence of Addison's wish to be adopted by the SPG, produced the desired result. Addison's appointment to Niagara was partly the result of his being available; it may have also been partly owing to his theological orientation. Inglis had hinted that a man of broadly based views on doctrine and liturgical practice would be the best candidate. Addison met this criterion. Charles Durand, who was baptised by Addison, remembered his parish priest as "no ritualist, no formulist." Incense and candles were not burned at the midday services. No one bowed east, and the church choristers were never dressed excessively. Addison's church and the services he conducted in it were simple and unadorned.[29]

The lateness of the season forced Addison to spend a dreary and interminable winter in Quebec. He finally surfaced in Niagara in July 1792. The place was bustling in anticipation of the long awaited arrival of Lieutenant Governor Simcoe and his wife, Elizabeth, and the opening of

The northeast façade of Lake Lodge, home of the Reverend Robert Addison. (Brox Co. Ltd. and J.K. Jouppien, heritage resource consultant)

Upper Canada's House of Assembly. Navy Hall was being restored for government use, new buildings were being erected, and living quarters for the Simcoes were being prepared. The Simcoes made a grand entrance on 26 July and took up residence in three specially prepared tents near the river. John Stuart, the chaplain to the Legislative Council, was also in town for the celebrations.[30] Addison and Stuart took the opportunity to have a long talk. It seems that Addison was appalled by Niagara's primitive appearance and crude society. The town was no gem, in his eyes, and the townspeople less than refined in their manners. Stuart, the veteran missionary, went out of his way to reassure the Cambridge graduate. The people were well disposed towards him, he told Addison, and Butler had repeated his pledge about the annual supplement of £100 above the sum that he was receiving from the SPG. When parliament opened its inaugral session, on 17 September, Stuart led the prayers in the Legislative Council, and Addison did the same in the House of Assembly, a sinecure he was to hold for many years.[31] Stuart, however, did not linger long in the capital, thinking it best to return to his home base in Kingston.

Addison was in sore need of Stuart's calming words. Niagara — or Newark, as it was now renamed — was a universe removed from the genteel atmosphere of Trinity and the leisurely life of a parish in the English countryside. The provincial capital had no church, and Addison learned quickly that prospects for one were dim indeed. He was obliged to conduct services in the Freemasons' Hall. Mrs Simcoe refers to this in her diary entry of 29 July 1792: "There is no Church here but a Room has been built for a Mason's Lodge where Divine Service is performed on Sunday."[32] Jacob Mountain, the new bishop of Quebec, made a similar observation two years later, but also mentioned a second place where people gathered for Sunday worship: "At Niagara there is a Minister, but no Church. The service is performed sometimes in the Chamber of the Legislative Council [Butler's Barracks], & sometimes at Free Mason's Hall, a house of public entertainment."[33]

This arrangement of using the Masonic Hall for something so unmasonic as reciting the Book of Common Prayer or conducting a communion service was not so out of place or without its rewards in the 1790s as one might imagine. A good number of the men in Addison's parish, including Butler and Hamilton, were active and conspicuous freemasons.[34] They saw no contradiction between the deism of their secret society and the traditional doctrines of revealed Christianity. Addison himself was oblivious to any inconsistency. He was happy to be the grand chaplain of Newark's masonic lodge.[35] Such were the spiritual adjustments some people made in the late eighteenth century.

In any event, Addison did without a church for seventeen years. This interregnum was embarrassingly long when one considers that a handsome chapel had been erected on the Grand River reserve as early as 1785,[36] and that other similar sized houses of worship had been built at Queenston in 1792,[37] The Twelve (St Catharines),[38] and The Forty (Grimsby) in 1803.[39] There are many reasons why the Anglicans of Niagara tarried so far behind their coreligionists in the outlying villages and crossroads of the peninsula, at least in the matter of building themselves a proper church of stone in the style he would have known best, the village churches of rural England. Posterity can thank him for his fine taste and sense of the romantic; present-day St Mark's looks and feels completely English. A sturdy stone church was a pretension, of course, and one most likely shared by the upper crust of his congregation. But pride of place in the backwoods of Niagara district was only a minor stumbling block when compared to the frightful parsimony of Addison's flock. He could count the Simcoes, the Butlers, the Hamiltons, and a fair number of other leading lights of Niagara society among his earliest members. Much has been made of this group in nearly all the published literature on the history of St Mark's. But what many authors have forgotten or overlooked is the incredible stinginess of the very people one would expect to be the most munificent supporters of the Church of England. Simcoe did absolutely nothing to assist in the building of a church. Mrs Simcoe all but ignored Addison, never referring to him even once in her diary. He was a nonentity. There is no evidence to suggest that Butler made any effort to have his cosigners live up to the seven-year bond they had voluntarily submitted to Bishop Inglis and the SPG. When Butler passed from the scene in 1796, the responsibility for the bond then fell to Robert Hamilton, who was equally negligent. Not even a personal rebuke from Bishop Mountain, on his visit to Niagara in 1795, proved sufficient to shame Hamilton and the others into action.[40] The cosignators to the bond never fulfilled their obligations to their minister, denying Addison for seven consecutive years the £100 supplement. During the same period, the people subscribed a mere £200, an insulting amount when one considers that no collection was taken for several of the years in question.[41]

Addison was placed in the awkward position of having to dun for his money. He became cynical. In October 1793, having spent but a year in his mission territory, he confessed to the SPG that "the humble Settler who labours on his land is kind to him: the rich Trader endeavours to be polite: but he is sorry to say that their subscription is likely to end in words."[42] It was an accurate assessment. Humble settlers do not build stone churches.

Nor do miserly merchants.

On a larger scale, the uncertain status of the Church of England in Upper Canada did little to help Addison assert his authority or validate his supposed prestige. The Constitutional Act of 1791, providing for the creation of Upper and Lower Canada as separate provinces, granted special privileges to the Church of England that had been previously recognized by the Colonial Office in its 1763 instructions to General James Murray and in the Quebec Act of 1774. These privileges were basically five in number. The first stated that no Protestant in either Upper or Lower Canada would be compelled to give tithes to the Roman Catholic Church. Where and when such tithes were collected, they would be used solely to support the Protestant clergy. The second set up the clergy reserves, whereby one-seventh of crown lands were to be reserved for the benefit of the Protestant clergy. The third allowed the monarch to authorize the governor or lieutenant governor to erect parsonages or rectories in the tradition of the Church of England and to endow them with land. It was understood by the framers of the constitution that these rectory endowments were distinct from the clergy reserves. The fourth made possible the appointment of senior clergy to the Legislative and Executive councils of the two provinces. The fifth placed the responsibility for ensuring the establishment of the church into the hands of the local legislature, and subjected all legislation concerning the established church to review in London.[43]

As it turned out, the established church was established in name only. The law was more theoretical than practical, making the so-called privileges more apparent than real. This was especially true during Addison's earliest years in Newark.

Initially, Simcoe was extremely adamant in regard to what he felt was the indispensable role of the established church in the province he governed. To his good friend Henry Dundas, he wrote on 6 November 1792: "I need not, I am sure, Sir, observe that the best security, that all just Government has for its existence is founded on the Morality of the People, and that such Morality has no true Basis but when placed upon religious Principles; it is therefore that I have always been extremely anxious, both from political as well as more worthy motives that the Church of England should be essentially established in Upper Canada ..."[44] What these "more worthy motives" were remains unclear. Perhaps Simcoe was genuinely fearful of sectarian strife if there were no official church dependent on government for its existence. The province was a haven for Roman Catholics, Lutherans, Presbyterians, Methodists, and an astonishing variety of dissenters originating in the United States, such as Moravians, Quakers, and Tunkers.[45]

Simcoe knew by heart the "party line" on religious establishment, and he repeated it, often vigorously, to his subordinates in the colonial administration; but he was essentially powerless to enforce his beliefs.

More realistic opinions, such as the one given by Richard Cartwright, went a long way to soften Simcoe's stand. Cartwright, a native of New York state, was a leading merchant, a legislative councillor, and a one-time business associate of Robert Hamilton. His advice to the lieutenant governor was blunt: "Where a new government is to be formed, as is the present case, among a people composed of every religious denomination, and nineteen-twentieths of whom are of persuasions different from the Church of England to attempt to give that Church the same exclusive political advantages that it possesses in Great Britain, and which are even there the cause of so much clamour, appears to me to be as impolitic as it is unjust."[46] Cartwright was commenting specifically on the Marriage Act of 1793, which reserved the solemnization of marriages to Church of England clergy, but his criticisms were aimed at the whole concept of establishment. Over time, Simcoe came to adopt a practical variant of the Cartwright

The Reverend Robert Addison's writing desk, made of local walnut. The country Chippendale chair is of the period. (Niagara Historical Society Museum, X970.565, 980.15.32)

position. He would allow each denomination to jockey for favour from the government, while treating his own church as if it were *de facto* first among equals and therefore not a denomination like the others. This was a clever strategy, one designed not to offend anyone but the most radical, and the radicals would not become a force in provincial politics for another generation. The favour in greatest demand was not religious toleration—that was a given — but land. It was plentiful, in effect the most common form of economic exchange, and its distribution rested in the hands of Simcoe and his Executive Council.

What effect did all this have on Addison? He was basically left to his own devices. Success or failure or just plain mediocrity in the mission field depended entirely on his own wits and powers of persuasion. He had the immense good fortune to realize this almost immediately upon his arrival in Upper Canada, and he was to react to his predicament in a positive fashion: he kept himself busy doing the Lord's work. Conscientious in the performance of his ministerial duties, he sought and found communities of believers in every settled part of the Niagara peninsula. Besides his home base of Newark, he visited Forty Mile Creek, Twenty Mile Creek, the Head of the Lake, Fort Erie and environs, the Grand River reserve, Chippawa, and even York (Toronto).[47] According to his own tabulations, as given in his reports to the SPG, he conducted 782 baptisms, witnessed 89 marriages, and buried 84 people from 1792 to 1799. In each place, he usually celebrated holy communion. He continued to visit the Six Nations Indians four times a year up to 1818, when the Reverend Ralph Leeming of Ancaster assumed this duty.

These facts help to draw a portrait of a man who overcame his natural indolence and diffidence of character.[48] He was exercising his priesthood in an apostolic way that would have been unimaginable to his clerical colleagues back in England. Nathan Bangs, the American Methodist, accused the Addison of later years of being a "poor drunken card-playing minister."[49] But, since Methodists loathed the clergy of the established church as a matter of course, Bangs's opinion should be taken with a good deal of scepticism. It certainly does not square with the energy and devotion which Addison displayed on his countless trips throughout the peninsula in the 1790s. In truth, Robert Addison was more of an itinerant than a resident missionary for the first decade of Upper Canada's history.

Poverty, however, was one aspect of missionary life Addison could not tolerate for long. The dignity of his office would not allow it. And he had to think of the social implications of his being the poor parson tramping about the countryside as if he were some ill-bred, half-educated Methodist circuit rider. That would not do. He was overworked, fatigued, and chronically short of money these years. To make matters worse, Newark was an expensive place to live. Isaac Weld the traveller remarked that "so sudden and so great has the influx of people, into the town of Niagara and its vicinity, been, that town lots, houses, provisions, and every necessary of life have risen, within the last three years, nearly fifty per cent, in value."[50] Weld was lucky, he was only passing through. Addison, meanwhile, had to live there. On numerous occasions, he aired his complaints to the SPG. If his patrons and parishioners would not give him the living he deserved, he would turn to the government for preferment. By doing so, Addison was merely doing what came naturally: he was looking after his own interests. He was also assuring himself, if only psychologically, that he was and would remain "first among equals" in the ranks of the local clergy. That is how the game was played, and he played it to the full.

Besides his post as chaplain to the House of Assembly, which he continued to occupy even after the government moved to York, he was made chaplain to the 5th Regiment, a source of income that was his as long as the regiment was stationed at Fort Niagara.[51] He was greatly disappointed when it left in 1796 along with Simcoe and the rest of the government. The SPG increased his salary by £20 to compensate for the extra hardships he endured on his trips to the Grand River.[52] He petitioned for land near Four Mile Creek, and he was granted the "old mill seat," which consisted of nine acres of choice property along the shores of Lake Ontario. Here he was to build "Lake Lodge," his home for the remainder of his life.[53] Over time, Addison was to acquire in grants and outright purchases more than 31,000 acres of property.[54] This was Addison the clever land speculator. He wanted some security not only for himself but also for his children, who had been denied any share in the land grants of 1797.[55] How much actual revenue he derived from his many land transactions is impossible to determine. He left no personal financial records. Lastly, Addison, who was touted as the most learned person of his day in Upper Canada, feared poverty so much that he purchased the lease to the salt springs in Ancaster for the term of his ministry in the peninsula. The lease was Simcoe's parting gift. The enterprise turned into an albatross for Addison. It eventually became the focus of a protracted legal wrangle that did little to enhance his reputation in the closing days of his career.[56]

During his initial seven years in the peninsula, then, Addison was the vicar of nothing and of everything. He had no church, little money, an insecure social standing, and only a transient friendship with the better classes of Niagara society, while he was expected by nearly everyone, Anglican or not, to be the living embodiment of English religion. It was an

St Mark's Anglican Church, Niagara-on-the-Lake, by G. D'Alamaine. This shows the church in 1834 after its reconstruction. Except for the belfry and steeple, this is the way it would have looked when it opened for its first service in 1809. (Niagara Historical Society Museum, 988.227)

The Reverend Robert Addison's silver chalice. The hallmark dates it London, England, 1768. (St Mark's Anglican Church, Niagara-on-the-Lake)

inauspicious beginning to a ministry that would not run its course until his death thirty years later, on 6 October 1829. But this is not the whole story. Addison's many trying experiences in the 1790s hardened him for future adversities and made him a wiser, more self-reliant man of the cloth. For instance, his spirit remained unbroken when his beloved stone church was burned on 13 December 1813 by the retreating Americans. Instead of collapsing in self-pity, he quietly persevered and finally rebuilt his church, which forms the nave of the current St Mark's. His magnificent library of 1,500 volumes is housed in the vicarage, and the communion plate he donated to his mission can be seen on display at the church. These same experiences made it possible for Addison to grow into an abiding presence, a familiar figure, in the overall religious milieu of Niagara as the province slowly developed and matured in the nineteenth century.

THE CHURCH OF SCOTLAND

The Church of Scotland could claim the largest number of adherents among religious believers in Newark and the surrounding area, and it would maintain its pre-eminence in town and country well into the 1820s. Presbyterians were not only numerous, they were flourishing, well organized, and blessed by an ecclesiology that encouraged lay initiative and independence. The laity and their elected representatives controlled the general direction of church government. They alone had the right to issue a call for a preacher, and they alone were responsible for founding a congregation and funding its operations. Whereas Addison's line of communication stretched from the Niagara peninsula to Quebec to London, the Presbyterians of Newark and their sister congregation in Stamford only had to turn to the presbytery in Albany, New York, when they were ready for a minister. Once they were given one, and the congregation and minister approved of each other following a trial period, the future well-being of the relationship was a purely local affair.

Reporting to Simcoe on 12 October 1792, Richard Cartwright wrote that "the Scots Presbyterians who are pretty numerous here And to which Sect the most respectable Part of the Inhabitants belong, have built a meeting House, and raised a subscription for a Minister of their own who is shortly expected among them."[57] Early attempts to chronicle the history of St Andrew's have taken this to be a reference to a meeting-house in Newark. Such is not the case. Cartwright was speaking about the Presbyterians of nearby Stamford, for a short while called Township No.2 or Mount Dorchester. Since 1785 they had been gathering for worship in private homes. Within six years, they had constructed "a modest edifice of logs, upon a stone foundation,"[58] and they had issued a call to the Albany Presbytery. In March 1791, John Young, of Schenectady, New York, was given the charge, but he unexpedtedly left for Montreal without the advance approval of either his congregation or the presbytery.[59] He was subsequently replaced by the Reverend John McDonald, who agreed to minister to the people of Stamford for "ten weeks including time on the journey."[60] The date of his appointment was September 1791. It is not known when his mission began. His name appears in church documents only once, as having baptised David, the son of Andrew Heron and Mary Kemp, in August 1792.[61] He may have come to the region more than once or stayed well beyond the original contract of ten weeks.

The focus of Presbyterian energy then shifted to the new provincial capital. Unable to support a minister for any reasonable period on their own meagre resources, the Presbyterians of Stamford joined forces with their coreligionists in Newark in issuing a second call. Each congregation submitted their own petition and subscribers' list dated 1 October 1794, agreeing to hire John Dun for a period of three years.[62] Dun was a Master of Arts from Glasgow University and a licentiate of the Albany Presbytery. While the contract was backdated 13 June, we should not automatically accept that as the date he arrived in Newark. More likely it indicates when he was first approached. From the flow of events as recorded in the church records, it seems that Dun appeared a few days before 1 October. Regardless, he showed up armed with a letter of recommendation from Richard Duncan, a merchant and legislative councillor,[63] and a willingness to accept a fixed salary of £100 per year, New York currency.

In preparation for his ministry, Newark's Presbyterians were busy laying the groundwork for a church. They wasted no time. On 23 September, a list of subscribers to a building fund was drawn up. It contained the names of seventy-eight men who pledged a total of £215, of which £160 had been paid.[64] The next meeting took place on 30 September at Hind's Hotel, where it was resolved that "as Religion is the foundation of all Societies, & which cannot be so strictly adhered to, without having a Place dedicated solely to Divine purpose, that a Presbyterian Church should be erected in the Town of Newark."[65] This resolution, which also mentioned payment for a clergyman, was signed by John Young, chairman; Ralfe Clench, clerk; and Andrew Heron, Robert Kerr, Alexander Gardiner, William McClelland, and Alexander Hemphile, all of Newark. The last named presented a bill of scantling (timbers) for a frame which called for 40 posts, 40 studs, 2 plates, 4 titles, 22 keepers, 6 beams, 26 rafters, and 18 collar beams.[66]

The meeting of 1 October at Andrew Heron's house was the opening session of the elders and congregation with John Dun as moderator. It ended with a resolution to petition the government for land. Time was at a premium, for John Clendenning had already agreed to build a frame, according to the bill of scantling, and to deliver it on the beach, pre-assembled and ready for raising. Dated 5 October 1794, the petition was presented on behalf of a "number of the Inhabitants of the Presbyterian Persuasion, in the Town of Newark" who are "desirous of Erecting a Presbyterian Church, a school house, and Parsonage house" on a square of four lots.[67] The petition was granted on 4 November but apparently not made known to the church committee until early December. The church records show that the committee discussed the possibility of building on a lot (no.45) that was owned by John Camp and situated near the front of the town. This discussion took place on the same day the government granted their petition.[68] The records also reveal that the committee was apprised of the grant by 11 December. They accepted the government's offer of lots 157, 158, 183, and 184. Before the day was finished, they decided that "the Church be built on the near line of Lots 157 & 184 facing the Street."[69] Andrew Heron, whose fine and bold signature can be found on every church document from 1794, was elected treasurer and given the task of collecting "the Subscriptions for the building of the Church as the Frame is shortly expected down."[70]

Construction began immediately and was completed by September 1795.[71] The church measured thirty-two feet by forty-five feet,[72] and boasted an impressive array of windows installed by William Dunbar, another member of the congregation. There were six windows with forty lights (panes) each; eight windows with twenty-four lights each; two Venetian windows, one on either side of the pulpit, with twelve lights each.[73] Dunbar was responsible as well for the doors, mouldings, shutters, and sashes. A belfry and steeple, the latter twelve feet square and rising approximately sixty to seventy feet in the air,[74] were added later in 1802 to house the bell donated by John McFarland.[75]

It seems that Heron had loaned the congregation a considerable sum of money as the meeting house took shape. To repay him and to set the finances on a more sure and steady footing, pews were let to rent, starting on 2 March 1796, "to the highest bidders, for one year, the largest sized Pews, not to let under Five Pounds NYC [New York currency] and the smaller ones not under Three Pounds NYC."[76] Twenty-four pews were rented, generating an income of £49. In October 1802, twenty-two pews fetched approximately £85.[77] This significant increase in revenue, after such a short gestational period, suggests a stability and prosperity unmatched by any other congregation in the vicinity.

One would think that Addison would have been vexed to no end by the almost instant success of the Presbyterians. But he was actually relieved to have someone assist him in looking after the spiritual needs of the settlers, an attitude perhaps encouraged by the broadmindedness of his religious beliefs. This is how the SPG journal of 27 August 1795 recorded Addison's impressions of Dun: "A Presbyterian Minister is settled among them, & is much caressed by the common people; but he still and heartily wishes he may be of use, as he seems liberal & well informed & must lessen Mr. Addison's toil of traveling about the country, as the greatest part are

First Presbyterian Church, Niagara-on-the-Lake, by Owen Staples (1866-1949). Finished in 1795 (the belfry and steeple were added in 1802–03, the church was destroyed by the Americans on 24 August 1813. (Metropolitan Toronto Library, T17050)

Presbyterians."[78] This generosity of spirit was not shared by Simcoe. Despite the advice of Cartwright, which had helped bring about a change in his policy towards those outside the pale of the established church, Simcoe had a difficult time shedding his prejudices about people like the Presbyterians. Their money and determination irked him greatly. To the Duke of Portland he wrote, on 8 November 1795: "Unfortunately the last year a Presbyterian Clergyman having arrived from Scotland the Inhabitants of all denominations built a place of worship, so that I apprehend very little assistance will be expected from them on the Erection of the Episcopal Church."[79]

Aside from the government's gift of four town lots, Newark's Presbyterians received "no allowance from any society, no endowment, no help from Home Government to build or pay a salary."[80] While it is true that Dun himself was allotted 1,200 acres,[81] any land he received was strictly for his personal use. The grant had nothing to do with the church over which he presided; it was not a means of paying his salary. Simcoe showed no favouritism in this regard; he treated ministers of other non-established churches in the same fashion. Land grants were awarded to Johan Conrad Brassell of the Lutheran Church, to George Levick of the German Church, and to the Moravians along the Thames River.[82] A similar policy was applied to the various denominations in Upper Canada. Each would receive sufficient land on which to erect a church, but no additional grants would be awarded. The Presbyterians, however, looked to their affiliation with the Church of Scotland, and they believed that since the mother church was co-established in Great Britain, so too were her offspring in Upper Canada. In his petition, Dun prayed for a part of the reserved or common land in Stamford where he proposed to build a parsonage next to the church. This was refused outright. So was the petition of 13 April 1796, presented by the congregation in the name of "Religion, Morality and Loyalty," asking that "some land be granted for the support of our Church."[83] Simcoe had to say no to such a request or else he would have opened up a Pandora's Box of religious claims upon the government that would have resulted in sectarian anarchy. Furthermore, according to his interpretation of the 1791 Constitutional Act, there could be but one state-supported church in the province and that had to be the Church of England.

Simcoe's rejection of their claim was only a minor irritant, a disappointment but not a disaster by any means. Presbyterians knew that the success of their religious enterprises depended wholly upon themselves. They had a church, a minister, a solid financial base, and, above all else, excellent lay leadership.

If they had looked at themselves in a mirror, collectively, they would have easily seen why they had done so well so quickly. During the capital period, Presbyterians were a relatively cohesive social group, defined in large measure by a distinctive social ethos. Among their membership they could count merchants, doctors, and politicians. Andrew Heron, the church treasurer and clerk of the session, was a well-known and respected Newark merchant who later founded the Niagara public library and published the Niagara *Gleaner*.[84] His leadership extended over many years, its durability providing a sense of continuity to the congregation. William Dickson and his brothers Robert and Thomas, cousins of Robert Hamilton, were also merchants. William's other pursuits were law and land speculation.[85] John McKay is described as a merchant in his land petition of January 1798.[86] James Crooks is listed as a merchant and local magistrate in his claim of 14 March 1797.[87] Thomas Clarke, another cousin of Robert Hamilton, was a merchant as well. His wife, Mary Margaret Kerr, was the daughter of Robert Kerr,[88] the most distinguished surgeon in the entire peninsula.[89] He was wealthy and generous and superbly connected in his marriage to Elizabeth Johnson, the daughter of Sir William Johnson and Mary Brant. Isaac Swayze was a member of the House of Assembly, representing the riding of 2nd Lincoln from 1792-96.[90] John McNabb was a road builder, a justice of the peace, and a member of the land board.[91] There was also Ralfe Clench. Married to Elizabeth Johnson, granddaughter of Sir William Johnson, he was a veteran of the American wars, clerk of the township of Niagara, colonel of the 1st Lincoln Militia, judge, farmer, and a charter member of Masonic Lodge No.19 in 1787.[92]

Lastly, we should not overlook John Butler and Robert Hamilton, the two men who had misled Bishop Inglis and the SPG on the relative strength of the Church of England and other denominations in the Niagara district. Ironically, Addison was the major victim of their gross exaggeration. And that was not all. The colonel and the merchant, and probably many others like them, were ambivalent about their attachment to any one religious denomination. They chose elasticity over strict adherence to any creed. Butler, the Anglican, was to purchase a pew in the Presbyterian church, and his heirs were careful to resubscribe in 1802, six years after his death.[93] Hamilton, a son of the manse, aligned himself more closely with the Anglicans than he did with the church of his youth and upbringing. He wanted to be an Anglican in a calculated bid to make himself and his family more respectable in colonial society. However, like Butler, he played both sides. To avoid offending his fellow Presbyterians he subscribed to the building of the church. An extremely modest £3 4*d* kept open an important door. His children were to be more magnanimous and consistent in their benefactions to what became St Andrew's.[94]

Freemasonry enjoyed an even higher profile among the Presbyterians than in Addison's congregation. As we have seen previously, both Butler and Hamilton were freemasons, the former a grandmaster and the latter a provincial deputy grandmaster.[95] Robert Kerr was deputy grandmaster of the Provincial Grand Lodge from 1797 to 1802.[96] At the local level, Ralfe Clench was a pioneer in spreading freemasonry's influence throughout the peninsula and no doubt in recruiting members from his church. His name appears in the *Upper Canada Gazette* as secretary to St John's Lodge No.19,[97] and later in the same capacity to St John's Lodge of Friendship No.2[98] The occasion for the last mentioned entry in the *Gazette* was the annual celebration of the Feast of St John the Evangelist. Members of the Grand Master's Lodge, who were from out of town, were required to meet at Thompson's

A page from the register of St Mark's Anglican Church showing the burial record of Colonel John Butler and signed by the Reverend Robert Addison (St Marks Anglican Church)

Hotel, and members of St John's Lodge of Friendship No.2 were to gather at Wilson's Tavern, at 10 a.m., Tuesday, 27 December 1796. Philanthropy Lodge No.4 was also present, as we read in this account of the day's events:

> Tuesday, the 27th ult. being the anniversary of the festival of St. John, Lodges No. 2 and No. 4 of Free and Accepted Masons, and a number of visiting brethren from other lodges, clothed in their respective badges of their masonic honors, and preceded by a band of music, playing Masonic airs, walked in procession to the presbyterian meeting-house of this town [Newark], where the Rev. Mr. J. Dun delivered a most excellent and philanthropic discourse, suitable to the occasion, calculated no less to instill the unalterable principles of piety and sound morality, than affection and reverence towards the royal craft; nor is it more than justice to observe that the deep attention paid by a crowded audience marked in the most unequivocal manner the merits of the discourse, and its effect upon the hearers.[99]

The following year, Lodge No.2 celebrated St John's Day in its new quarters at Queenston.[100] In 1799 the Grand Lodge and its guests met at the home of Charles Fields prior to marching to the Presbyterian church where the sermon was delivered by the "Rev. Bro. Addison, Grand Chaplain."[101]

John Dun abandoned the ministry six months short of completing his three-year term. Nothing was recorded concerning his reason for leaving. His petition for a town lot, dated 28 December 1796, the day after his speech to the masons, cryptically alludes to "certain discouraging circumstances"[102] and to little else of substance. One of these circumstances might have been isolation. The nearest Presbyterian minister was John Bethune at Williamstown in Glengarry County. Another factor was his lack of ordination when he came to Niagara. At the bidding of his two congregations he went to Montreal where he asked the presbytery there to accept his two charges into their connection. The Montreal Presbytery not only agreed to his proposal but they also ordained Dun so that "he might be immediately capacitated to administer the ordinance as well as preach the Gospel."[103] His problems in this respect should have been solved. However, the Albany Presbytery, to whom he still owed allegiance, took a dim view of such irregular proceedings. When Dun reported to them in person, in September 1796, his superiors sympathized but the minutes do not exactly show a vote of confidence in their man. Dun simply gave up.

Although he resigned from the pulpit, John Dun remained a member of the congregation in good standing, renting a pew and participating in the general governance of the church. To make a living he joined the ranks of the local merchant class. He was a bookseller, regularly advertising in the pages of the *Gazette*,[104] and later a general merchant, town assessor, and pound keeper. His rise to modest social prominence was cut short when he went down with the sloop *Lady Washington* in Lake Ontario, on or about 6 November 1803.[105] He died intestate, his debts amounting to £1,400. Oddly enough, his successor to the ministry at Newark was John Young, a close friend and the man who was offered the Stamford call in 1791. Young came in 1802, and he probably preached Dun's funeral sermon.

NOTES

1   Stuart Ivison and Fred Rosser, *The Baptists in Upper and Lower Canada* (Toronto: University of Toronto Press, 1956), 22-7.

2   Janet Carnochan, *History of Niagara* (Belleville, Ont.: Mika Publishing, 1973), 76.

3   The first entry in the Register of St Vincent de Paul's parish, Niagara-on-the-Lake, is 2 January 1827. On 3 April 1831 a meeting was called to open a subscription for a church.

4   For additional information on Desjardins, Le Dru, Burke, and Puisaye, see Michael Power, *A History of the Roman Catholic Church in the Niagara Peninsula 1615-1815* (St Catharines, Ont.: 1983), Chapters 12, 13.

5   George H. Cornish, *Cyclopedia of Methodism in Canada: Containing Historical, Educational, and Statistical Information, Dating From the Beginning of the Work in the Several Provinces of the Dominion of Canada and Extending to the Annual Conference of 1880* (Toronto: Methodist Book and Publishing House, 1881), 264.

6   Wilfred D. Warner, *The Accounts Register. Niagara Circuit Methodists 1795-1823. Additions Compiled by Wilfred D. Warner* [Niagara Falls], 181. His birthdate may be only an inference based on the date of death given on his tombstone.

7   Thomas Webster, *History of the Methodist Episcopal Church in Canada* (Hamilton: Christian Advocate Office, 1870), 33.

8   George F. Playter, *History of Methodism in Canada* (2v., Toronto: Wesleyan Conference Office, 1862), 1:15. Sometimes his family name was recorded as "Neill."

9   Mrs Stanley C. Tolan, "Christian Warner — A Methodist Pioneer," *Ontario Historical Society Papers and Records* (*OHSPR*), 38 (1942), 71.

10   Ibid., 75.

11   Playter, *History of Methodism in Canada*, 1:41-2.

12   John Carroll, *Case and His Cotemporaries; or The Canadian Itinerants' Memorial Constituting a Biographical History of Methodism in Canada, From its Introduction into the Province till the Death of Rev. William Case in 1855* (2v., Toronto: Samuel Rose, 1867), 1:38.

13   Playter, *History of Methodism in Canada*, 1:65.

14   Cornish, *Cyclopedia of Methodism*, 264.

15   Arthur E. Kewley, "Some Early Sites of Methodist Camp Meetings in the Niagara Peninsula," *Religion and Churches in the Niagara Peninsula* (St Catharines, Ont.: Proceedings Fourth Annual Niagara Peninsula History Conference, Brock

University, 17-18 April 1982), 74.

16 *Book of Accounts of the Contributions of the Methodist Church in Niagara Circuit Established 1795*. Microfilm, University of Victoria College, Toronto.

17 "Addison, Robert," *Dictionary of Canadian Biography (DCB)*, 6 (Toronto: University of Toronto Press, 1987), 3. This is the most complete and accurate biographical information on Addison in print.

18 Arthur P. Addison, "Robert Addison of Niagara," *Canadian Journal of Religious Thought*, 1 (1924), 421.

19 Ibid.

20 "Petitions for Grants of Land in Upper Canada, Second Series, 1796-9," *OHSPR*, 26 (1930), 101.

21 National Archives of Canada (NAC), A-157, Society for the Propagation of the Gospel in Foreign Parts (SPG), Journals, 1792-97, 25:360.

22 Ibid., 361.

23 "Ogilvie, John," *DCB*, 4 (Toronto: University of Toronto Press, 1976), 586.

24 Cyril de M. Rudolf, "St. Mark's Early History," Publications of the *Niagara Historical Society (NHS)*, 18:4.

25 Ernest Hawkins, *Annals of the Diocese of Toronto* (London: Society for Promoting Christian Knowledge, 1848), 7-8.

26 NAC, SPG Journals, 25:120-1.

27 Ibid., 273-7.

28 Rudolf, "St. Mark's Early History," 4.

29 *The History of the Diocese of Niagara To 1950 A.D.* (Hamilton: 1950), 19.

30 NAC, SPG Journals, 26:71-9.

31 Alexander Fraser, ed., "Journals of the Legislative Assembly of Upper Canada," Archives of Ontario (AO) *Report*, 6 (1909), 3; AO *Report*, 7 (1910), 1.

32 Mary Quayle Innis, ed., *Mrs. Simcoe's Diary* (Toronto: Macmillan of Canada, 1965), 75-6.

33 E.A. Cruikshank, ed., *The Correspondence of Lieut. Governor John Graves Simcoe ...* (5v., Toronto: Ontario Historical Society, 1923-31), 3:91.

34 Bruce G. Wilson, *The Enterprises of Robert Hamilton: A Study of Wealth and Influence in Early Upper Canada, 1776-1812* (Ottawa: Carleton University Press, 1983), 143.

35 "Addison, Robert," *DCB*, 6:5.

36 NAC, SPG Journals, 25:121. This is how the Reverend John Stuart described the Mohawk chapel: "The Church about 60 feet in length & 45 in breadth, — built with squared logs and boarded on the outside and painted — with a handsome steeple and bell, a pulpit, reading desk & communion table, with convenient pews."

37 *St. Saviours Brock Memorial Church, Queenston, Ontario, Canada: A Short History* (Queenston: 1988), [1]. This church is first mentioned in Addison's letter of 27 August 1795. See NAC, SPG Journals, 27:37.

38 John N. Jackson, *St. Catharines, Ontario: Its Early Years* (Belleville, Ont.: Mika Publishing, 1976), 127n.4. See also *History of the Diocese of Niagara*, 19.

39 R. Janet Powell, *Annals of the Forty 1783-1818* (Grimsby Historical Society, 1950), 22-3, 39-40. Early historians claim 1794 as the date of the first church in Grimsby, but

the evidence at hand suggests that subscriptions were not taken until 1800 and that a church was not constructed until 1803.

40 NAC, SPG Journals, 27:60.

41 Ibid., 451.

42 Ibid., 26:217.

43 J.J. Talman, "The Position of the Church of England in Upper Canada, 1791-1804," *Canadian Historical Review*, 15, no.4 (1934), 361-3, 366-7.

44 Cruikshank, *Simcoe Correspondence*, 1:251.

45 Mary Beacock Fryer, *Elizabeth Posthuma Simcoe 1762-1850* (Toronto: Dundurn Press, 1989), 60. A group of Moravians had settled near Niagara Falls. See P. Campbell, *Travels in the Interior Inhabited Parts of North America in the Years 1791 and 1792*, ed. H.H. Langton (Toronto: Champlain Society, 1937), 153.

46 Cruikshank, *Simcoe Correspondence*, 2:88.

47 Janet Carnochan, "Early Records of St. Mark's and St. Andrew's Churches, Niagara," *OHSPR*, 3 (1901), 9-17, 53-7, 66-7.

48 Hawkins, *Annals of the Diocese of Toronto*, 46.

49 J.S. Moir, "Early Methodism in the Niagara Peninsula," *Ontario History*, 43, no.2 (1951), 53n.5.

50 Isaac Weld, *Travels Through the States of North America* (2v., New York: Johnson Reprint Corporation, 1968), 2:90.

51 Cruikshank, *Simcoe Correspondence*, 3:369.

52 A.H. Young, "The Rev. Robert Addison and St. Mark's Church," *OHSPR*, 19 (1922), 160.

53 Cruikshank, *Simcoe Correspondence*, 4:320-1.

54 "Addison, Robert," *DCB*, 6:4.

55 "Petitions for Grants of Land in Upper Canada, Second Series 1796-99," 101.

56 Ernest Green, "The Search for Salt in Upper Canada," *OHSPR*, 26 (1930), 419-26.

57 Cruikshank, *Simcoe Correspondence*, 1:236.

58 Ernest Green, "Township No. 2 — Mount Dorchester — Stamford," *OHSPR*, 25 (1929), 257. See also *Stamford Presbyterian Church 1784 — 200th Anniversary — 1984* [1984], 8-9. This work describes the church as 56 feet in length and 45 feet in depth. It then continues with a detailed description of the fabric. However, I am not sure if the author is describing the church as it first appeared or after it had undergone extensive renovations. The source consulted for this congregational history was a manuscript by G. McMicking, an early member. The church is built on lot 45. See "Partial Redrawing of Plan of Township No. 2, believed to have been made in 1791," *OHSPR*, 25, opposite 260.

59 *Minutes of the Albany Presbytery*, March 1791, "Niagara," 29. See also "Young, John," *DCB*, 6:822-3.

60 *Minutes of the Albany Presbytery*, September 1791, 41 [?].

61 Carnochan, "Early Records of St. Mark's and St. Andrew's Churches, Niagara," 81. The first entry in the Register and Session Book of the Stamford Associate Presbyterian Church is 12 April 1827. See Janet Carnochan, "Early Churches in the Niagara Peninsula, Stamford and Chippawa, with Marriage Records of Thomas Cummings, and Extracts from the Cummings Papers," *OHSPR*, 7 (1907), 147-225.

62 Archives of St Andrew's Church (Niagara-on-the-Lake, Ontario), Record Book of the

Presbyterian Congregation at Newark, 1 October 1794, 3. The original of Stamford's petition of 1 October 1794 belongs to the congregation. It is reproduced in *Stamford Presbyterian Church*, 13.

63   "Dun (Dunn), John," *DCB*, 5 (Toronto: University of Toronto Press, 1983), 279-80.

64   St Andrew's Records, 7-8.

65   Ibid., 1.

66   Ibid., 2.

67   NAC, RG 1, L1 (Upper Canada State Papers, Land Board Records), Upper Canada Land Book A, 215, Microfilm Reel C-100. See also Alexander Fraser, "Grants of Common Lands, Etc., in Upper Canada 1792-1796," *AO Report*, 18 (1929), 93.

68   St Andrew's Records, 6.

69   Ibid., 9.

70   Ibid.

71   Ibid., 13.

72   *History of St. Andrew's Presbyterian Church 1791-1975*, [1975], 5.

73   St Andrew's Records, 5-6.

74   *History of St. Andrew's*, 5.

75   St Andrew's Records, 26.

76   Ibid., 15.

77   Ibid., 22.

78   NAC, SPG Journals, 27:38.

79   Cruikshank, *Simcoe Correspondence*, 4:134-5.

80   Janet Carnochan, *Centennial St. Andrew's Niagara 1794-1894* (Toronto: William Briggs, 1895), 20.

81   NAC, RG 1, L1, Upper Canada Land Book A, 215, Microfilm Reel C-100. See also "Petitions for Grants of Land, 1792-6," *OHSPR*, 24 (1927), 57; Cruikshank, *Simcoe Correspondence*, 5:204, petition no.62. This petition was granted on 4 November 1794. The grant was not patented until 31 December 1798. Dun received 800 acres in Ancaster Township and 400 acres in Pelham Township.

82   Cruikshank, *Simcoe Correspondence*, 5:192.

83   NAC, RG 1, L1, Upper Canada Land Book B, 52, Microfilm Reel C-101. See also "Petitions for Grants of Land in Upper Canada, Second Series," 275.

84   Carnochan, *Centennial St. Andrew's*, 21, 32; "Early Records of St. Mark's and St. Andrew's," 18-21.

85   "Dickson, Robert," *DCB*, 6:209. See also "Petitions for Land Grants, 1796-9," 163.

86   "Petitions for Grants of Land in Upper Canada, Second Series, 1796-9," 250-1.

87   Ibid., 146.

88   "Clark (Clarke), Thomas," *DCB*, 6:147-50.

89   "Kerr, Robert," *DCB*, 6:374-5.

90   "Swayze (Swayzie, Sweezy), Isaac," *DCB*, 6:246-7.

91   "Petitions for Grants of Land in Upper Canada, Second Series, 1796-9," 252-3.

92 "Clench (Clinch), Ralfe (Ralph, Rolfe)," *DCB*, 6:374.

93 Janet Carnochan, "Names Only But Much More," *NHS*, 27:10-11.

94 Ibid., 9.

95 Wilson, *The Enterprises of Robert Hamilton*, 143.

96 "Kerr, Robert," *DCB*, 6:374.

97 J. Ross Robertson, *The History of Freemasonry in Canada from Its Introduction in 1794* (2v., Toronto: George F. Morang, 1900), 1:276.

98 *Upper Canada Gazette or American Oracle*, 21 December 1796.

99 Ibid., 4 January 1797.

100 Ibid., 9 December 1797.

101 "Extracts from Niagara Papers," *NHS*, 32:15-16.

102 NAC, RG 1, L1, Upper Canada Land Book B, 200-1, Microfilm Reel C-101. See also Alexander Fraser, "Grants of Crown Lands, Etc., in Upper Canada 1796-1797," *AO Report*, 19 (1931), 86.

103 *Minutes of the Albany Presbytery*, September 1796.

104 *Upper Canada Gazette*, 27 September 1797, 25 November 1797, 2 December 1797, 9 December 1797.

105 "Dun (Dunn), John" *DCB*, 5:280.

CHAPTER
FIVE

MUSLIN GOWNS
AND MOCCASINS

Elizabeth Severin

John McBride, an apprentice in the Niagara area, ran away from his master in the spring of 1797. The advertisement that promised a ten-dollar reward for his return did not mention the colour of his eyes, his height, or his age. How would people recognize him some weeks after his disappearance? The colour and style of his clothes would give him away. Clothing was scarce and expensive in the Niagara peninsula in the 1790s; a poor boy could not change his appearance with a new wardrobe. It would be easier to change the colour of his hair than to change his "clouded nankeen coat, brown cloth waist coat, and fustian trousers."[1] He ran away in his only suit and chances are that he was found wearing the same clothes.

When Lieutenant Governor John Graves Simcoe and his wife, Elizabeth Posthuma Gwillim, arrived in Niagara (Niagara-on-the-Lake) in the summer of 1792, they brought many suits of clothes which reflected their wealth and station. Fine clothing was not vanity for them; it was pomp and majesty, the embodiment of the British society which they hoped to establish in Upper Canada. The Simcoes had prepared for their trip to Canada as a modern traveller might for a trip to the Amazon basin. They brought all the ceremonial, household, and personal goods necessary to maintain the family in a land where civilization had an uncertain hold on the edges of the rivers and lakes. Because they did not expect to find suitable clothing there, Mrs Simcoe brought a dress made specially in London for the opening of the first parliament, several pairs of new shoes, and a full set of scarlet and gold regimentals for the lieutenant governor. And she was not unusual. When

Elizabeth Simcoe assured a friend in England that there were "as many feathers, flowers and gauze dresses at our balls [in Niagara] ... as at a Honiton Assembly,"[2] she was describing the contents of trunks brought by government officials and their relations, such as the Jarvis family, Peter and Elizabeth Russell, and William Osgoode.

In between these extremes of rich and poor were settlers such as the Servos family. Daniel J. Servos, miller and merchant, had a wardrobe that was simple and practical. A waistcoat and britches of buff colour, a coat, a great coat, stockings and shoes, linen and calico shirts, a handkerchief to wear as a neck cloth, a penknife, and a pocket-book fitted him out nicely.[3] He had little need for elaborate silk or lace clothing; a fine hat and a pocket watch with a seal were sufficient to show his status.

A few glimpses of clothes worn by the poor, the rich, and the middle class in the Niagara area in the late eighteenth century slip down to us through the cracks in time, but there are many difficulties in analysing these details. Since that period, words have disappeared from use, or acquired different meanings; for instance, clouded nankeen was a sturdy cotton fabric with a variegated colour, and a pocket-book was a wallet, not reading material. Moreover, many of our attitudes about clothing would have astounded Mrs Simcoe. Today, we can buy clothes anywhere, in different sizes and colours, suitable for every occasion and every season. We have access to custom-tailored suits or bargain-basement mark-downs. When we are bored with our clothes, or they start to look shabby, we throw them away. Within some economic limits, we dress as we wish, and people all over Canada, indeed all over the world, look remarkably similar.

In the 1790s, ready-made garments were rare. The Niagara area, like other newly settled parts of Upper Canada, had few skilled tailors or dressmakers. The wealthy maintained connections in England who filled orders for new suits, but clothing was costly and difficult to acquire regardless of one's economic means. Cloth itself was expensive, especially in Upper Canada where nearly every yard was imported. Woolen fabric for a jacket cost at least 15 shillings, the buttons and linings 4 or 5 shillings more. The tailor's charge for making the garment was only 3 shillings. Modern equivalents are difficult, but the records of the Servos mill suggest that, in 1990 dollars, one might pay about $500 for enough cheap cotton and coarse wool flannel to make a very ordinary shirt and coat. Those who could afford to do so saved money by purchasing cloth in quantity. A bolt of muslin, calico, or fine cambric linen made many shirts, shifts, and handkerchiefs over the years. Good cloth was valued highly. Rich and poor alike cut garments carefully to minimize waste, recycled them into new uses, and patched or darned them with great skill. Robert Hamilton, an immensely successful Queenston merchant, had a fine silk waistcoat trimmed with

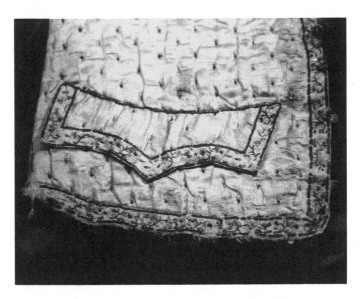

This well-worn waistcoat, adapted from an earlier style, belonged to Robert Hamilton of Queenston. Although he was a very prosperous merchant, his clothes show many signs of the renovations that were common practice in the late eighteenth century. (Niagara Historical Society Museum, 972.65)

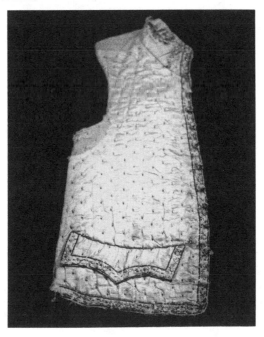

steel beads which was neatly pieced and adapted from an earlier style.[4] Elizabeth Russell, who came to Upper Canada with her brother, Peter, the receiver general, asked for an extra yard and a half of fabric to match the muslin and calico gowns she ordered from England, "to repair with."[5]

Clothing was a clear indication of class and economic status in this period. The poor and much of the middle class had a few worn and faded clothes in the practical styles and drab colours that had proven their utility to many generations of millers, farmers, and housewives. Changes at the whim of fashion were rare among the conservative and frugal rural class. Even the wealthy were slow to change the basic cut and silhouette of their clothing, but they displayed their status by having great quantities of clothes, which were made from fine fabrics, beautifully trimmed or embroidered and embellished with precious jewellery. An inventory of Elizabeth Russell's rings, pins, and necklaces took up three closely written pages.[6]

Elizabeth Simcoe, entirely representative of the government élite in Newark (Niagara-on-the-Lake), was practical in her attitude to clothing.

This informal portrait of Samuel Peters Jarvis, son of Hannah and William Jarvis, shows him dressed in Indian leggings and moccasins. (Royal Ontario Museum, Toronto, 985-178.1)

Her diary and correspondence reveal that, while she played the role of lieutenant governor's lady with discipline and ceremony, she was prepared to adapt to the circumstances of the country. She wore her London gown for the opening of the first parliament, although she was pregnant again and the fit was less than perfect. Later she was pleased to receive a corset, a muslin gown with the new higher waist, some shoes, a straw hat, and silk stockings from her friend Miss Burges in England.[7] For the cold weather she had a warm hood, "a kind of Calech lined with eiderdown, a very comfortable head-dress,"[8] a woolen great coat, and a fur tippet, or scarf, which she had made herself out of a faun skin brought to her by one of her husband's aides.[9] Walking on ice was perilous, but Mrs Simcoe was not forced indoors, for she discovered that "cloth shoes or coarse worsted stockings over shoes prevents slipping."[10] Colonel Simcoe also adapted to the weather and the local wisdom on occasion; for a trip to the Mohawk settlement on the Grand River he wore "a fur Cap tippet & Gloves and maucassins."[11] Their son Francis was dressed in Indian-style clothes, a rifle shirt, and sash at his third birthday party, red leggings and a cloak on another occasion.[12] For the Simcoe daughters at home in England, their mother sent moccasins, souvenirs of Canada.

Elizabeth Russell had more difficulty than Mrs Simcoe in adapting to the complications that faced her in Canada. She declined an invitation to a ball in Montreal to honour the king's birthday "as I have no cloathes with me but my Travelling Dress,"[13] and attended none of the parties during her first winter in Newark since there was no room in her small house where she might dress and it was "a great deal of trouble" to unpack her trunks.[14] Her disappointment upon learning that fur caps, tippets, and linings were very expensive in Canada was echoed by subsequent nineteenth-century travellers looking for a bargain. There is no mistaking the querulous tone of her comment to a friend in England that, because of the lack of an acceptable maid-servant, she was forced to be her own chambermaid, housekeeper, and dressmaker.[15]

The Jarvis family also came to the Niagara area as part of Simcoe's entourage. They have probably left the most enduring image of their class since they had their portraits painted before their departure from England.[16] Hannah Jarvis is the perfect image of Georgian composure in her spotted muslin gown with dark sash, sheer fichu, lightly powdered curls, and direct gaze. Her two small daughters are also dressed in light muslin, with wide silk sashes just below the gathered square neckline and tucks in the skirts for easy adjustment of the length. Colonel William Jarvis wears the green and silver of the Queen's Rangers, Simcoe's regiment during the American

Revolution, and his son has a perfect small version of his father's finery, plus the long hair and lace-trimmed collar which were suitable to a four-year old.

When Elizabeth Russell finally found a marten-skin cap to her liking, it came from Montreal. When Colonel Jarvis wanted morocco slippers, kid gloves, ribbons, beaver hats, coloured feathers, or toothbrushes for his family, he ordered them from York or Kingston.[17] When a Niagara farmer, bricklayer, or tailor needed clothing, he dealt with a local merchant who could also grind his grain and sell his flour, someone like Daniel Servos. It is through the records of his mill that we gain an insight into the clothing of the middle class in the Niagara area in the 1790s.

The mill dealt in the sturdy practical fabrics needed by working families — osnaburg, nankeen, linen, calico, fustian — as well as warm woolens such as blanket cloth, stroud, cassamere, flannel, cadu, and calimanco. Woolen textiles were so important that they were often called simply and generi-

Hannah Peters Jarvis and her daughters posed for this portrait before their departure from England. (Royal Ontario Museum, Toronto, 981-79.2)

This page of Daniel Servos's personal account book, dated 1779, records the purchase of one pair of stockings for 3s 6d, one yard and a half stroud for 15s, four yards of calico for 12s, three yards of linen for 9s, and "mowkisons" for 3s.(Niagara Historical Society Museum, FA69.3 .108)

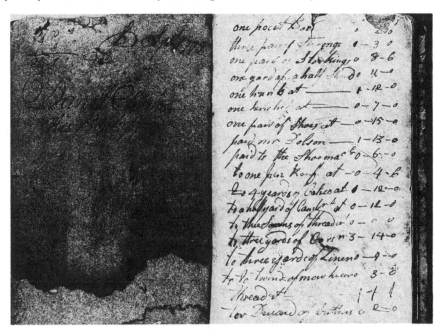

cally "cloth." Daniel Servos often clothed his family by bartering the services and products of his mill for the skills of his customers. He bought great coats and jackets (one in superfine brown wool), many pairs of boots, shoes and slippers, mittens, moccasins, waistcoats, and many pairs of "overhals." He arranged for the replacement of boot legs and soles, and the weaving of many blankets and yards of linen. Occasionally he sold a luxury item, such as a skein of silk for 1 shilling, a dust cap for 48 shillings, a red silk handkerchief for 10 shillings, or a "necklas & earrings" that cost more than 3 pounds for the future wife of one customer.[18]

Most of the cloth sold in the Niagara area was imported from England; thousands of yards of woolens and linens were brought into Canada by Montreal agents. Cloth was an important part of the goods that were given to His Majesty's loyal Indian allies to secure their support or to obtain their land. Although some of the presents were symbolic — silver brooches, silver armbands, hats with ostrich feathers, silk handkerchiefs — most were highly practical trade goods. Robert Nelles, a settler and merchant near Hamilton, delivered the following goods "to the Missasaga Nation for a Piece of Land, Aug 24th 1797":

In May 1790, Jacob Vanalstine bought at the Servos mill "one Shirt Calico," "one pair Mockisons," "one pint Rum," "3 yards Linen," and "one Coffin." (Niagara Historical Soceity Museum, FA69.3.108)

Mr Jacob Vanalstine Dr

May	On Settlement Dr	£ 7	4 4
16	To one Shirt Calico /16		" 16 "
1790			
" 24	To one quart Rum /4		" 4 "
27	To half pound Tobaco /3		" 3 "
Jun 1	To Cash Paid Minerdbratt		
	On order of Larraway /16		" 16 "
17	To one pair Shuepakt/6		" 6 "
20	To one pound & half Tobaco/6		" 9 "
July 4	To one pair Mockisons /4		" 4 "
13	To Cash /2		" 2 "
15	To 3 yards Linen /5		" 15 "
29	To one lb Tobaco /4		" 4 "
30	To pair Spurs boh /16		" 16 "
August 2	To 31 flower		1 2
	To one pint Rum /2		" 2 "
	To one Sheet /10		" 10 "
	To Two gallons Rum		1 1 "
	An order on Crooks		
	To making one Coffin		1 2 "
	Nails with boards		
Sept 6	To 30 lb flower		" 8 "
10	To yd & half Irish Sheting		
3	To one Lofe of Bread /2		" 2 "
22	To 40 lb flower /10		" 10 "

Blankets   {32 Blankets 2 points
             {22 Do 1½ points
             {36 Do 2½ points
             49 yards Blue Strout
             40½ yards Black Strout
             79 yards Linnen
             90 yards Calico
             9 Dozen of Indian Knifes
             47 pound of Brass Kettles[19]

Such trade goods had an obvious effect on the clothing of the native people in the Niagara area. Joseph Brant, war chief of the Mohawks, once came to dine with the Simcoes wearing a fur cap and "an English Coat with a handsome Crimson Silk blanket lined with black & trimmed with gold fringe ... round his neck he had a string of plaited sweet hay."[20] Mrs Simcoe considered a group of Ojibwa extremely handsome in "black Silk handker-

The Servos mill records reveal that Jacob Vanalstine bought on 3 February 1790 "one Pair Mitings" for 6s, "a half pound Tobaco" for 3s, "one Pair Shoes" for 16s, and "one Peticoat Striped" for 20s. (Niagara Historical Society Museum, FA69.3 .108)

chiefs covered with silver Brooches tied right round the head, others silver arm bands, & their shirts ornamented with brooches, scarlet leggings or pantaloons, & black, blue, or scarlet broadcloth Blankets."[21]

Some of the Indians Mrs Simcoe met were destitute. We know little of their appearance or clothing, and even less about the rest of the poor in the Niagara area. The temporarily poor, like the refugees from the American Revolutionary War who arrived in Upper Canada with nothing, were given clothing by the British government. One group of "invalid loyalists" received, for each man, 7 yards of linen, a pair of leggings or 1 1/2 yards of course cloth, a blanket, a pair of stockings, a pair of mittens, 1/2 yard of fearnaught (a heavily felted woolen cloth) for a cap, a hat, and a pair of shoes. Each woman received 8 yards of linen, a blanket coat or a blanket, a pair of stockings, another blanket to make into a petticoat, a pair of mittens, and a pair of shoes.[22] Since the British crown was not renowned for its charity in North America, this probably represented the minimum wardrobe required for survival.

There were no easy ways for the poor to acquire clothes. There were no second-hand clothing markets in Upper Canada, and no organized charitable societies. Home-made cloth was not practical for many. To make linen, cleared land had to be planted with flax rather than food crops. Special tools, special skills, and many hours of labour were required to finish the cloth. Wool was even more difficult to produce since it depended on sheep, which were costly, temperamental, and disease-prone. For those at the bottom of a society where goods were expensive and money was scarce, the only solution was the never-ending cycle of reusing, repairing, and remaking clothing until it literally fell apart. Shoes wore out especially quickly on the rough terrain, and the moccasins that Daniel Servos sold for one day's labour were not a charming souvenir but a necessity for the poor. Little of this ordinary clothing has survived; consequently it is as rare and valuable to the museums that collect it as it was to its original owners.

When we try to summon up the appearance of the Servos family, John McBride, or Colonel and Mrs Simcoe, to understand their attitude to clothing and self-image, and to place textiles, shoes, and jewellery in the context of the late eighteenth century, there is very little information available to us. Early travellers in Upper Canada were more interested in the state of trade, agriculture, or navigation than in the appearance of the people. Portraits and diary references refer to the wealthy and the literate, not the majority of the population. Newspapers describe the occasional runaway, but contain very few advertisements and no social notes for the Niagara area. Merchants' account books are cryptic. A bill of sale at the

Servos mill which records the purchase of "one Pair miting, /6; one pair shoes, /16; one Petticoat striped 1/0" is helpful but rather terse.[23] Clothing was too mundane to receive much notice in the records of the 1790s.

Like a thrifty housewife we try to stitch together 200-year-old scraps of information. The pattern that results is complex and diverse. Besides reflecting the economics, technology, politics, social structure, trade, and communications of an era, clothes retain a personal quality. A muslin gown or a pair of moccasins are not just articles of clothing, they are keys to understanding the Niagara area in the 1790s.

NOTES

1   *Upper Canada Gazette*, 24 May 1797.

2   Mary Quayle Innis, ed., *Mrs. Simcoe's Diary* (Toronto: Macmillan, 1965), February 1793, 87.

3   Niagara-on-the-Lake Public Library, Historical Resource Centre (NPLHRC), RG 2, Servos Personal Accounts, 1779.

4   Niagara Historical Museum, Robert Hamilton's Waistcoat (acc. no.X972.65).

5   Metropolitan Toronto Library, Baldwin Room (MTLBR), Elizabeth Russell Papers, 21 May 1799.

6   MTLBR, Elizabeth Russell Papers, Miscellaneous Papers.

7   Mary Beacock Fryer, *Elizabeth Posthuma Simcoe* (Toronto: Dundurn Press, 1989), 66, 130-1, 154.

8   Innis, ed., *Mrs. Simcoe's Diary*, 25 December 1791, 44.

9   Ibid., 4 November 1792, 81.

10 Ibid., 18 November 1791, 39.

11 Ibid., 4 February 1793, 85.

12 Fryer, *Elizabeth Posthuma Simcoe*, 104, 111.

13 MTLBR, Elizabeth Russell Papers, 2 June 1792.

14 Ibid., 8 January 1793.

15 Ibid., 27 November 1793.

16 Royal Ontario Museum, Canadiana Department, acc. nos.981.79.1 and 981.79.2.

17 MTLBR, William Jarvis Papers, Personal Accounts, 1797.

18 All the references to cloth and clothing in this paragraph are from NPLHRC, RG 2, Servos Mill Records, 1.

19 NPLHRC, RG 2, Section E, Robert Nelles Papers.

20 Innis, *Mrs. Simcoe's Diary*, 9 December 1792, 82-3.

21 Ibid., 9 August 1793, 103.

22 National Archives of Canada, RG 8, C Series (British Military Records), 1331:55.

23 NPLHRC, RG 2, Servos Mill Records, 1, account of Jacob Vanalstine, 96.

CHAPTER
SIX

VICTUALS AND VIANDS
IN THE NEW PROVINCE
OF UPPER CANADA

Dorothy Duncan

When Lieutenant Governor John Graves Simcoe, his wife, Elizabeth, and two of their six children, Sophia and Francis, arrived in the newly created province of Upper Canada in 1792, they found a sparsely populated land of astonishing harshness, beauty, and bounty. The inhabitants included the First Nations, fur traders, military officers and men, surveyors and their crews, settlers in search of land, entrepreneurs, merchants, and a few professionals. They came from every walk of life and many cultural and religious backgrounds. For some, this land had been their home for centuries, while for others it was only a resting place on the way to somewhere else.

Food was of primary concern to them all — finding it, preserving it, and storing it so that it was readily available to serve their specific needs. The newcomers brought with them memories of the ingredients, recipes, and food traditions of their homelands, but their hope that this culinary heritage could be transplanted to Upper Canada soon vanished. Confronted with a harsh climate, new and often unknown vegetation, primitive transportation, and the necessity of clearing the virgin forest and of procuring seeds to plant in the newly cultivated gardens and fields, the newcomers soon grew to appreciate the knowledge and skill of the First Nations in utilizing the indigenous plants for food, beverages, and medicines. Eventually, everyone who stayed and prospered in Upper Canada could attribute their success, at least in part, to their ability to combine their own knowledge and skill with that of the native people, and to apply the best of both to the task of solving the daily round of challenges that they faced in the New World.

THE FIRST NATIONS

For centuries, large areas of North America, from the Gulf of Mexico to the Great Lakes and beyond, had been occupied by native peoples who, in varying degrees, had depended on agriculture to survive. Samuel de Champlain was among the first to comment on the farming practices of the First Nations in the area that was to become Ontario. Early in the seventeenth century he described a tribe of Algonquins growing squash, beans, and corn (called the three sisters by the natives) in the Ottawa River valley. As he travelled into the Huron country, stretching from Lake Simcoe to Georgian Bay, he found true native farmers, dependent on growing crops, rather than on hunting, to survive. Although corn was their most important crop, which they roasted and used in making bread, pudding, and soup, they also grew sunflowers, for oil and soup, as well as beans and squash. Europeans arriving in the rich, fertile Niagara area in the seventeenth century found the Iroquois living in bark houses which were usually grouped together in permanent villages or settlements. They had already developed a basic system of agriculture and were growing and storing beans, corn, pumpkins, and squash, thus ensuring a food supply over the harsh winter months.

The First Nations taught the settlers how to improvise with cooking utensils so that they could utilize whatever natural material was available. For example, a traditional method of baking was to cut pieces of bark from a chestnut tree to use as a container. The food was then placed on the inside of the bark, and moved in front of the fire to bake. The flavour of the chestnut bark and the wood smoke enhanced the flavour of the meal. The natives also taught the settlers self-sufficiency on the trail or in the woods, including the art of building a campfire on dirt or sand or in a shallow pit, away from dry brush or grass. If the woods were wet, natives showed the newcomers how to start a fire with the lower dead branches of jack pines or with the pitch-filled deadwood in split-open old pine stumps. The First Nations taught them, too, how to build a roaring blaze and let it burn down to a thick bed of coals before starting to cook, and how flat rocks placed around the fire to heat could be used to keep food hot for long periods. To roast, they would have shown them the technique of digging a hole, filling it with small sticks, setting them afire, and, when the fire died down, placing the roast in the pit and covering it with coals, ashes, and dirt for several hours until it was finished.

144

Another lesson the First Nations taught the newcomers was how to extract the sweet sap from the sugar maple, a tree that many immigrants from Britain and Europe had never seen before. When European explorers first arrived they found the First Nations managing maple groves, tapping the trees, gathering and evaporating the sap, and consuming maple syrup. The newcomers were not long in imitating them, and later improving on their methods. The next step, of course, was further refinement of the sap to make maple sugar, a concentrated, easily carried, high-energy food that was useful for barter or cash sale. A typical advertisement for the latter appeared in the *Canadian Constellation* at the end of the eighteenth century:

> For Sale
> A quantity of pork and maple sugar, the first at twenty dollars per barrel of 200 lbs and the other at 1s 2d York per lb. by the barrel. Cash only will be received in payment as they are an assignment, Clark and Street Queenston Sept 12.[1]

FUR TRADER'S FARE

The wealth of furs to be found in the Canadian interior brought individual trappers and traders, as well as the great fur giants such as the North West Company, into the area long before the province was created. Food was as important to these entrepreneurs as gasoline is to a modern airline, since they needed food both for themselves and for use as trade goods.

Two entries from a gentleman's journal kept while on a visit to the Niagara area confirm the involvement of the local residents in the lucrative fur trade:

> The Niagara is not navigable higher than Queenston, consequently there is a portage from this place to Chippewa, which employs numerous teams, chiefly oxen; each cart being drawn by two yoke of oxen, or two horses. I passed great numbers on the road, taking up bales and boxes, and bringing down packs of peltries.[2]

> I sold my horses to Mr Innis for one hundred dollars. Mr Innis did not want them; he was on the point of setting out for the Grand Portage, and expected, therefore, that in consequence of their low price he could afford to pay for their keep till his return.[3]

The Grand Portage to which Mr Innis was going was the inland headquarters of the North West Company until Jay's Treaty required the British to give up posts on the American side of the boundary by 1796. Its successor was the newly constructed Fort William (Thunder Bay), which remained the inland headquarters until the North West Company merged with the Hudson's Bay Company in 1821.

Records of the provisions that were transported by canoe from Montreal through the new province to be used as trade goods and as supplies for the headquarters of the North West Company at Grand Portage are detailed in this inventory of 1794:

> 10 kegs, sugar
> 8 kegs, salt
> 32 kegs, butter
> 80 kegs, pork
> 230 kegs, grease
> 40 kegs, beef
> 400 kegs, high wines
> 50 kegs, rum
> 10 kegs, port wine
> 10 kegs, brandy
> 20 kegs, shrub
> 3 kegs, sausages
> 17 bags, green peas[4]

In stark contrast to the provisions they were carrying in the Montreal canoes was the sustenance that fuelled the French Canadian canoemen who paddled and portaged the 90- to 100-pound packs over the 1,000 miles between the two points. A report in 1784 to General Frederick Haldimand, governor of Quebec, gives us a graphic description of how these men survived:

> The Inland navigation from Montreal, by which the North-West business is carried on, is perhaps the most extensive of any in the known World, but is only practicable for Canoes on account of the great number of Carrying places. To give your Excellency some Ideas of which, there are upwards of ninety from Montreal to Lake du Bois only, and many of them very long ones.
>
> Two setts of men are employed in this business, making together upwards of 500; one half of which are occupied in the transport of Goods from Montreal to the Grand Portage, in Canoes of about Four Tons Burthen, Navigated by 8 to 10 men, and the other half are employed to take such goods forward to every Post in the Interior Country to the extent of 1,000 and 2,000 miles and upwards, from Lake Superior, in Canoes of about one and a-half Ton Burthen, made expressly for inland service, and navigated by 4 to 5 men only, according to the places of their destination ... Their general loading is two-thirds Goods and one-third

Provisions, which not being sufficient for their subsistence until they reach winter Quarters, they must and always do, depend on the Natives they occasionally meet on the Road for an Additional Supply; and when this fails which is sometimes the case they are exposed to every misery that it is possible to survive, and equally so in returning from the Interior Country, as in the Spring provisions are generally more scanty. In the winter Quarters, however, they are at ease, and commonly in plenty, which only can reconcile them to that manner of life, and make them forget their sufferings in their Annual Voyage to and from the Grand Portage.[5]

MEALS FOR THE MILITARY

The military garrisons in Upper Canada provided not only security but also considerable stimulation to both the economy and the social life of the developing communities across the province. Fort Niagara was surrounded by gardens and fields in an attempt to make it self-sufficient. In addition to the fresh vegetables and fruits that could be grown there, a commissariat officer was responsible for buying, either from farmers or local markets, whatever was needed to augment the daily provisions of food and spirits for the soldiers and their officers. For the rank and file, who had taken the king's shilling to join the British army, meals were a monotonous round of tea and bread for breakfast, and meat, pease, and bread for an early dinner — their main meal of the day — at 1 p.m. The soldiers rotated as "cook of the day," gathering the allotted supplies from the commissary, stewing them up over the fire in the regimental cookhouse, and then carrying the resulting cauldron of stew to the barracks to be doled out. Their regular ration of rum was augmented with additional rations when it was wet, or cold, or when they were fatigued with work. In contrast, an officer, who had purchased his commission in the army, found that his social life revolved around dining in the regimental mess in the late afternoon. The officers contributed to a mess fund, which, among other things, provided for a mess steward who was responsible for preparing and serving their meals. Many of the officers had leisure time for hunting and fishing and this produced welcome additions to the daily rations. When the officers sat down to dinner in the late afternoon, about 3:30 to 4 p.m., the fare served on the fine china and gleaming crystal rivalled the best in the new province. Soup would have been followed by fish, beef, ham, fowls, a variety of vegetables, depending on the season, savoury, sweet puddings, and cheese, the last served at the end of the meal with nuts and sweetmeats. Beverages would have included wine, punch, claret, madeira, port, and sherry. Tea, coffee, and chocolate

147

would have all been available to the officers at this period and would have demanded a full complement of accoutrements for their preparation and serving, including chocolate pots, tea chests and caddies, sugars, creamers, and mixing bowls.

SURVEYORS AND THEIR CREWS

Following the American revolution, and prompted by the flood of refugee loyalists, the first township in what is now southern Ontario was laid out in 1783. In quick succession, nine "Royal Townships" were laid out along the St Lawrence, with the first five located from Cataraqui (Kingston) to the Trent River. A year later, more land was acquired, west of the Niagara River, and surveys were carried out in the area. With the creation of the new province, and in order to place the deputy surveyors of Upper Canada on the same rates of pay as those in Lower Canada, Simcoe in 1792 ruled that one-quarter of a dollar a day be allowed "to find your own ration." For a "coasting survey," any number of men could be employed not exceeding ten; for an "inland survey," not more than twelve. The allowance for axemen was 1/6 of a (Halifax) shilling a day; and for chain-bearers, 2 1/2 (Halifax) shillings a day. For the daily quarter-dollar allotment the deputy surveyor was obliged to deliver one and a half pounds of flour, twelve ounces of pork, and a half-pint of pease (peas) to each person employed on his party. "If you are furnished with a Battoe, axes, tomahawks, camp kettles, oilcloths, Tents, Bags for the King's Stores," Simcoe's instructions continued, "you will be allowed only ten pence rations for your party."[6]

For surveyors and their crews, the frugal and unchanging rations of bread, pork, and peas were augmented by whatever the forests and streams yielded, such as berries and fruit, passenger pigeons, partridges, wild ducks, geese, and fish netted or speared in the streams, lakes, and rivers. Despite their attempts to have adequate provisions on hand, they often found their supplies dwindling. When this happened, part of the crew was inevitably sent for more, which slowed down their work tremendously. One writer has noted that "the running of the line of Dundas Street from Burlington Bay to the forks of the Thames, a distance of about eighty miles, took from September 16 to October 17, 1792. One full week of this was spent waiting for provisions."[7]

Local farmers and merchants vied for what they considered to be lucrative contracts to supply the flour, salted beef and pork, peas, and other foodstuffs to the British army, the survey parties, and the newly arrived settlers. Potential customers were always suspicious of the freshness of the food they were buying, and those selling would do their best to reassure them in their advertising:

For Sale
30 barrels of CORN and 20 ditto salted BEEF, in excellent order to be held by J McKay in Niagara August 9, 1799.[8]

EATING ON THE MOVE

The new arrivals coming into the province often found themselves running short of provisions and were dependent on living off the land or buying meals at the unpredictable inns and taverns that dotted the few roads that had been built. Elizabeth Simcoe was often a traveller and she describes some of her meals:

> We dined in the Woods & eat part of a Raccoon, It was very fat & tasted like Lamb if eaten with Mint sauce.[9]

> His Excellency & suite eat Raccoons & Porcupines which were good the latter like Pork.[10]

> The black Squirrel is large and quite black. It is as good to eat as a young Rabbit.[11]

> Wild Ducks from Lake Simcoe which were better than any I have ever tasted, these Birds are so much better than any in England from their feeding on wild Rice.[12]

Mrs Simcoe's diary contains scores of other references to foods found locally, including gooseberries, apples, dried apples, strawberries, raspberries, plums, wild grapes, whortleberries, watermelons, wild geese, turkey, partridge, wild pigeon, woodcock, snipe, elk, caribou, moose, venison, bear, pickerel, cod, eel, black bass, pike, herrings, and rattlesnake,[13] as well as imported foods such as Shaddocks, a species of orange from the West Indies.[14] Of the bounty to be found in Upper Canada she leaves no doubt:

> The sturgeon is about six feet long. Those that are caught here are infinitely better than those which go to the Sea. Cooks who know how to dress parts of them cutting away all that is oily & strong, make excellent dishes from Sturgeon such as mock turtle soup, Veal Cutlets & it is very good roasted with bread crumbs. The 5th Regt. have caught 100 Sturgeon and 600 whitefish in a day in Nets.[15]

> The Indians are particularly fond of fruit. We have 30 large May Duke Cherry trees behind the House & 3 standard Peach trees which supplied us last autumn for Tarts & Deserts during 6 weeks besides the numbers the young Men ate. My share was trifling compared to theirs & I eat 30

149

in a day. They were very small but high flavoured. When tired of eating
them raw Mr Talbot roasted them & they were very good.[16]

In stark contrast she also describes the desperate decisions that travellers
often had to make when confronted with the prospect of starvation. For
instance, she noted how the lieutenant governor and his party once started
out on a five-day march to York with only two days' provisions. "The Gov
had recourse to a Compass & at the close of the day they came on a
Surveyor's line & the next Morning saw Lake Ontario. Its first appearance
Coll Simcoe says was the most delightful sight at a time they were in danger
of starving & about 3 miles from York they breakfasted on the remaining
Provisions. Had they remained in the woods another day it was feared Jack
Sharp would have been sacrificed to their hunger. He is a very fine
Newfoundland Dog who belonged to Mr Shane ..."[17]

All too often, travellers' accounts of the meals provided in local inns
confirmed that they left much to be desired. This comment, referring to the
Niagara area, comes from the gentleman's journal mentioned earlier: "I sat
down to a miserable dinner at Fairbank's Tavern and after dinner sent my
introductory letter to Colonel Hamilton from his friend Mr Bache of New
York, which procured me an invitation to supper. The goodness of my
supper made amends for the badness of my dinner — Col Hamilton has a
good house and garden."[18]

Because of the uncertain quality of accommodation for travellers,
Simcoe ordered the building of the King's Head Inn at Burlington, which
served travellers for many years before it was destroyed during the War of
1812. Mrs Simcoe describes a meal there: "They prepared me some refreshment at this House, some excellent Cakes baked on the coals, Eggs, a boiled
black squirrel, tea & Coffee made of Peas which was good, they said
Chemists Coffee was better. The Sugar was made from black Walnut Trees
which looks darker than that from the Maple, but I think it is sweeter."[19]

CARVING FARMS OUT OF THE WILDERNESS

Although the new province of Upper Canada could boast few settled
communities — Kingston, Newark (Niagara-on-the-Lake), and the French
settlement opposite Detroit — visitors as well as those in search of a
permanent home were arriving in a steady stream, lured by the abundance
of good, accessible land.

It was imperative to those settlers that they become self-sufficient as
quickly as possible in order to survive the wildly fluctuating seasons in
Upper Canada, the difficulty of transport, and the scarcity of ingredients

and supplies. Following the example of the First Nations, the new arrivals turned to farming to ensure a steady food supply. Every family would have kept a cow or two to provide milk, butter, and cheese, and a few fowls. They would also have cleared and planted their fields, gardens, and orchards as quickly as possible to produce grain, fruit, and vegetables for their tables.

To achieve cleared fields, orchards, and garden plots from the virgin forests of Upper Canada was a herculean task that demanded strength, skill, and courage. Using a sharp axe, the settler felled a stand of trees in the early summer and let them lay where they fell until early fall, when the area was set ablaze to eliminate the small branches, dried leaves, and underbrush. When the fire died down, he cut the remaining trunks into lengths and pulled them, using a yoke of oxen if he was fortunate enough to own one, into a heap, where, again they were set afire and reduced to a pile of potash that could be used for soapmaking. The stumps were sometimes left, and the seeds sown among them, but more often the farmer used the yoke of oxen and a stump puller to remove the stumps and move them to the perimeter where they could be piled in rows to form the fence. This was slow and difficult work and it is believed that the average farmer cleared about three acres a year.

Those who carved a farm out of the forest felt justifiably proud. In 1794 Elizabeth Russell, half-sister of Peter Russell, the receiver general of Upper Canada, wrote to her friend Elizabeth Kiernan in England: "We are comfortably settled in our new House and have a nice little Farm about us. We eat our own Mutton and Pork and Poultry. Last year we grew our own Buck weat and Indian corn and have two Oxen got two cows with their calves with plenty of pigs and a mare and Sheep. We have not made Butter yet but hope soon to do so."[20]

The importance of a successful harvest was manifest to everyone in those early years, and it must have taken every ounce of ingenuity for many of the members of the first legislature, which met at Newark in September 1792, to persuade their neighbours, friends, and family to look after their farms so that they could leave to attend the sessions. As one writer has said, "the members of the Legislative Assembly found no slight difficulty in leaving their farms at a season when their crops needed their undivided attention; but sufficient of them gathered together, having travelled in some cases hundreds of miles in canoes and through trackless forests to permit the business of the country to be done."[21]

Realizing the importance of agriculture to the success of the province, Simcoe appears to have been instrumental in forming and supporting the first agricultural society in Upper Canada. It was created in 1793 at Newark

"Great pains should be taken to arrive at perfection in cooking fish," cautions The Housekeeper's Book. *"The kettle for boiling fish should be roomy, with a trainer to lay the fish upon ... when the water boils, stand the fish kettle by the fire and let it simmer gently."* (Una Abrahamson)

If this copper? kettle could speak, it could provide detailed descriptions of everyday life in the Servos household when a supply of boiling water was constantly in demand. (Servos collection, Niagara Historical Society Museum, FA69.3.13)

This group of solid silver teaspoons, handcrafted by an English silversmith in the late eighteenth century, were treasured possessions that would have graced the family table, and, in an emergency, could be bartered or sold for currency. (Niagara Historical Society Museum, 980.15.89)

Tea was not only a beverage but also a medicine in colonial Canada and this rosewood tea caddy or chest with a lock reflects its importance and its value. These chests were fitted with compartments for storing the imported teas and bowls for blending the special mixtures. (Niagara Historical Society Museum, 970.570)

Burl bowls, hand hewn from the wart-like growths on native Canadian trees, were popular in kitchens and larders because of their extraordinary strength. It is believed that the bowl on the right was carved from a burl on a walnut tree on the Whitmore farm, Niagara Township, 1792. (Niagara Historical Society Museum, FA69.3.74, FA69.3.87)

Elizabeth Simcoe describes the food traditions of the First Nations in her diary and in this sketch captures the details of a gathering in the Niagara area. (Archives of Ontario, Simcoe sketch # 175g)

and attracted a broad membership. A visitor to Newark in 1793 described the group:

> They had monthly meetings at Newark at a house called "Freemason's Hall," where they dined together. It is not supposed that in such an infant settlement, many essays would be produced on the theory of farming or that much time would be taken up with deep deliberation. Every good purpose was answered by the opportunity it afforded of chatting in parties after dinner on the state of crop, tillage, etc. Two stewards were in rotation, for each meeting, who regulated for the day. The table was abundantly supplied with the produce of their farms, and plantations. Many of the merchants and others, unconnected with country business were also members of this society. All had permission to introduce a visitor. The Governor directed ten guineas to be presented to this body for the purchase of books, — a countenance honourable to himself and to the Society.[22]

Newark's agricultural society flourished for some time, but by 1796 it was losing some of its members and several years elapsed before other local societies were formed. Although farming remained primitive in this early period, agricultural societies appear to have been popular and important social organizations and eventually paved the way for the Agricultural Association of Upper Canada, established in 1846.

Much of the fruit, such as cherries, plums, and grapes, for which the Niagara region became famous in later years, was native to the region. Peter Kalm, the first person to describe Niagara Falls in English from his personal observations, portrayed the bounty this way: "The wild grapevines grow quite plentifully in the woods. In all other parts of Canada they plant them in the gardens, near arbors and summer houses. The latter are made entirely of laths, over which the vines climb with their tendrils and cover them entirely with their foliage so as to shelter them entirely from the heat of the sun."[23]

As early as the seventeenth century two Sulpician missionaries described attempts to make wine from local fruit on the north shore of Lake Erie: "I will tell you, by the way, that the vine grows here [near Port Dover, Paterson's Creek] only in sand, on the banks of lakes and rivers, but although it has no cultivation it does not fail to produce grapes in great quantities as large and as sweet as the finest of France. We even made wine of them, with which M Dollier said holy mass all winter, and it was as good as *vin de Grave*. It is a heavy dark wine like the latter. Only red grapes are seen here, but in so great quantities, that we have found places where one could easily have made 25 or 30 hogsheads of wine."[24] Local grape growers and farmers in the area made wine for their own consumption and for sale, but the first commercial winery was not established until 1871. The Niagara Falls Wine Company, based in Toronto, was formed in 1874 and later moved to Niagara Falls and changed its name to T.B. Bright and Company. Today it can claim to be Ontario's oldest continuously operating wine company.

Knowledgeable farmers and gardeners improved their orchards by grafting the native trees and shrubs with cuttings of imported, proven varieties. In his statement of losses during the War of 1812, Robert Kerr confirms the success of those early residents in developing gardens and orchards:

> A garden with every sort of fruit Trees, four Vineyards, and a large nursery of grafted and innoculated Fruit trees of all Descriptions; (Cut down by order of Lt Philpots of the Royal Engineers). The best garden in the province; to which every Gentleman in the district will Certify. £250.0.0
>
> A List of Fruit Trees etc in Robert Kerr's Garden — Almonds, Apricots two sorts, Plumbs six sorts, nectarines two sorts, Cherries four sorts, Peaches Eleven Sorts, Pears five sorts, Apples twelve sorts, Currants three sorts, seven sorts of Gooseberries, Strawberries three sorts, Raspberries, four Vineyards, Flowers & Medicinal Plants, Flowering Shrubs, and Ornamental Trees.[25]

THE NEW CAPITAL

The capital at Newark was a frontier community that had been influenced both by the American revolution and by the United Empire Loyalists. The strong military presence in the area was evidenced by Fort Niagara; Navy Hall, erected to accommodate naval officers wintering at Niagara; and Butler's Barracks, which had been built to house Butler's Rangers. In addition, many pensioned military officers had settled nearby. An early traveller described the scene:

> Niagara is the present seat of Government in Upper Canada ... This settlement may be divided into Niagara, properly so-called, and the village of Newark. The former comprehends the fort, and a few houses erected at the bottom of the eminence on which the fort is situated. On the other side of the river Niagara is Newark, where the Governor, and principal persons in office reside. This is a poor wretched straggling village, with a few scattered cottages erected here and there as chance,

156

convenience, or caprice dictated. The Governor's house is distinguished by the name of Navy Hall ...[26]

Close to those "few scattered cottages" there would have been the all important garden called the "house," "yard," or "kitchen" garden. Plots would be selected where the soil was fertile and rich, or placed on a slight southern slope to trap the early spring sun, making it possible to work the land early in the spring. The drainage would be good, and the garden would be protected from early frosts in the fall. Because of the difficulty of clearing land, it was planted close to the house and protected by a fence from the free-ranging animals. As restoration architect Peter John Stokes has written, "Besides the rail fences of the backyard and the drystone walls or fieldstone piles common to the fields, the gardens of Niagara were usually closed off from the street by a neat painted fence. Often in the Town of Niagara itself an early building is built on the street line, and formed part of the enclosure."[27]

As well as having a carefully tended and much needed garden by the door, the early settlers at Newark, like settlers throughout the colony, roamed through the woods and along the streams and roadsides looking for wild plants suitable for food and medicine. These plants included dandelions, plantain, puffballs, wild fruits, and fiddleheads. Many of the plants found in Upper Canada were unknown to the newcomers, such as the May apple discovered in the Niagara area and described by Mrs Simcoe:

> I send you May apple seeds. I think it the prettiest Plant I have seen, the leaves extremely large of a bright green the flower consists of 5 white petals of the texture of orange flowers but 3 times larger, 10 yellow chives round a large seed vessel which becomes a fruit of the colour & near the size of a magnum bonum Plumb, the seeds resembling a melon. The flower is on a short foot stalk one or two sitting between the leaves. They grow near the roots of old Trees in good land. The fruit is ripe in August.[28]

THE DAILY ROUND

Growing or finding food was necessary not only for the daily unending round of meals, but also to accumulate a surplus which could be preserved for the long winter ahead by drying, pickling, salting, or smoking. Drying and cold storage were the easiest methods of preservation for vegetables such as beets, cucumbers, and cabbage which could be stored in barrels or casks in cold areas, either underneath the house or in storage areas built into the side of a hill. Root vegetables were often packed in earth or sand (root end up). It was also important to dry and store seed for the next year's crop. The dried seeds were kept from year to year in small, handmade linen bags and carefully stored high and dry away from the rodents. Herbs would have been cut and hung to dry from the rafters and then ground and stored in crocks with closely fitting tops made of beeswax, animals' bladders, and cloth.

Housewives were dependent on memory, handwritten recipes, or recipe books brought with them from their former homes to preserve vegetables, fruit, and meat, prepare meals for their families, and cure the sick. The first Canadian cookbook was not published until 1831, when James Macfarlane, a Kingston printer, reprinted an American cookbook entitled *The Cook Not Mad; or Rational Cookery*, originally published the year before in Watertown, New York, by Knowlton and Rice.

For the Upper Canadian housewife in the late eighteenth century, a prized recipe book, if she could have afforded one, would have been written by Elizabeth Raffald, of Manchester, England, or one of her contemporaries. Raffald's book, *The Experienced English House Keeper*, was published in 1769 and was so successful that by 1810 a total of fifteen authorized versions had been issued. Raffald signed every copy of the first edition, but despite this precaution, twenty-five pirated editions also appeared. Two recipes follow, typical of her simple writing style that any cook or kitchen-maid could readily understand:

To Make Syllabub Under the Cow

Put a bottle of strong Beer, and a Pint of Cyder into a Punch Bowl, and grate in a small Nutmeg. Sweeten it to your Taste, then milk as much Milk from the cow as will make a strong Froth, and the Ale look clear.

Let it stand an Hour, then strew over it a few Currants, well washed, picked, and plumped before the Fire. Then send it to Table.

To Make A Drunken Loaf

Take a French Roll hot out of the Oven, rasp it, and pour a Pint of Red Wine upon it. Cover it close up for half an Hour.

Boil one Ounce of Mackarony in Water, 'till it is soft, and lay it upon a Sieve to drain. Then put the size of a Walnut of Butter into it, and as much thick Cream as it will take. Then scrape in six Ounces of Pumasant cheese [Parmesan cheese], shake it about in your Tossing pan, with the mackarony 'till it be like a fine Custard. Then pour it hot upon your Loaf; brown it with a Salamander, and serve it up.

It is a pretty Dish for Supper.[29]

Elizabeth Raffald, as she appeared in The Experienced English Housekeeper, *was one of many Englishmen and women writing and publishing a steady stream of cookery books to satisfy growing local and North American markets. (Una Abrahamson)*

MRS RAFFALD.

The homes dotting the Upper Canadian landscape ranged from humble shelters of canvas, bark, and boughs to well-constructed dwellings of wood, brick, or stone with appendages such as summer kitchens, woodsheds, bake ovens, smoke houses, and driving sheds. It would not have mattered whether the home was large or small, or the family rich or poor; the kitchen with its cooking fireplace of stone or brick was the heart of the home at this period. A crane was built into the side of the fireplace and from it hung the trammel, kettles, and cauldrons needed for cooking, heating water for dishes, laundry and bathing, melting tallow for candles, and a multitude of other tasks. Fortunate was the cook who had either a bake oven built into the side of the fireplace, or one outside, close to the kitchen door. More often bake stones, bake pots or earthenware ovens were pressed into service to make the daily scones, biscuits, bread, and puddings.

In these surroundings, with unlimited ingenuity and primitive hand-made iron and tin utensils such as long-handled forks, ladles and skimmers, some extra cauldrons and pots of various sizes, a skillet, and a trivet, the womenfolk produced at least three meals daily and accomplished a round of domestic chores. A typical day would have started with lighting the fires by 5 or 6 a.m., preparing the family breakfast, clearing it away, and washing up. Sleeping areas would have then been tidied, the beds made, slops emptied, wood chopped and water brought, rubbish and ashes disposed of, and the midday meal prepared, cooked, and on the table for 12 noon. Once eaten, it would have been cleared away, the washing up done, utensils cleaned and polished, the kitchen put in order, candlesticks cleaned, other rooms dusted and cleaned (if needed), guests received and entertained, the evening meal prepared, eaten, cleared away, dishes washed, and the kitchen tidied again. Depending on the day of the week, there might have been bread to knead and set to rise in the doughbox beside the fireplace, clothes to make or mend, medicines to be mixed and administered, and letters to be written before bed.

Breakfast, the first meal of the day, broke the fast since tea or supper the day before. In a humble home this meal could have been a plate of gruel or porridge and a cup of weak tea, and would have been eaten after the chores in the barns and outbuildings were finished. Breakfast would be taken at a later hour in middle- and upper-class homes and could have included thinly sliced smoked bacon, fresh eggs from free-ranging fowl, poached smoked fish, freshly baked bread or rolls, butter, preserves, honey, and tea.

The main meal of the day was dinner, taken at midday, and again the menu would vary dramatically with the economic and social circumstances of the family. One main dish, either soup, stew, or pudding with bread and tea, could comprise the meal in a humble home. For the well-to-do, the meal could be both hearty and elaborate, consisting of soup, fish, joints of meat, vegetables, puddings (both sweet and savoury) fruit, and cheese.

The last meal of the day was variously called high tea, tea, or supper. It

This English softpaste porcelain tea set is typical of those that could have been used at tea tables in the developing communities in Upper Canada in the late eighteenth century. (Niagara Historical Society Museum, 988.122.1)

was served from 5 to 6 p.m. and included cold leftovers from dinner at noon or simple fare such as biscuits, cheese, preserves, fruit, and confections.

"Taking Tea" was a favourite occupation in the capital for it was an opportunity to combine a light meal in the late afternoon with good conversation and fellowship. Many times during her residence in Newark, Mrs Simcoe wrote of having "taken tea" with her many friends, and in many locations, such as in the marquee, in a very large bower composed of oak boughs, with the ladies of the Queen's Rangers at the Landing, and at the mess.[30]

Tea was not always the only beverage offered to visitors, as this traveller confirms:

> The inhabitants of this country are very hospitable. Soon after the entrance of a visitor, spirituous liquors, and madeira are almost always introduced. Usages of this kind appear singular to Europeans. They are however founded in reason. Among a people, where the cold is extreme a considerable part of the year, where covered carriages are unknown, and the roads indifferent, with few houses of accommodation, it may be presumed that such refreshments cannot be unacceptable. Indeed, if

there is occasion to employ any of the lower ranks, there is small progress
to be made, without the aid of liquors. Pay what you will to them for any
little service performed, the compact is never acknowledged as just one,
unless there is an appeal to the rum bottle, in the *dernier resort* ...[31]

The closely knit society to which the Simcoes belonged must have entertained a good deal, for Mrs Simcoe comments on 27 May 1793: "We dined
alone for the first time since we left Quebec. The Gov. having no business to
attend to & the weather delightful we crossed the water & drank tea on a
pretty green bank from which there is a good view of Navy Hall & we
enjoyed this half holiday amazingly."[32]

As Newark grew and became a social centre as well as the political hub
of the province, merchants imported and advertised teas, provisions,
spirits, and tableware to serve the needs of those wanting to entertain. Rum,
brandy, Geneva wine, English goods, green and Bohea tea, soup ladles,
tablespoons and teaspoons, and sugar tongs were advertised in the *Upper
Canada Gazette* at Newark during this period.[33]

For those who did not have cash, merchants and mill owners such as
Daniel Servos carried out a lively business in barter with the families of the
community. Customers exchanged butter, duck eggs, turnips, cabbages,

*New arrivals brought family treasures with them to their new homes and this European coffee
pot is tangible evidence of the diversity of goods that came into the province with the settlers.
(Niagara Historical Society Museum, 982.1.89)*

peas, apples, and venison for imported provisions of coffee, salt, sugar, Bohea, Hyson and green teas, and spirits such as port wine and rum.[34]

It would have been at community and social events that many specially prepared dishes were served, such as cakes, sweetmeats, cold tongue, chowder, pumpkin pie, mock turtle soup, and some very good cakes,[35] and this is confirmed by the following descriptions of evening gatherings at the capital:

> At Niagara, as in all parts of Canada, they are much attached to dancing. During winter, there are balls once a fortnight. These entertainments are not like many English Assemblies, mere bread and butter billets, where nothing is to be met with but cold tea and vapid negus, but parties at which the exhausted dancers may recruit with a substantial supper, and extend their diversion beyond the tame limits of eleven, and twelve o'clock, hours at which a company only begins to enter into the spirit of amusement.[36]

> Mrs Macaulay gave me an account of a Subscription Ball she was at which is to be held in this Town of Niagara (not at the fort) every fortnight during the winter. There were 14 couples a great display of gauze, feathers & velvet, the Room lighted by Wax Candles & there was a supper as well as Tea.[37]

The food patterns that were either established or brought into the new province of Upper Canada were neither predictable nor constant. In a pioneer society, good food and good fellowship were both important elements of community life. During its years as the capital of Upper Canada, Newark appears to have been a closely knit, social community that dined, supped, and took tea together almost daily, and as such it set a high standard for the rest of the province. However, those who lived or travelled at a distance from the meagre chain of settled communities spread across the colony often needed every ounce of ingenuity and skill available to them to be assured of their next meal.

NOTES

1   *Canada Constellation* (Niagara), 12 September 1799.

2   *Visit to the Falls of Niagara in 1800: A Faithful Copy of a Gentleman's Journal ...* (London, 1827), 159.

3   Ibid., 160.

4   National Archives of Canada (NAC), Hudson's Bay Company Papers, Scheme for the North West Outfit, 1794, North West Company Correspondence, 1791-99.

5   NAC *Report*, 1890, 50-1.

6   General Instructions for Deputy Surveyors in the Province of Upper Canada, 1792, 1, cited by Don W. Thomson in *Men and Meridians*, 1 (Ottawa, 1966), 227.

7   W.H. Breithaupt, "Dundas Street and Other Early Upper Canada Roads," *Ontario History*, 21, no.8 (1924), 8.

8   *Canada Constellation*, 9 August 1799.

9   Mary Quayle Innis, ed., *Mrs. Simcoe's Diary* (Toronto: Macmillan, 1965), 112.

10 Ibid., 88.

11 Ibid., 78.

12 Ibid., 109.

13 Ibid., various pages.

14 Ibid., 79.

15 Ibid., 81.

16 Ibid., 97.

17 Ibid., 109.

18 *Visit to the Falls of Niagara in 1800*, 160.

19 Innis, *Mrs. Simcoe's Diary*, 184.

20 Metropolitan Toronto Library, Baldwin Room, Elizabeth Russell Papers, 24 February 1794.

21 T.G. Marquis, ed., *Great Canadians* (Toronto, 1903), 183.

22 Gerald Craig, ed., *Early Travellers in the Canadas 1791-1867* (Toronto: Macmillan, 1955), 6.

23 Peter Kalm, *Travels into North America 1753-61*, cited by Mary Alice Downie and Mary Hamilton in *And Some Brought Flowers: Plants in a New World* (Toronto, 1980), 54.

24 René de Bréhant de Galinée, *The Journey of Dollier and Galinée, 1669-70*, cited by Downie and Hamilton in *And Some Brought Flowers*, 54.

25 NAC, RG 19 E5(a) (War of 1812 Losses Claims), 3741:file 3.

26 Craig, *Early Travellers in the Canadas*, 6.

27 Peter John Stokes, *Early Architecture of the Town and Township of Niagara* (Niagara, 1967), 112.

28 Innis, *Mrs. Simcoe's Diary*, 80.

29 Elizabeth Raffald, *The Expererienced English House Keeper* (London, 1769), cited by Eric Quayle in *Old Cook Books* (New York, 1978), 106.

30 Innis, *Mrs. Simcoe's Diary*, various pages.

31 Craig, *Early Travellers in the Canadas*, 8.

32 Innis, *Mrs. Simcoe's Diary*, 96.

33 *Upper Canada Gazette* (Newark), 10 June 1794 and 10 December 1794.

34 Niagara Historical Resource Centre, Niagara-on-the-Lake Public Library, Servos Mill Records, 1794-95.

35 Innis, *Mrs. Simcoe's Diary*, various pages.

36 Craig, *Early Travellers in the Canadas*, 7.

37 Innis, *Mrs. Simcoe's Diary*, 83.

CHAPTER SEVEN

AT HOME IN EARLY NIAGARA TOWNSHIP

Peter Moogk

Ten years after the town's destruction, Thomas Powis, former owner of the Niagara Coffee House, vividly recalled the horror of 10 December 1813 for the commission investigating compensation claims for property lost during the War of 1812. "O may the commissioners in due compassion, consider the distresses of Niagara being burnt ... consider — four hours notice when in flames, no Carts horses not ten friends and those divided — That what was saved nearly Destroy'd and the Unfortunate in Debth of Winter from Affluence reduced to a birth [sic] in snow, the Enemie pilphering the small remains."[1] The deliberate destruction of St Davids and Niagara (Niagara-on-the-Lake) by the Americans and their allies in 1813, the havoc of fighting around Queenston the year before, and the depredation of township farms by both warring armies scarred the manmade landscape created after the arrival of the American loyalists in the 1780s. The war left a searing memory among the population. When John Goldie visited the area in 1819 he observed that "many people are not yet in such circumstances as they were before the war — Many of the Inhabitants here hate the Yankies, as the Devil, and wish to have another opportunity of shooting a few of them."[2] By then, several victims of the war had removed themselves to less vulnerable regions of Upper Canada. The delay in paying militiamen for wartime service and in compensating those who had lost property created political discontent in the district. Seventy-two-year-old Thomas Powis, who had been ruined by the war and yet remained at Niagara, could not understand the commissioners' procrastination in providing financial help to those who had suffered in the conflict.

For historians of material culture, who did not share Powis's pain, the War of 1812 had a benefit. It generated an incomparable record of the material life of the first generation of European settlers who lived in Niagara Township. Their stories are contained in a series at the National Archives of Canada innocuously titled "RG 19, E5(a), Department of Finance, Upper Canada: War of 1812 Losses Claims." These exceptionally precise accounts from the whole range of society provide information that is missing in other historical sources.

Travellers' narratives of the 1790s give general impressions of the well-cultivated Canadian shore of the Niagara River and the regularity and neatness of the hundred or so buildings of the first capital. "Several," wrote William Berczy in 1794, "are well and elegantly built."[3] Other visitors, such as the Duke of La Rochefoucauld-Liancourt, added a few details on the most notable structures. In 1795 the duke observed that at Newark (Niagara-on-the-Lake) "about a hundred houses, mostly very fine structures, have already been erected ... In point of size and elegance, the house of Colonel [David William] SMITH, lieutenant-colonel in the fifth regiment, is much distinguished from the rest. It consists of joiner's work, but is constructed, embellished, and painted in the best style; the yard, garden and court surrounded with railings, made and painted as elegantly, as they could be in England. His large garden has the appearance of a French kitchen-garden, kept in good order."[4] The architectural drawing of Smith's splendid home has been published in several works.[5] Some War of 1812 losses claims have been used by social historians; the detailed inventory presented by William Dickson, executive councillor, in his claim for property lost in the war has been quoted as though it were representative of furnishings in Upper Canada.[6] Dickson was given £2,672 in Halifax currency as restitution — more than any other Niagara Township claimant. The average award was £320.

Although wealth does not always correspond to social status, there was a social hierarchy in the sums awarded for lost property. Awards above £1,000 were restricted to government officials, merchants, and gentlemen. Below them, other occupations were arrayed in this order:

£700-1,000   Stonemason
Merchant-soapmaker
Printer
Miller
Innkeeper

166

£400-675	Butcher
	Farrier-blacksmith
	Surgeon
	Soap and candle-maker
	Baker
£100-275	Cabinet-maker
	Minister of religion
	Spinning-wheel maker
	Farmer
	Brewer
	Cooper
	Saddler
	Blacksmith-wheelwright
Under £100	Blacksmith
	Carpenter
	Weaver
	Labourer
	Servant
	Shoemaker

This listing also reflected the amount of capital required to carry on certain trades.

As can be seen from this list, the losses claims permit one to reconstruct a picture of the everyday possessions of the humble as well as of the mighty. Petitioners might be tempted to exaggerate the value of their lost property, and the government assessor assumed that most had done so, but the listing of domestic furnishings, even if inflated, was drawn from their experience of what might plausibly be found in a Niagara Township home. Claimants itemized household effects, such as kitchen utensils, that travellers thought unworthy of note. Furthermore, since that property was accumulated over the years, the record is not just a snapshot of life in Niagara Township in 1812; it describes a way of life that developed during the 1790s and the first decade of the nineteenth century.

The completeness of the records was proportionate to the destruction. Houses and their contents at Niagara and in St Davids are described in great detail. Queenston was so badly shot up in 1812 that deliberate burning seemed gratuitous; one resident, hearing of the other villages' destruction, dispatched his "housel Fourniture ... to Mr. David Clows in the Beach woods on the mountain for Safty" where, alas, the American soldiers of General McClure found it.[7] Rural households are not so well documented.

The township's farmers, who often received the property of those close to the frontier for safekeeping, fared much better than the villages. An exception to this pattern occurred when the British troops, colonial militia, and Indian allies encamped at the Crossroads on Four Mile Creek from July to October 1813; they ravaged nearby farms. Split-rail fences were torn up for firewood, and the army's horses consumed crops of wheat, oats, corn, and buckwheat or trampled them. Soldiers cut hay for bedding and dug up the potatoes; they and their Indian allies stole hogs, sheep, and beehives (for the honey). Some buildings were appropriated as barracks and a few farmhouses were ransacked in the absence of the male occupants.

Farmer Peter Bowman complained that, when he was called away to rebuild a bridge at Chippawa Creek, "the Indians Frightend my familly and together with the Troopes plunderd my House." Native warriors helped themselves to men's and women's apparel, cloth, and pillow cases.[8] Farmers were conscripted to work as teamsters transporting supplies, building materials, and the wounded. For the retreat to Burlington in the autumn of 1813 all available horses, saddles, harnesses, and waggons were appropriated for government service. Still, the township's cultivators did not suffer as greatly as residents of the frontier villages, whose homes were set ablaze. As a consequence of the countryfolk's relative good fortune, there are few records of the nature or contents of rural dwellings. From 205 claims I have constructed a composite portrait of the typical Niagara Township house, particularly in the villages. Another thirty claims from the adjoining townships of Grantham, Thorold, and Stamford served as a comparative standard.

An early-nineteenth-century visitor to the town of Niagara — "Newark" dropped out of usage after Lieutenant Governor John Graves Simcoe's departure — and to the village of St Davids would have seen widely spaced houses. "Straggling" was the term used by some travellers to describe the distribution of the buildings. Residential lots at Niagara were frequently one-half acre in area. Each dwelling and its garden were commonly enclosed by a fence of pointed pickets or pales. Six-foot-high board fences enclosed the balance of town lots. Rural split-rail fences might stand in for a board fence, especially on the largest lots. Outbuildings, such as a smoke house, stable, and carriage shed, occupied the balance of the lot. A few residents kept winter "pleasure sleighs" or "carrioles" in their sheds along with a saddle, bridle, and cart. The stables of William Claus, Indian superintendent, contained "a Waggon, a Phaeton and a Gigg, Three Pleasure Sleighs, one lined, and one [with] lined & covered Cushions ... A Wood Sleigh ... [and] Perambulator." "Beaver and Buffaloe Robes" were available to protect riders in cold weather (Vol.3751, #1070).

Town life had a strong rural flavour: nearly everyone had a horse, many kept a milk cow, and a few residents referred in their claims to hogs, chickens, turkeys, geese, and rabbits. Several complained that their kitchen and herb gardens were destroyed in the war; few described their nature. Claimants mentioned the cultivation of "Vegetables of Every Kind" or "Cabbage & Roots" in the kitchen gardens (Vol.3739, Daniel Place; Vol.3744, #305). Peas, potatoes, and turnips were also present. Flowers and ornamental plants were not mentioned. Orchards were already a matter or pride; residents grieved at the loss of apple, cherry, peach, and plum trees. British troops cut down the fruit trees to deprive enemy landing parties of cover. James Crooks, who lived along One Mile Creek at Niagara's edge, boasted that his "Crookston" estate had quince, pear, apricot, and nectarine trees in its orchard as well as a "copse and ornamental wood."[9]

"Crookston" also had a two-storey, brick dwelling which was, at the time, unusual. The well-known claims of William Dickson and David William Smith include elevations of their elegant brick homes with an incised stucco finish imitating cut stone.[10] An 1818 collective letter from fifteen of Niagara's residents complained that a British officer had appropriated "the stone brick and other remaining Materials of the destroyed Buildings" to build Fort Mississauga when the town was reoccupied.[11] This document gives the impression that stone and brick homes were common in the town, but in fact some of these petitioners lived in frame houses with brick chimneys and stone foundations. The first signatory, Alexander Mackie, described his two dwelling houses at Niagara as:

> No.1.   A Frame House — one Story high 18 by 18, Lathed & plastered [with] A good Chimney with a Stone & Lime foundation ...

> No.2.   A Frame House 36. by 20. feet & one & half Story high Completely finished that is to say — A Good Stone Cellar at Least 7 feet in the clear, A Large double stack of Chimneys & filled in with Brick — Lathed & plastered above & below (Vol.3741, #62) ...

Almost 80 per cent of the houses described in the claims were of wooden frame construction, covered in weather-boarding and roofed with shingles. The three appraisers employed to verify losses at Niagara were all carpenters: George Young, John Monro, and James Tinlin. There were very few brick or stone residences in pre-war Niagara. Stone construction was slightly more frequent in Queenston and St Davids, close to the Niagara Escarpment, where stone was quarried. In the second village David Secord owned "a Stone House 1 1/2 Story high 40 by 24 feet with a Cellar" with a stone kitchen wing and an attached, frame summer kitchen (Vol.3741, #50).

Some frame dwellings were the second house to be erected on the site. Although John Burch's sawmill at Niagara Falls was completed in the late 1780s, making lumber available to local builders, many early settlers erected a small log structure as the first house. Even Upper Canada's original receiver general, Peter Russell, had to live in a two-room log cabin. The provincial registrar, William Jarvis, wrote that upon his arrival at Niagara in 1792 "I was obliged to pay $140 for a log hut with three rooms (two of which are very indifferent) with half an acre of ground." By 1796 he was building a new home, measuring "40X24 with two wings 36X18 which would admit us to have a bedroom for the children and ourselves, the kitchen and offices, two sitting rooms and a room for a friend occasionally." The old log house then became an office.[12] David Harkman, a baker at Niagara, had "one hewed Log house 20 by 16 ft." on his lot in 1812. His home, however, was a "Frame House 24 by 24 ft. 1 1/2 Story well finished above and below" (Vol.3738, D. Harkman). Samuel Bunting was then using the old twenty-by-sixteen-foot log house on his property as his cooperage (Vol.3743, #213), while on David Secord's lot there was still "a House built of round Logs 20 feet square." The earliest log cabins were demoted to outbuildings or they became the kitchen wing off the back of a later frame house. Such was evidently the case with William Claus's "frame dwelling House [with] squared log Kitchen" at Niagara (Vol.3751, #1070). Legal officer Ralfe Clench was building his new frame house when the war struck and was still living in "a round log dwelling House 2 Rooms above & below, well lathed and Plastered within — Brick Chimney 2 fire places — Cup Boards &c." His kitchen, root house, and fowl house were also of round log construction. He added, rather defensively, that this "was as good and convenient [an] estate as any in the Town" (Vol.3744, #324). Since the older log structures were often covered with weather-boarding, visitors could easily mistake them for frame buildings.

Looking at the typical frame house of the pre-war period, one would have seen a one-and-a-half-storey structure, with a façade twenty-two to thirty-six feet across, fronting onto the street. In depth, it measured eighteen to twenty-four feet. Weather-boarding or clapboarding provided the usual exterior finish. The colour, when painted, was seldom noted in loss claims. One claim spoke of a white exterior (Vol.3743, #254). Niagara's spinning-wheel maker, John McKay, occupied "the Yellow House Lot," which suggests that a yellow house was a distinct rarity (Vol.3745, #361). There was also a Yellow House Tavern at Niagara. The one listing of paints in a merchant's store spoke only of kegs of "Blue, white & Red" paint and one of powdered red lead (Vol.3740,#5).

Walking up the path to the centre door of a Niagara house, one ascended steps. In a few cases the steps led to a "gallery" or verandah and, less frequently, to a porch. John Ball's house had an eight-foot-wide verandah running the full length of the twenty-eight foot façade (Vol.3740, #19). John Sanders, cabinet-maker of Niagara, occupied a smaller "frame House 22 ft. by 18, one Story & Half with a Porch in front & 'stoop' behind ... with a good Cistern and Cellar" (Vol.3742, #151). The verandah and back "stoop" came with the American loyalists from New York and "stoop" was really the Dutch word *stoep*, meaning a flight of steps. British visitors were intrigued by these appendages which they later associated with tropical colonies. Elizabeth Simcoe described the "gallery" of Robert Hamilton's Queenston home as "a delightful covered walk both below & above in all weather."[13] The verandah provided shade and allowed the windows to be left open to catch the cross breeze on sultry days.

Opening the panelled front door, the visitor usually entered a centre

Floor plans for a 26-foot by 24-foot, one-and-a-half-storey, framed dwelling house and an adjacent cooper's shop at Niagara. The notations seem to be in the handwriting of James Tinkin, Niagara carpenter. This small house with workshop was probably leased to a craftsman by the owners, who were merchants. (National Archives of Canada, RG 19, E5 (a), 3741:61)

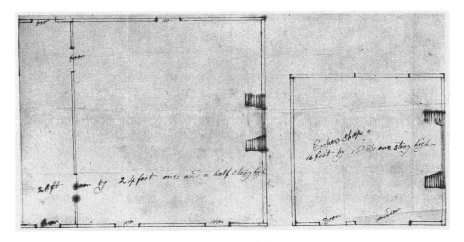

hall or "lobby". The interior walls consisted of smooth plaster over split lath wood nailed to studs. The woodwork might be painted in dark brown, red, or blue, and the upper walls could be enlivened with stencilwork. The floors would be thick pine boards, like those in Samuel Boyd's house at St Davids, torn up by men of the Royal Scots Regiment for firewood (Vol.3743, #212). To the right of the main entrance was the parlour in "genteel" homes.

Elevation of a 24-foot high, two-storey, wooden frame shop and dwelling house with clapboarding that belonged to William MacKearn and John McEwen, Niagara merchants. This building also had an attic, brick chimney, and stone foundation. (National Archives of Canada, RG 19, E5 (a), Vol.3741:61)

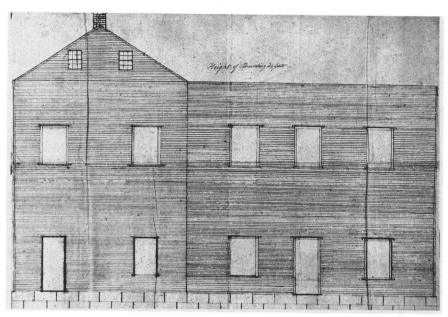

Floor plan for a 36-foot by 24-foot, one-and-a-half-storey, framed dwelling house with centre hall and one hearth. This Niagara home was a leasehold property owned by the merchants MacKearn and McEwan. (National Archives of Canada, RG 19, E5 (a), 3741:61)

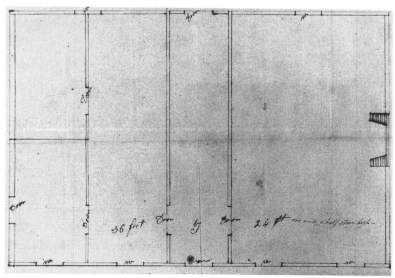

Village craftsmen and merchants placed their retail shop in this room, which would have had a counter and be lined with shelves to display the seller's wares. Workshop and living quarters were generally accommodated in one building. Surgeon James Muirhead had an apothecary shop in his home, and merchant Robert Campbell, who was living on Niagara's Prideaux Street, close to Mississauga Point, kept shop in his house. Campbell recalled that "on the day of Queenston Battle (13 Oct'r. 1812) two hot Shot passed through the Store ... [and] Cut away two shelves ... on all which stood cut Glass Decanters, Tumblers, Glasses & Crokery which was thrown down Broke and destroyed." When Niagara was put to the torch, he tried to rescue as much as he could from the cellar — the upstairs shop had been ransacked by American soldiers. He wrote that what he could not carry out, "sundry heavy articles of pot Metal, Pottery Ware &c [were] Burnt and Split in the Cellar when the [burning] House fell into it." He did not long retain the salvaged goods lying about in the snow: "On the day after the Conflagration the People from the Country and some of our Militia came in with sleds and carried off a number of heavy articles thrown out of the Cellar [:] Jars, Casks, Iron Bars &c." (Vol.3743, #247).

Robert Campbell dealt primarily in hardware while Secord's store at St Davids specialized in cloth and foodstuffs. David Secord had just loaded his remaining stock of green tea, tobacco, sugar, port wine, flannel, and "merchandize consisting of Broad Cloths, Calicoes, Blankets &c" in a horse-drawn waggon when the American troops arrived and seized the lot (Vol.3741, #50). Such a mixed stock, especially liquor, was security against the changeable wants of their customers.

Local craftsmen who lost their accumulated stock and raw materials, such as Alex Mackie the soapmaker and John Grier the tanner, had separate structures for their work. The merchant tanner was reduced to farming for a living despite being "far advanced in life." Grier described himself as "imbittered with the destruction of all his property & reduced ... to contend with the numerous inconveniences of want" (Vol.3741, #60).

Writing-desks appeared in the households of merchants, gentlemen, and military officers and might have found a place in the front room. George Lawe of Niagara reportedly had "a Mahogany letter Case with Pidgeon Holes and Drawers" (Vol.3740, #21). The chesterfield, couch, or sofa which graces modern living-rooms was scarcely to be seen in the early period. Only two "sophas" appeared in the lists of lost furniture. One was in the home of Mrs Catherine Forsyth of Niagara before the "British Indians" carried it off. It may have furnished her parlour along with her cherrywood and mahogany tables and "Oil Cloth Carpet." Oil-painted floor cloths matched the number of rugs and carpets in the few households that could afford them. James Secord senior of Queenston listed his two carpets separately from "6 Rugs & Blankets," indicating that the "rugs" could have covered his beds or have been placed over his knees rather than on the floor (Vol.3743, #235).

In nearly every fireplace were andirons, which locals called "dog irons" or "hand irons." A shovel and tongs were equally indispensable instruments for tending fireplaces and were found in most homes. Few had a "wire fender" (Vol.3740, #11) or fire-screen to catch flying sparks, as did Catherine Forsyth. A fine wood mantelpiece was the central ornament of many later Niagara parlours, yet only three claims mention mantelpieces — one valued at £4.[14] By 1812 open fires were being superseded by more efficient cast-iron stoves, described as having so many "plates," which suggested that they could be disassembled in warm weather. The smoke was carried upward in pipes which were allowed to wander before entering a chimney flue so as to release more heat. Two or three box-shaped iron stoves would be in one home and the parlour was an appropriate location for one. A "Franklin Stove of Eleven Plates" (Vol.3741, #164; cf. Vol.3740, #5) may have come from the United States, while a "six plate carron stove" (Vol.3741, #59) and "3 [enclosed] Canada Stoves & Pipes" (Vol.3742, #174) suggest manufacture in Scotland or the Canadas.

Moving from heating to seating, Mrs Forsyth had a dozen undefined

Two ladder-back chairs flank the tavern table of an early Niagara family (McClelland). (Niagara Historical Society Collection, X 990.006, X 990.005, X 970.561)

chairs. Other claims distinguished between "Windsor chairs" and "common chairs" — the latter were possibly slat or arrow-back chairs made locally. Chairs seem to have been sold in multiples of six since only one claimant had less than six chairs and the highest number in a private home was thirty. Catherine Forsyth would not have had anything so crude as a slat-back sidechair in her parlour, but we can only guess whether her formal armchairs were upholstered or not.

The amusements available in winter for those sitting before the hearth fire or stove are suggested by the presence of a card table at Mr John Powell's (Vol.3740, #11), or the books listed in a number of other claims. Ann Butler, widow of Thomas, owned "1 family Bible" and "1 Set of Humes History of England" (Vol.3741, #64). In the bombardment of Fort George in November 1812 Dennis Fitzgerald, adjutant of the 41st Regiment, said that he lost a Bible, a prayerbook, "4 Volumes Chesterfields letters," and a gazetteer (Vol.3743, #231). Ben Holmes of Niagara possessed a "Testament and 1 Spelling Book" as well as a "Cookery Book," though he, like some others, could not sign his own name (Vol.3740, #9). The reading of Timothy Street, a St Davids tanner-currier, reflected his piety: two large Bibles and a pair of psalm books as well as "a Quantity of Books" (Vol.3741, #79). At Niagara, where Anna Jameson in 1836 saw plenty of taverns and no bookseller, the population was still able to buy books, possibly from general merchants. Widow Jemima Stewart had twenty books (Vol.3744, #256) while the surgeon James Muirhead claimed to have had an "extensive Medical Library with a Number of other Valuable Books" (Vol.3741, #63). The substance of William Claus's library is equally elusive; he had "upwards of 500 volumes of Books, Maps, Atlas" valued at £400 (Vol.3732, II, #1070). William Dickson must have had a substantial number of works in his "neat new Book case made of Cherry, with Glass sliders," although he lived only his "large Bible" separately. When he lifted his gaze from a book, Dickson could look upon "6 Prints, Admirals [portraits and Nelson's] Victory of the Nile; a fine Print Salgre & Traveller; 2 Views of Malsbury Abbey; 2 Ditto. Gentleman & farmers family" (Vol.3740, #5). No other claimant described the nature of the "prints" (Vol.3743, #235) or pictures on the walls. Sergeant William Lowe listed a miniature portrait among his wife's jewellery, which indicates that it was for personal adornment and not hung as a picture (Vol.3745, #385).

In daytime the light by which one read books or admired prints came from windows with twelve, fifteen, twenty, and twenty-four glass panes. Window curtains are listed in the memorials, but only enough for one or two rooms — one set would certainly go to the master bedroom for privacy and

warmth at night. Artificial light came from candles in brass candlesticks —
very common items. Dennis Fitzgerald also had "1 Pair Snuffers & Stand"
to go with his four candlesticks (Vol.3743, #231). The three brass candlesticks belonging to Rosannah Fields were supplemented by "6 tin sconces"
which could be attached to the wall; she also made her own candles from
tallow and wax, as her "1 set [of] candle moulds" testified (Vol.3740, #14).
There is not one reference to a candelabrum in a private home, not even in
the magnificent Dickson residence with its imported English furniture and
damask curtains.

William Dickson could admire himself in his "Parlour Looking Glass."
About a quarter of houses had one or two mirrors; that belonging to widow
Elizabeth Thompson, a loyalist, was a "Large Looking Glass (Gilt frame)"
worth £8 15s (Vol.3743, #248). The mirrors could have been in a bedroom or
the main hallway as an assist to dressing or to increase the light available by
reflection.

A possible yet unlikely fixture of the parlour would be a billiard table.
One was present in the Niagara Coffee House, which is not surprising, but
they also graced two households. The one owned by John Emery had two
spare cloths, which suggests heavy usage (Vol.3741, #78; cf. Vol.3471, #98).
Billiard players probably amused themselves in another ground-floor room
next to the parlour.

Crossing the hallway from the parlour to the dining-room, one would
have espied the best table in the house: a large dining table made entirely of
walnut wood or even with a mahogany top. Local cabinet-makers favoured
black walnut wood. The dining table could be extended by raising drop-
leaves or by attaching half-round ends. Many households had "sets" of
dining tables which could have been placed end-to-end to accommodate a
large number of guests. No chairs were specially designated for the dining-
room, although this would be a natural location for Windsor chairs in
homes where they coexisted with "common chairs."

Tea was certainly consumed in the dining-room and other rooms of
Niagara homes. Tea tables are noted in a few homes along with tea pots,
cups, saucers, silver tea spoons, and even a tea tray. Copper and iron tea
kettles even appeared in inventories presented by craftsmen and poor
widows. "Hyson" and "green" tea were stocked by merchants; farmer John
McFarland claimed to have had fifty-two pounds of tea at his house
(Vol.3743, #254). Tea was, without doubt, the most popular beverage,
followed at some distance by chocolate and coffee.

Tea was served with varying degrees of refinement. Ben Holmes
measured out his tea from tea chest and cannister. He boiled the water in a

tea kettle over the fire; water and tea were then blended in a special pot. To serve his guests he had "12 Cups & saucers, with Teapot, Sugar Bowl, Slop Bowl & Cream Jug" (Vol.3740, #9). At the home of James Muirhead, surgeon, the silver service included sugar tongs and teaspoons (Vol.3741, #63). Elizabeth Campbell, widow of Fort George's major, fled under fire with her children to the Dickson house from the fort, where she had lost "20 Tea Spoons" and "1 Tea-board & 1 Doz'n. tea cups and Saucers" (Vol.3742, #174). Dutch-speaking farmer "Garret" [Gerrit] Slingerlandt served his green tea from pewter and Delftware teapots (Vol.3742, #158). He also possessed pewter and Delft plates, but no tea cups. Pewter plates and basins appeared in a scattering of other homes. The Dutch are almost as fond of beer as are the Germans, and for Niagara's German-speaking baker, tea was no substitute for a malty brew. Karl Gisso had no kettle or crockery for tea; he kept ten-gallon kegs of beer and cordial in the back of his house for himself and guests. Karl was a hospitable fellow: he owned thirty-six table settings of plates, knives, and forks (Vol.3744, #307). A distinction was made between everyday cutlery and that reserved for special events. Charles Ryan of Queenston referred specifically to his "Knives & Forks for Day use" (Vol.3749, #2050). The Lawe family's "2 Knife Cases containing 3 1/2 Dozen of Knives" suggest choice cutlery (Vol.3740, #21). There is only one submission that lists table-cloths to cover the dining table (Vol.3743, #231).

The best dinnerware was displayed. Rosannah Fields had a glazed corner-cupboard for this very purpose as well as a large cupboard with folding doors and a plain cupboard. Timothy Street of St Davids had in his dining-room "1 Co[r]nner Cubboard containing tea Cadie plates dishes spoons knifes & forks" (Vol.3741, #79). The claimants' valuable dinnerware was given a cursory description: China, blue-printed, Delft. A corner cupboard might have contained the tumblers and wine glasses that appear in some ten lists. Two claims cite "black bottles" among the stolen valuables (Vol.3740, #9; Vol.3741, #78). They may have been the equivalent of decanters since the two items do not appear together in any one list. The Fields family's decanters were of one pint and two quarts' capacity (Vol.3740, #14).

Decanters were usually placed on a sideboard, a furnishing of well-to-do homes or of those that had known prosperity. William Robertson of Queenston had "a Large cherry sideboard and mounting compleat" which cost him £12 (Vol.3742, #164); that of Elizabeth Thompson at Niagara was made of walnut wood and equipped with drawers and doors (Vol.3743, #248). Farmer George Lawe owned two sideboards "with [linen] Presses underneath" (Vol.3740, #21). On the top with the decanters would be the cruet stands with bottles possessed by two claimants (Vol.3740, #9; Vol.3742, #174) and, perhaps, a mustard pot for which Elizabeth Campbell had a ladle. The sideboard drawers would be a natural resting place for her silver "Plate [:] 10 Table Spoons, 10 Desert Do., 20 Tea-Spoons, 1 Soup Ladle, 4 Salt-spoons & Mustard Ladle, 2 Silver cups" (Vol.3742, #174). Muirhead the surgeon matched her with his silver service: "8 table spoons, 11 Desert Ditto, 2 silver Goblets, 6 tea spoons, 2 pairs of sugar tongs, 4 salt spoons & 1 silver fish knife" (Vol.3741, #63). All of this was far removed from the world of humble folk who, at best, counted a few silver spoons among their treasures. Nor did such people customarily eat in a dining-room; the kitchen was the scene of their repasts.

The domestic kitchen was connected to the dining area by a doorway; it might be an adjoining room at the back of the house or the kitchen could occupy a wing extending from the building's rear as an L's foot or the stem of a T. Putting the kitchen in a wing spared household occupants from the additional heat in summer. The kitchen's warm air was scented with wood-smoke, dried herbs, and by various provisions stored there. The broad, open, brick hearth might have a crane for suspending the iron cooking pots that everyone owned. Gridirons, frying pans, brass (called "bell metal") pots, and copper kettles were also in universal use. James Muirhead did not even take the trouble to list them; they were simply "Culanary Utensils of the Kitchen" worth £15 in all, twice the value of his "small Still with a pewter castwork and tub" (Vol.3741, #63). A select number of homes had additional amenities — not stills — such as a plate warmer, a Dutch oven, or a roasting oven. One "Double Stove" could have been designed to heat the owner's "2 pair [of] smoothing Irons" while cooking food (Vol.3743, #231). Ben Holmes, who may have been William Dickson's cook, gave a meticulous count of his kitchenware: "6 Tin Tumblers, 4 Quart Measures, 1 Pint do. ... 1 Dozen Tart pans & 1/2 Dozen Tin Platters, 8 Flat Tins for Baking ... 3 Brass Cocks [taps], 1 Frying Pan ... 6 Earthen Bowls ... 1 Tea Kettle, 3 Dozen Black Bottles ... 1 Set of Scales and Weights ... 1 Cookery Book." Ben also had a "lanthorn," which likely hung on a peg by the back door ready for going out at night (Vol.3740, #9).

By the door or over the kitchen mantel in the households of gentlemen and farmers one might see a "fowling piece" or shotgun, and a musket which claimants called a "fusee" or "fuzee," from the French *fusil*. A powder-horn and shot bag would be nearby. Niagara storekeeper and former gunner Charles Koune owned a brace of pistols, four swords, and three fowling pieces (Vol.3741, #71). Colonel Claus bid adieu to "Two Rifles, 1 d[ou]ble. barreled Gun and one single Do., one pair Pistols, and English

Saddle and Bridle with Holster Pipes" (Vol.3751, #1070). The widow of township farmer James Oliver possessed a more conventional array of arms: musket, shot bag, and powder-horn (Vol.3747, #502).

A large kitchen would have been an appropriate location for the spinning-wheels and weaving-looms belonging to those who were still old-fashioned enough to make their own cloth and linen rather than buy the superior textiles on sale at merchants' shops. The farmhouse of John Collard contained "Weaving tackling, 2 little wheels [for] spinning, 1 large spinning wheel" when it was "destroyed by a Detachment of the Enemy under the command of the Traitor [Joseph] Willcocks on the 22nd day of July 1814" (Vol.3748, #639). Most of the villagers wore imported, manufactured cloth. Queenston's weaver Charles Ryan probably made woollen bed coverlets. Making bed quilts was a respectable feminine avocation. A quilting frame had no social stigma and a Queenston merchant did not hesitate to list his own frame (Vol.3743, #235).

A rough table and plain chairs sufficed for the kitchen. Earthenware and wooden bowls were there for mixing and serving food. Rosannah Fields had two "Japan servors," which sound like painted and varnished tin trays for carrying food into the dining-room (Vol.3740, #14). On the kitchen floor or on low shelves were small barrels or earthenware crocks filled with flour, salt, vinegar, lard, butter, and sugar. Animal fat and grease were kept for soapmaking. Sugar was bought in a "soft" form or as a conical "loaf" from which the day's needs were scraped. The Slingerlandts had an additional crock of pickled pork (Vol.3742, #158); pork was also preserved by smoking it. More savoury were the boxes of tea and chocolate. In addition to these, John Emery had "2 boxes Raisons ... 1 do. of Alspice, A barrel of Gin ... 1 Kegg tobacco, 100 lb. of Cheese" as well as a barrel of cider (Vol.3741, #78). Perishable vegetables and fruit ought to have been stored in a cooler place, such as root house or root cellar. William Jarvis described his winter provisions in 1793 as "a yoke of fattened oxen ...; 12 small shoats [hogs] to put in a barrel occasionally ... about 60 head dunghill fowl; 16 fine turkeys and a dozen ducks ... In the root house I have 400 head of good cabbage, about 60 bush. potatoes and a sufficiency of very excellent turnips. My cellar is stored with 3 barrels of wine, 2 of cider, 2 of apples, and a good stock of butter. My cock loft contains some of the finest maple sugar I ever beheld ... also plenty of good flour, cheese, coffee, loaf sugar, etc."[15]

Kitchen sinks there must have been, yet no one mentioned them. The listed "wash tubs" were more likely intended for laundry. Perhaps the stone inset sinks of the period were treated as an integral part of the house. The same may be true for bake ovens, although bread was available from

Niagara's two commercial bakers, Harkman and Gisso. When day was done and washing-up concluded, John Emery had a warming pan into which he could place the last embers of the kitchen fire to take the chill out of his bed. He then retired, bearing the warming-pan and a candlestick, to a cosy bed upstairs. Since only five clocks are mentioned (Vol.3741, #64; Vol.3742, #151 [2 brass]; Vol.3748, #639; Vol.3751, #1104), people probably consulted watches, which were twice as common, or their own fatigue as a guide to bedtime. At the top of the wooden staircase were at least two bedrooms with small twelve or fifteen light gable windows and, perhaps, dormer windows for additional illumination in daytime. Bed clothing and night dresses are mentioned so it seems that day clothes were removed for sleep. Clothing was usually stored in a chest or trunk at the bed's foot; few had a bureau or dresser and no one mentions bedroom cupboards or closets for what folk called their "wearen apparel."

The parents' place of repose was a bedstead made of black walnut or, less frequently cherrywood. The Streets of St Davids also had a black-walnut cradle for an infant. Cots would do for servants. The bed-frame ends had knobs or holes to secure the cordage, providing a net-like support for the mattress. Two beds in George Lawe's house were described as being "sacken [sacking?] Bottomed" (Vol.3740, #21). Three-quarters of the mattresses described were filled with feathers rather than straw, which was a nest for vermin. Nonetheless, Isaac Leech, a Niagara shoemaker, was outraged when "a straw Bed and English Mattress, 2 Sheets and Pillows [were] taken [on 18 December 1813] by an American officer who was sick at his House" (Vol.3759, #1952). Sheets and blankets overlaid every mattress; a favoured few had an additional quilt or counterpane. Retention of body heat and the exclusion of drafts were assisted by the bed curtains and canopies mentioned, in passing, by four petitioners. Widow Campbell had an astounding range of bedroom furniture: "1 Large four post bedstead ... 1 Traveling bedstead ... 2 Coach roof bedstead[s] ... 1 small bedstead ... 1 Wash Stand ... [and] 2 Toilet Glasses" as well as a chest of drawers.[16] At an earlier date Major Campbell's straight razor may have rested beside the basin on the wash-stand. Gerrit Slingerlandt mounted black-walnut bed-steps to get into a typically-Dutch enclosed bed which he called (as the English-speaking clerk heard it) his "slepbenk" (Vol.3742, #158). A *slaapbank* is really a sofa bed. Mijnheer and Mevrouw Slingerlandt had flannel sheets for winter, instead of linen; their heads rested on pillows (probably filled with down from their own geese), and under their chins they tucked English and home-woven blankets, topped by "Calhire [calico?] Bed Spreads."

Rather than venture outdoors at night, people had a chamber-pot under the bed for pressing matters. Although there were no indoor latrines, the humble chamber-pot is never listed in losses claims, possibly because of its low value. Squeamishness was not the cause; widow Elizabeth Thompson of Niagara included a "New Bidette" among her bedroom furnishings (Vol.3743, #248). Thus we leave our typical resident of Niagara Township: tucked into bed and insured against the night-time hazard that afflicts such capacious tea drinkers.

The War of 1812 losses claims reveal that Niagara Township had passed

This late eighteenth-century slant-front desk is made of walnut with maple-string inlay. As it belonged to an early Niagara family, it probably was in use during the capital years and survived the burning of the town in 1813. The brass candlesticks and the looking glass are of the period. (Private collection, photograph, William Severin)

beyond the pioneering stage of development. Few people dwelt in log houses with rustic furnishings and tools of their own making; the era of simple self-sufficiency—if it ever existed—was past. The early-nineteenth-century population belonged to a commercial society and purchased most of its needs. All classes dressed in imported fabrics and ate meals from decorated British earthenware. The local merchants who supplied the crockery, cutlery, glassware, spices, cooking utensils, textiles, and European wines and spirits acted as distributors for Montreal wholesalers.

The variety of trades among the claimants bespoke a diversified economy. The furniture, leather goods, and cast-iron stoves used in the township were products of colonial industry and craftsmen. Flour mills and sawmills were driven by streams descending the Escarpment. Literacy was sufficiently widespread to provide employment for a printer at Niagara, a town with 500 to 700 residents on the eve of the war. Newspapers, books, and prints kept the population abreast of ideas and fashions in the mother country.

British tastes did not mean uniformity: the township had a leavening of German, Dutch, and French-speaking people as well as of American immigrants. A small number of artisans and servants were of African ancestry. At least a dozen religious creeds were professed in addition to "nondescript" beliefs. Our typical Niagara home *circa* 1812 was not an intellectually isolated and rough prison in the boreal forest; it was an outpost of European civilization with its own New World cosmopolitanism.

This article is dedicated to the memory of my recently-deceased father, Willis John Moogk, who imparted his own enthusiasm for Niagara's history to me.

APPENDIX

Sample Claim: Mrs Ann Butler of Niagara Township, NAC, RG 19, E5(a), Vol.3741, No.64.

Mrs Ann Butler of Niagara, widow of the late Thomas Butler of Niagara Esquire, deceased for corn and hay growing on the farm near Niagara for the following articles left in her House, which was destroyed by the Indians serving with His Majesty's forces during the late war, That is to say:

18	Acres of Wheat	100 / - £ 90 - 0 - 0 [sic]
10	Acres of Oats	50 / - 25 - 0 - 0
6	Acres of Pease	0 / - 21- 0 - 0
4	Acres of Corn	100 / - 20 - 0 - 0
100	Bushels Potatoes	2 /6 12 - 10 - 0

UNPUBLISHED DOCUMENTS USED

National Archives of Canada, Series RG 19, E5(a)

Vol.3728, File 4 (Military campaign expenses, Niagara District)
Vol.3732, Folio registers of claims: II (claims 1-420), III (claims 367-1874)
Vol.3738, Alphabetic collection of incomplete or rejected claims (A-H)
Vol.3739, Same (J-Y)
Vol.3740, Claims 1-49
Vol.3741, Claims 50-125
Vol.3742, Claims 126-180
Vol.3743, Claims 181-255
Vol.3744, Claims 256-320
Vol.3745, Claims 321-399
Vol.3746, Claims 400-478 in three parts
Vol.3747, Claims 479-550
Vol.3748, Claims 551-649 in 2 files
Vol.3749, Claims 650-800 in 2 files
Vol.3750, Claims 801-999
Vol.3751, Claims 1000-1139
Vol.3752, Claims 1140-1215
Vol.3758, selected Niagara District claims
Vol.3759, same

Note — The registers of claims use "Niagara" for both the township and for the district, necessitating examination of each document to identify those from the township alone.

NIAGARA TOWNSHIP CLAIMANTS, including those whose residence after 1813 was elsewhere.

Vol.3738 (These claims are ususally numbered, but when they were rejected or questioned, the number was reassigned to an acceptable claim. The result, if one relies on numbers, is confusion.): S. Casaday, J. Clement, E. Cooper, J. Crooks, Joshua Cudney, W. Dorman, J. Duval, J.B. Duté, J. & H. Freel, C. Fink, J. Eggleston (see 157 below), D. Harkman, J. Horn.

Vol.3739: P. Lampman, Widow Lee, Widow Leighton, M. Loughen, A. McDonnell, C. McNabb, D. Martin, M——, D. Place, T. Powis, S. Pritchard, L. Stanley, A. Stevens, M. Thompson, J. Whitten.

Vol.3740: Nos. 5 (W. Dickson), 9 (B. Holmes), 10 (S. Cassidy), 11 (J. Powell), 12 (J. Secord), 13 (C. & R. Fields), 15 (J. D. Servos), 16 (M. McBride), 19 (G. Ball), 20 (P. Ball), 21 (G. Lawe), 22 (B. Fry/Trey), 20 (O. Cockerell), 25 (J. Wilson), 26 (J. Whitmore), 44 (J. Cushman), 49 (R. Woodruff).

Vol.3741: Nos. 50 (David Secord), 51 (J. Lawrence), 53 (F. Markle), 55 (G. Shaw), 57 (A. Gardner), 58 (J. Secord & J. Crooks), 59 (Daniel Secord), 60 (J. Grier), 61 (W. McKearn & J. McEwan), 62 (A. Mackie), 63 (J. Muirhead), 64 (A. Butler), 65 (C. Forsyth), 66 (J. Burns), 67 (A. Heron), 68 (T. Merritt), 71 (J. Koune), 78 (J. Emery), 79 (T. Street), 80 (I. Vrooman), 87 (H. Waters), 97 (C. Cores), 99 (A. Brown), 109 (B. Pickard), 110 (J. Bunting), 125 (R. Kerr).

Vol.3742: Nos. 126 (W. Kerr), 131 (I. Ryan), 132 (J. Secord), 133 (M. Berninger/Bellinger), 134 (D. Martin), 135 (W. Robbins), 138 (A. Secord), 145 (J. Jones), 151 (J. Sanders), 157 (J. Eagleson/Eggleson), 158 (G. Slingerlandt), 159 (L. Farris), ? (J. Wagstaff), 163 (R. Hamilton), 164 (W. Robertson), 165 (J. Hawn), 173 (J.G. de Puisaye), 174 (Elizabeth Campbell), 175 (Edward Campbell).

Vol.3743: Nos. 181 (R. Allison), 182 (J. Lutz), 186 (J. Monro), 197 (S. Quick), 198 (C. Lowell), 199 (J. Stephens), 201 (W. Chriseler/Crysler), 203 (C. Lambert estate), 208 (R. Donaldson), 212 (S. Boyd), 213 (S. Bunting), 214 (Jane Bunting), 215 (estate of John Bunting), 216 (P. Bowman), 217 (J. Page), 218 (E. Horten/Horton), 227 (Presbyterian congregation), 228 (T. Powis), 230 (R. Addison), 231 (D. Fitzgerald), 233 (P. McCabe), 235 (J. Secord), 246 (W. Jarvis), 247 (R.

Campbell), 248 (E. Thompson), 254 (estate of John McFarland), 255 (M. Miller).

Vol.3744: Nos. 256 (J. Stewart), 257 (J. Winterbottom), 275 (J. Friesman), 276 (J. Rogers), 305 (J. Thomas), 307 (K. Gisso), 313 (J. Cain), 314 (E. Scott), 316 (Major Slater), 317 (J. Haines), 318 (John Boyce), 319 (Jacob Boyce/Boise).

Vol.3745: Nos. 323 (J. Levell/Lovell), 324 (R. Clench), 325 (estate of A. Rogers), 330 (estate of G. Forsyth), 333 (A. Meneth), 356 (J.S. Baldwin), 361 (estate of J. McKay), 369 (W. Kent), 384 (W. Lawe).

Vol.3746: Nos. 405 (estate of Ezekiel Cudney), 406 (J. Cudney), 414 (D. Cudney), 422 (G. Young), 426 (R. Jupiter), 449 (D. McPherson).

Vol.3747: Nos. 469 (J. Tinlin father and son), 502 (estate of J. Oliver), 521 (W. Dunbar).

Vol.3748: Nos. 590 (J. Brown), 591 (S. Baldwin), 618 (B. Collard), 620 (W. & J. Crooks), 621 (E. Collard), 627 (estate of D. Clow), 637 (E. Cudney), 639 (J. Collard).

Vol.3749: Nos. 683 (J. Chisholm), 711 (J. Durham), 746 (B. Fairchild), 758 (J. Fox), 764 (F. Goring), 791 (J. Corbin), 792 (A. Cameron).

Vol.3750: Nos. 847 (G. Kirby), 850 (J. Kemp), 853 (M. Sporbeck), 867 (J. Jackson), 879 (P. Lee), 892 (W. Lyons), 897 (estate of M. McLellan), 957 (J. Newkirk), 987 (E. Phelps).

Vol.3751: Nos. 1000 (D. Rose), 1033 (I. Swayzie), 1035 (J. Symington), 1060 (C. Wanner/Warner), 1067 (J. Smith), 1070 (W. Claus), 1073 (E. Wright), 1081 (E. Vanderlip), 1080 (S. Vrooman), 1094 (E. Wynne), 1104 (J. Smith), 1111 (J. Thompson/Thomson), 1115 (J. Woolman), 1123 (H. Woodruff), 1126 (J. Young), 1127 (P. Wanner), 1132 (C. Warner), 1135 (P. Wanner).

Vol.3752: Nos. 1161 (A. Burns), 1167 (A. Hutt), 1177 (G. Field), 1183 (Grant & Kirby).

Vol.3758: Nos. 1663 (estate of Johnson Butler), 1876 (E. McKenney), 1911 (C. Acker), 1952 (I. Leech), 1977 (J. Pell).

Vol.3759: Nos. 2044 (W. Holmes), 2046 (James McFarland), 2050 (C. Ryan).

NOTES

1   National Archives of Canada (NAC), RG 19, E5(a) (War of 1812 Losses Claims), 3743:228, Thomas Powis to Robert Nichol and John Clark, 29 December 1823.

2   John Goldie, *Diary of a Journey through Upper Canada ... 1819* (Toronto: 1967), 33.

3   Archives de l'Université de Montreal, Collection Baby, Papiers Berczy, boite 11442, dossier S\22: "The Traveller: ... An expedition in Upper Canada," 26.

4   William R. Riddell, ed., *La Rochefoucauld-Liancourt's Travels in Canada 1795 ...*, Archives of Ontario *Report*, 13 (1917), 49.

5   Publications of the *Niagara Historical Society*, 11 (1914), frontispiece; Janet Carnochan, *History of Niagara* (Toronto: William Briggs, 1914), opposite 21.

6   Jeanne Minhinnick, *At Home in Upper Canada* (Toronto: Clarke Irwin, 1970), 33. Notwithstanding this comment, Minhinnick's book is an excellent source, especially for the post-1815 period, and it inspired this article's title.

7   NAC, RG 19 E5(a), 3739:file 4, letter M, anonymous claim.

8   Ibid., 3743:216, Peter Bowman to J.B. Macaulay, 8 January 1824.

9   Ibid., 3738:12 (on folder; document itself numbered 54).

10 Peter J. Stokes, *Old Niagara on the Lake* (Toronto: University of Toronto Press, 1971), 10.

11 NAC, RG 8, C Series (British Military Records), 93:19-21, letter to Capt. Henry Vavasour of the Royal Engineers, 5 May 1818.

12   Mary Agnes Fitzgibbon, "The Jarvis Letters," Publications of the *Niagara Historical Society*, 8 (1919), 28, 37.

13   Mary Quayle Innis, ed., *Mrs. Simcoe's Diary* (Toronto: Macmillan, 1965), 76.

14   NAC, RG 19 E5(a), 3743:212 (Samuel Boyd) and 235 (James Secord the younger, also of St Davids, and in the same file as his father's claim, 3747:521).

15   Fitzgibbon, "The Jarvis Letters," 33-4.

16   NAC, RG 19 E5(a), 3742:174; this claim is quoted in Publications of the *Niagara Historical Society*, 11 (1914), 28-9.

CHAPTER EIGHT

EARLY INNS AND TAVERNS

*Accommodation, Fellowship,
and Good Cheer*

Richard D. Merritt

> There is nothing which has yet been contrived by man, by which
> so much happiness is produced as by a good tavern or inn.[1]

Samuel Johnson's tribute to eighteenth-century inns sums up the importance attributed to the inns and taverns of Newark (Niagara-on-the-Lake)
by both travellers and local citizens. This paper will begin by exploring the
connection between Newark's early inns and the evolution of the area's
transportation system. It will then describe the early inns and taverns as
well as their proprietors, and examine the significant role of the early inns
in the social development of the first capital of Upper Canada.

In Britain there was a distinct difference between an "inn" which
provided lodging and board and a "tavern" which served only food and
drink. In the Thirteen Colonies and later the United States, "tavern" was the
usual all-inclusive term used in New England and New York state; in
Pennsylvania, "inn" was more common, while in the South the term
"ordinary" was generally used.[2] In the Newark of the 1790s, however, the
designation inn, tavern, ordinary, public house, house of entertainment,
ale-house, tippling house, half-way house, and hotel seem to have been
used interchangeably, although the last usually referred to a slightly larger
establishment which hoped to attract more "genteel" patrons.

187

REST FOR THE WEARY

One of the prime functions of the early inn was to provide accommodation and refreshment for the weary traveller. Hence the establishment of Newark's early inns closely parallelled the development of the formative transportation network of the Niagara peninsula. In order to succeed, the early innkeeper had to cater to the needs of the travelling public. To understand who these travellers were and how they reached Newark in the 1790s, one has to look at the transportation routes of the period. Andrew Burghardt, in his landmark paper on the subject,[3] points out that prior to the American revolution (when there was essentially no permanent white or Indian settlement in the Niagara peninsula), several major Indian trails crossed the region. The most important, the Iroquois Trail, was part of the major east-west route of eastern North America. In the Niagara peninsula the trail stretched from the Niagara River at Queenston to present Hamilton, where it climbed the Niagara Escarpment. (Most of this route is today followed by York Road and Highway 8 or Regional Road 81.) It followed the narrow Iroquois terrace immediately at the foot of the escarpment, but still above the marshy clay plain some ten to fifty feet below; along this dry terrace the

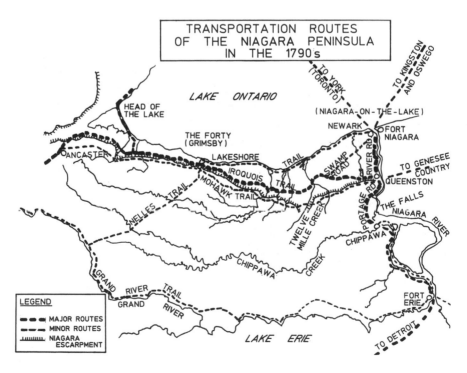

streams were narrow and relatively easy to ford. This was in contrast to a much less important Indian trail which, in following the lake shore from the Niagara River to the Head of the Lake, had to cross the wide estuaries of several large creeks. The shifting sandbars of these creeks were constantly being eroded by the pounding waves of Lake Ontario, and so the trail frequently had to be relocated. Another Indian trail, the Mohawk Trail, led from the Queenston crossing of the Niagara River and followed the crest of the escarpment before rejoining the Iroquois Trail near present-day Ancaster. North-south trails consisted of two Niagara River trails, one on each side, extending from the mouth of the river to where it emerges from its deep gorge at Lewiston-Queenston. The Indian portage trail around Niagara Falls, however, ran only along the east bank of the river.

The most important entry point for the Indians from the east, according to Burghardt, was at Queenston-Lewiston with its dry terraces on each side and easy access to the banks of the constricted river where the current declines in velocity — a good crossing site. The mouth of the river was significantly less important, with most traffic approaching by water from the east.

After the revolution the Indian entry points served as the originating points for white penetration as well. In the 1780s loyalist refugees, congregating at Fort Niagara, crossed over to the fertile plains of the west bank; throughout the 1780s and 1790s thousands of American settlers crossed at Lewiston-Queenston; others crossed at Black Rock (Buffalo)-Fort Erie while significantly fewer crossed at the mouth of the Welland River (Chippawa). Private ferries were apparently available to transport these settlers, their wagons, and livestock, and so on across the river. It was not until 1793 that Lieutenant Governor Simcoe introduced strict government regulations for the operation of ferries at Newark, Lewiston-Queeston, and Fort Erie-Black Rock.[4]

The main route of penetration by the settlers naturally followed the Iroquois Trail. By 1785 it had been widened from a trail to a width sufficient for wagons as far as Ancaster, and in the 1790s it was the most important east-west road in the peninsula. To meet the needs of early travellers, several inns were soon erected along the Iroquois Road. George Adams opened a tavern stand in 1797 where the road crossed the Twelve Mile Creek. It was subsequently bought by Paul Shipman and for years the community which grew up around the tavern was known as Shipman's Corners rather than by its present name, St Catharines.[5] The enterprising David Secord erected an inn where the Iroquois Road crossed the Four Mile Creek (the future site of St Davids, making Secord the only local innkeeper to have been elevated to sainthood). In 1798 some local inhabitants met at one of Newark's inns to plan construction of the Black Swamp Road[6] (later the Niagara Stone Road), which eventually cut through the Black Swamp in the middle of Niagara Township from Newark to join up with the Iroquois Road near present Homer.

The British knew that eventually they would have to hand over the jurisdiction of Fort Niagara on the east bank of the Niagara River to the Americans and thus encouraged settlement and construction of roads on the west bank. The river road on the east bank fell into disuse, while the road on the west bank from Niagara to "the Landing" (Queenston — apparently so named because the Queen's Rangers encamped there in 1792) was improved. Not only was it the major land connection between Niagara and all points south, west, and even northwest at the time but it was already recognized as one of the most scenic drives in North America. As a traveller in 1793 wrote: "Nothing can be more romantic than a road which leads from it [Niagara] to a place called 'The Landing' about nine miles distant ... in the summer evenings, it is the usual resort of those who seek air and exercise,

"The Landing," watercolour by Mrs Simcoe, c. 1792. The Landing or Queenston, eight miles upstream from the mouth of the Niagara River, was the lower terminus for the Portage Road. Ships, unloading supplies for the British posts of the upper Great Lakes and loading furs from the interior of North America, docked here rather than at Newark. The Queen's Rangers were also stationed here; hence, the need for many taverns at "The Landing." (Archives of Ontario, BK2 M54)

and aided by the mild radiance of a setting sun, takes in at every open, landscape worthy of the pencil of Claude."[7] As early as 1792 loyalist Gilbert Field[8] had established an inn on the River Road halfway between Newark and the Landing.

The new international boundary agreed upon at the conclusion of the American revolution had placed the old portage route on the American side. Consequently, the British government in 1788 began construction of a new portage road for the transportation of British goods on the west bank from Queenston to Chippawa. A group of merchants headed by Robert Hamilton of Queenston was granted a lease to operate the portage in 1790 on the understanding that local settlers would be employed to haul the goods. The importance of the Portage Road in terms of the local economy and as the lifeline for all British settlements to the west and northwest cannot be over-emphasized. That it was the busiest road in Upper Canada during the 1790s is supported by a description in 1794: "There [Queenston] have I seen four vessels of 60 and 100 tonns burden, unloading at the same

"Gilbert Field's House," watercolour by J. Cotten, c. 1913. Gilbert Field's house (tavern), built c. 1799 on the River Road, still stands on the present-day Niagara River Parkway, halfway between Niagara-on the-Lake and Queenston. (Metropolitan Toronto Library, J. Ross Robertson Collection, T17081).

time, and sometimes not less than 60 waggons load in a day, which loads they carry ten miles to the upper landing."[9]

Inns quickly sprung up along the Portage Road to refresh travellers and drivers alike. Whirlpool House at Stamford, built as early as 1800 by Andrew Rorback, still stands today. Another early inn at Stamford was kept in the 1790s by Mrs Christina Tice,[10] widow of Gilbert Tice who had served as Sir William Johnson's trusted innkeeper in the Mohawk valley prior to the revolution.[11] Loyalist Charles Wilson apparently deserves credit for being the first innkeeper on the Canadian side of Niagara Falls, but one early traveller of 1796 was not impressed by Wilson hospitality, simply noting on his descriptive map of the Falls, "Wilson's a poor tavern."[12]

In the 1790s even the best roads, recently hacked through the wilderness, were still full of stumps, rocks, and deep holes. In the spring these roads were morasses of deep tenacious mud, in the summer they were choking with dust, and in early winter they were lined by deep frozen ruts. The designation "road" was used very liberally. One reason for the sad state of the early roads was the fact that owners of the property through which the road passed were responsible for the maintenance of that portion of the road. Local town councils appointed "overseers of roads" to encourage improvement but these officials were often ignored.

Winter was the best time to travel, usually by open sleigh drawn by one or two horses — a mode of transport which particularly fascinated Europeans.[13] Gliding over the smooth snow and snuggled down under fur robes, the passengers usually found such travel most exhilarating.

During the rest of the year most travellers walked, rode horseback, or travelled in open wagons or carts drawn by horses or oxen. Another popular vehicle of the day was the calèche or "calash," which was a gig on grasshopper springs with a seat for two passengers. Mrs Simcoe describes driving a calèche herself, with only her four-year-old son as companion, along the entire length of the Portage Road.[14]

Given the traffic on the Portage and River roads it is not surprising that by 1798 two competing stage-coach lines were established between Newark and Chippawa — the first in the province. (One could not travel to York from Niagara by coach until 1816.) Significantly, both of these lines were established by enterprising innkeepers. John Fanning, a Chippawa innkeeper, advertised:"My stage coach is as easy as any in the province and the goodness of the horses and the carefulness of the drivers are exceeded by none. And customers will not be overcrowded in my coaches, for generally four, not exceeding five passengers will be admitted while, for the better accomodation of the aristocratic passengers, way passengers will not be taken up but by the request of the passengers."[15] Meanwhile, two other aggressive innkeepers offered a more democratic service:

> J. Fairbanks and Thomas Hind acquaint friends and the public that their stage will continue to run between Newark and Chippawa on Mondays, Wednesdays and Fridays; to start from Newark at 7:00 a.m. on each day and return the same evening, provided four passengers take seats by 4 in the afternoon. Otherwise to start from Chippawa at 7 o'clock the following morning and return the same evening. Each passenger is allowed 14 pounds of baggage, and to pay one dollar. Way passengers to be taken up at six pence a mile York currency. Letters 4d. each.[16]

The Newark town council for 1798 quickly responded to the challenge of increased traffic by passing a by-law which stipulated that "all Teams, Carriages etc. coming to town, should keep the road, and those going from Town to turn out for them."[17] (Another by-law passed the same day allowed "hogs to run at large.")

Although the coach operator tried to be very accommodating, travel by stage-coach on the early roads could be a horrifying experience. Descriptive terms such as "bone-jarring," "head-cracking," and "limb-dislocating" were often used. Patrons were advised to travel with a hat to prevent direct contact between one's head and the low roof of the carriage! Often passengers were compelled to help push the coach out of the mud or up a hill. It was not uncommon for passengers to be thrown out of their carriage if a wheel should strike a large stump or boulder. The early carriages, because of their ovoid design, were often very cramped inside, made worse by all the luggage being stored inside as well. Moreover, if the passenger list included an "uppity Britisher" and an "upstart Yankee," there was bound to be tension throughout the trip. No wonder passengers were happy to hear the blast of the driver's horn as they pulled up to a tavern for refreshments and a change of horses. However, after each stop at a tavern the mood inside the coach often became more boisterous. As Margaret McBurney and Mary Byers have noted: "At the best of times a formidable experience, the journey often became a rollicking, noisy and occasionally dangerous adventure. Nor was it unknown for the driver to become somewhat unsteady as well, since it was customary for the tavern keepers to treat him to free drinks in exchange for his continued patronage."[18] The mental image of passengers staggering out of their coach upon finally reaching their destination would often have been an accurate one.

Water transport, by virtually any form of craft that would float, was far superior to land transportation in the 1790s. As previously noted, a ferry crossed the Niagara River at Newark between the garrison at Fort Niagara (still in British control until 1796) and a dock situated on the beach half-way between the foot of present-day King Street and the government wharf at Navy Hall (the official residence and offices of the lieutenant governor and his family). Many of the local inhabitants simply rowed across the mouth of the river at their leisure, at least until the Americans established custom houses along the border in 1799. Ice, jammed at the mouth of the river in late winter and early spring, reduced this traffic to those impetuous few who were foolhardy enough to cross over on the ice. Boats ranging in size from simple rowboats and four-horse paddle-boats[19] to 100-tonne schooners — the latter carrying cargo from Kingston and Oswego to Queenston's storehouses — plied the Niagara River between Newark and the Landing. Thomas Talbot, Simcoe's private secretary, often paddled his canoe along this portion of the river.[20]

"H.M. Schooner, Onondaga," black and white sketch. As the Onondaga *was the flag ship of the Provincial Marine on Lake Ontario, many travellers and government officials arrived at Newak aboard this ship. (Metropolitan Toronto Library, J. Ross Robertson Collection, T34630)*

Shipping on Lake Ontario in the 1790s was controlled by the Provincial Marine, which in turn was under the direct control of the British government. Established for military purposes, the ships (of which there were only five in 1792) were allowed, if not otherwise engaged, to transport private cargo of merchandise as well as passengers across the lake during the seven-month shipping season. The flag-ship of this little fleet was a two-masted schooner, the *Onondaga*.[21] The fleet was based in Kingston with other ports-of-call being Newark, York (Toronto), and, until 1796, Oswego. The Provincial Marine also allowed two or three private vessels on Lake Ontario provided they did not exceed ninety tons. The Newark-Kingston trip of 160 miles could take almost one week depending on the wind but on one occasion the *Onondaga* arrived at Newark twenty-two hours out of Kingston.[22] Mrs Simcoe describes one trip from York to Newark taking only three hours and forty-five minutes.[23] Isaac Weld, who travelled from Kingston to Newark in September 1796, took a cabin berth at a cost of 2 guineas and reported: "The cabin table on board this vessel was really well served, and there was an abundance of port and sherry wine, and of every sort of spirits, for the use of the cabin passengers."[24] Because of lack of winds, Weld was eventually forced to land at Mississauga Point in a yawl — after he had changed his clothes so as "to be proper to appear in at the Capital of Upper Canada, and at the centre of the beau monde of the province." He then goes on to relate: "On arriving at the town, we were obliged to call at no less than four different taverns, before we could procure accommodations, the people at the first places we stopped all being so severely afflicted with ague, that they could not receive us."[25]

THE INNS' CLIENTELE

Most of the European travellers on their grand tour of North America, as well as the various government officials coming to Newark to take up their official posts, arrived by ship from Kingston and Oswego. A few Europeans such as the Duke of La Rochefoucauld-Liancourt and most American tourists travelled overland from Philadelphia and New York, crossing at Fort Erie and eventually reaching Newark via the Portage and River roads.

Although these genteel travellers and a host of artists[26] as well came to Newark and paid their respects in the little capital of Upper Canada, for the most part their prime motivation for coming to the area was to experience Niagara's falls. Imagine the excitement and anticipation of the passengers who could see from aboard ship on Lake Ontario, still fifty to sixty miles distant from Newark, the cloud of mist rising from the great Falls. Even in the little settlement of Newark, depending on the direction of the wind, one could hear the thunder of the Falls eighteen miles away. Edmund Burke, the eighteenth-century British statesman and philosopher, had popularized the concept of the emotional experience of the "sublime" — the almost supernatural thrill one experiences when exposed to terror and awesome beauty at the same time. Certainly the great Falls of Niagara met these criteria and its effect on people was further accentuated by the ever-present magestic eagles and the often-seen rattlesnakes at Table Rock. The only other venue in North America where one could truly experience the

"Sir Alexander Mackenzie," oil on canvas by Sir Thomas Lawrence, London, c.1800–02. Alexander Mackenzie (1764–1820), fur trader and partner of the North West Company, discovered the river which now bears his name, having followed its course to the Arctic Ocean. In 1793 he became the first European to cross continental North America and reach the Pacific Ocean. In September 1794 he passed through Newark, giving the first official report of his discoveries to Simcoe at Navy Hall. During his visit, he stayed at Hind's Kings Arms Hotel. (National Gallery of Canada).

sublime was the Arctic. For eighteenth-century Europeans, the trip to the Falls of Niagara represented a philosophical and spiritual pilgrimage. For Americans, the Falls became a symbol of America's limitless potential — an icon for the growing United States which would not be replaced by the Statue of Liberty until the late nineteenth century.[27]

Few American tourists reached the Falls of Niagara, however, until the completion of the Genesee Road and Erie Canal two decades later. The fact is that even in the 1790s tourists in the Niagara area were quite infrequent. Although they generally stayed in the local inn, they were often invited into private homes or entertained by the commanding officer of the local garrison. John Maude reports that, after a "miserable dinner" at Fairbanks' Tavern (Queenston), he was invited to Robert Hamilton's mansion where he enjoyed a supper which "made amends for the badness of my dinner."[28]

Other travellers of the day included merchants and fur traders, some of whom were on their way to Detroit or the northwest. One traveller who seemed to make a point of visiting Newark was the famous explorer Alexander Mackenzie, who stopped there in 1794 on his way home to Montreal, fame, and a knighthood. He received an audience with Simcoe at Navy Hall on 8 September at which he reported on his recent explorations to the Arctic and Pacific oceans and officially enunciated for the first time his concept of a British transcontinental mercantile empire.[29] Simcoe asked him to write an official report, and Mackenzie complied with his request while staying at Hind's Tavern in Newark.[30]

Another interesting visitor was William Berczy, artist, architect, and land developer. While in Newark in June 1794 to negotiate with Simcoe for a grant of land for a group of German settlers immigrating to Upper Canada, he sketched the view from his hotel room (Wallace's Tavern) the only streetscape of Newark to have survived this period.

Although the appointed government officials established residences in the capital, most of the members of the Legislative Council and House of Assembly lived scattered throughout the province, travelling to Newark for the three-to-four week session of parliament each year. Some may have stayed with friends, but most probably boarded in local inns and frequently gathered for animated political conversation in the taprooms.

Many of the clientele in Newark's taverns were one-day visitors to town. Not only was Newark the capital of Upper Canada but it was also the administrative centre for the entire Niagara peninsula, a position it retained even after York became the capital. Although the thousands of incoming settlers passed to the south at Queenston and Fort Erie,[31] sooner or later these settlers and/or their representatives would have to come to Newark to present their petitions for land and return later to obtain their crown patent. It was at Newark that all licences were issued and court cases held. Moreover, since the town was the commercial centre of the peninsula, most of the merchants and early artisans established their shops either at Newark or Queenston.

As early as 1792 Simcoe had proclaimed that a market was to be held weekly in Newark; moreover, an annual fair would be held in town during the second week of October during which the toll for ferries was to be suspended.[32] Local farmers were thus regularly seen on the roads bringing their produce to town. Once the day-tripper had completed his intended business in town he would be tempted to stop at a local tavern for refreshments; there he could also learn the latest news, renew acquaintances, and perhaps indulge in a few games before the long trip home through the wilderness.

Another group well represented in the taprooms of Newark was the military. The officers enjoyed the convenience and camaraderie of their mess. The enlisted men had their canteen but frequented the taverns of "the

"Part of Newark taken from Valaces Tavern the 9th June 1794," pen and ink sketch by William Berczy. Berczy spent considerable time at Newark negotiating with the government for land for a group of German immigrants from Genesee County (New York). The inscription on the sketch may have been added later from memory. The view is more suggestive of that from the back of Hind's Hotel looking up present King Street rather than from Wallace's Tavern on present Prideaux Street. This is the only known streetscape of Newark during the capital years. (Agnes Etherington Art Centre, Queen's University)

Bottoms"[33] — a collection of buildings outside the garrison of Fort Niagara on land now occupied by the United States Coast Guard. There general merchant stores, grog shops, taverns, brothels, and so on catered to the needs of the ordinary soldier, sailor, settler, and Indian alike. In 1794, in an effort to discourage any further development on the east bank, the commandant of Fort Niagara ordered the Bottoms's taverns and liquor stores closed.[34] The result was that the soldiers and sailors began frequenting the Canadian taverns, which became even more convenient once the British military command abandoned Fort Niagara in 1796 and began construction of Fort George on the military reserve (that portion of crown land behind and to the west of Navy Hall). Not all of Newark's citizens were pleased, however. In 1798 several townspeople complained that, while the Protestant soldiers were attending church on Sundays, the Catholic soldiers were permitted to attend their favourite tavern.[35] Interestingly, the local tavernkeeper was entitled to a "gratuity" of a dollar for every able-bodied young man he could persuade (perhaps with a little help from the bar) to enlist in the Provincial Marine.[36]

When the land board met on 24 June 1791 to plan the new town of Newark, one of its first acts was to "authorize a public house to be built on the corner lot at the east end of town adjoining the river, and a Masons Lodge on the next to."[37] Almost all the members of the board were masons: presumably the majority also appreciated the importance of a public house in a growing community. The Masonic Lodge, or Freemasons' Hall as it was generally called, was quickly erected, probably on lot 33 at the northwest corner of present King and Prideaux. Described as "a neat compact building of wood and plaster,"[38] it was a two-storey building in which the rooms upstairs were reserved for the two lodges of masons active at Newark during the 1790s.[39] The public rooms downstairs were used for divine services by the Church of England,[40] dinner meetings of the Agricultural Society, and courts of justice before the court house was completed. It also served as a ballroom and even an Indian council room (before the Indian Council House was erected on the commons). The opening of the first parliament of Upper Canada was probably held there as the renovations of the old Butler's Rangers barracks were incomplete. In many respects the inns competed with the Freemasons' Hall for public functions. The two lodges of masons in Newark, although their regular meetings were held in the Freemasons' Hall, occasionally marched in procession, often accompanied by a band, to one of the taverns for dinner to celebrate such special occasions as the Festival of St John the Evangelist on 27 December.[41] Almost all the early innkeepers as well as most of the other adult males in Newark of the 1790s were members of these fraternal lodges.

The public house authorized by the land board was built on lot 1 at the corner of the present Front and King streets. Francis Crooks, who had emigrated from Scotland and established a store at the Bottoms, was its owner but not its operator; rather, as was very common during this period, he leased out the building as a tavern, which was known as the Yellow House, presumably because of its exterior colour. Several other inns quickly followed to meet the growing needs of the community. It is difficult to keep track of the tavernkeepers and the location of their tavern stands in this early period because they seem to have often moved around from one stand to another, frequently changing the name of their inn as well. Indeed the innkeeper was kept busy with one eye on the bar and the other watching his competitors down the street.

There were at least six taverns in Newark by 1794, when the legislature finally passed "An Act for regulating the manner of Licensing Public Houses, and for the more easy convicting of Persons selling Spirituous

Upper Canada Gazette, 21 December 1796. The hotels and taverns of Newark were busy on 27 December 1796 entertaining the masons who were celebrating the Festival of St John. (Ontario Legislative Library, Toronto)

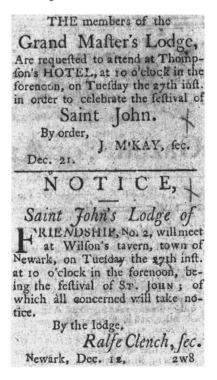

THE members of the
Grand Master's Lodge,
Are requested to attend at Thompson's HOTEL, at 10 o'clock in the forenoon, on Tuesday the 27th inst. in order to celebrate the festival of
Saint John.
By order,
J. M'KAY, sec.
Dec. 21.

NOTICE,

Saint John's Lodge of
FRIENDSHIP, No. 2, will meet at Wilson's tavern, town of Newark, on Tuesday the 27th inst. at 10 o'clock in the forenoon, being the festival of ST. JOHN; of which all concerned will take notice.
By the lodge,
Ralfe Clench, sec.
Newark, Dec. 12, 2w8

Liquors, without license."[42] To apply for a licence, the prospective inn-keeper, upon paying a registration fee of one shilling, was required to swear allegiance to the king and provide character references. If approved, he then paid an annual fee of 56s. The local magistrate could restrict the number of inns in his locality although this apparently was not necessary during the 1790s. Breach of a licence could result in suspension for three years. For a minor offence an innkeeper could end up in the town's stocks for a day. The revenue collected from taverns, shops, and still licences, as well as from the duty on wine, was used to pay the salaries of the members of the Legislative Council and House of Assembly.[43] The secretary of the province, William Jarvis, was responsible for collecting the licence fees. In April 1797 Jarvis reported that he had issued 114 tavern and retail liquor licences in the preceding year.[44] In Newark, his home district, Jarvis personally kept lists of the licences issued;[45] unfortunately, these were inaccurate. Throughout the rest of province Jarvis appointed the licensing agents — considered a plum position.[46] It was not until 1803, however, that inspectors of taverns, shops, and stills were appointed and accurate records kept.

The land board's stipulation that a tavern be erected first, even before any government or religious buildings, bespeaks the importance that the officials placed on the local tavern. So does the fact that, in early Newark as in most early communities in Upper Canada, the churches often seemed to have enjoyed a certain symbiotic relationship with the local inns. Members of the Church of England, the officially "established church," did not actually start construction of their church until 1804,[47] remaining content until then with the Freemasons' Hall. The more numerous and aggressive Presbyterians, however, held their inaugural meeting at Hind's Hotel on 30 September 1794 to draw up a subscription list to build a meeting-house and support their chosen minister, the Reverend John Dun.[48] The following day the members of the previously founded Presbyterian congregation at Stamford journeyed to Newark (and presumably met at the same inn) to sign a similar subscription since they were to share Dun's services.[49] The innkeepers of both communities were generous supporters of these congregations. As early as 1793 the Sons of St Andrew's celebrated St Andrew's Day at Wallace's Tavern — the festivities lasted two days.[50] In most early communities, taverns were often built near the churches and meeting-houses. Worshippers, often chilled during the long church services of winter or parched during the hot humid summer meetings, could seek refreshment and rest in the nearby tavern before travelling home. By providing spiritual and physical sustenance, the churches and the taverns met the needs of the pioneer struggling to survive in a harsh environment.

The Agricultural Society, first of its kind in Upper Canada, enjoyed the patronage of the lieutenant governor and usually met at the Freemasons' Hall, but on occasion the members held their banquets at one of the inns.[51] This was probably one of the few occasions that Simcoe actually entered a public house. (Interestingly, Simcoe, on writing to a friend at home, compared his offical residence at Navy Hall to an English ale-house.[52])

The Simcoes held several grand balls at Navy Hall to celebrate the king's or queen's birthday, descriptions of which have survived.[53] The guest

A blank innkeeper's licence for 1793 signed by both Simcoe and Jarvis (Archives of Ontario, 1792 # 65)

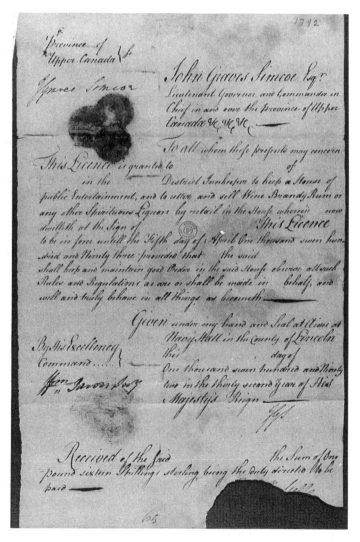

list usually consisted of members of the government, military and merchant classes, and visiting dignitaries. These were very formal affairs where a strict code of social etiquette was observed, although country dances were often more popular than the formal minuets. Open to a larger segment of Newark's population were the bi weekly subscription dances known as the "Niagara assemblies," which were held at the Freemasons' Hall and several of the local inns. During the long, cold, and lonely winters, these assemblies were apparently gay affairs where music, dance, food, and drink were enjoyed often until dawn — so long as enough ladies attended! The first attorney general, John White, whose wife was still back in England, complained in his diary on 8 February 1793 that "only four ladies came."[54] On another occasion one observer, describing the local assembly, dryly noted, "The Ladies from the country are coming in, literally in cart-loads."[55] One of an innkeeper's greatest aspirations was to have a ballroom in his establishment — usually on the second floor — to host such events. This large room could also accommodate auctions, court cases, town meetings, polling stations, and, on at least one recorded occasion in a Queenston ballroom, cock-fights.[56] One meeting held in a Newark hotel, however, was to have greater significance. Pursuant to a recently passed provincial act,[57] ten practitioners of law met at James Wilson's hotel on 17 July 1797 and established the Law Society of Upper Canada,[58] which continues today in Toronto as the governing body of the legal profession in Ontario.

Although these special occasions were important in the social life of the capital, it was the day-to-day operations of the local tavern which had the most impact on the average citizen. In a society where a rigid class structure was still very evident, the local tavern provided a refuge where patrons were treated as equals. (No doubt certain taverns in Newark were popular with soldiers and sailors while others catered to the farmers or the merchant and professional class.) There for a few hours one could meet with friends, escape problems at home, and hear the latest gossip; indeed, the tavern was the news centre of the community in the 1790s. Public announcements were posted as broadsides at the front of public houses; the weekly newspaper, the *Upper Canada Gazette or American Oracle*, first published at Newark in April 1793, was undoubtedly available at the tavern. Newly arrived guests often brought news from near and far. Before merchant Joseph Edwards was appointed postmaster at Newark in 1796,[59] the mail, which included newspapers from Europe (and, to Simcoe's discomfort, from republican Philadelphia and New York), was "left at bars of taverns or counters of shop-keepers."[60] At these taverns, business deals were hatched and political manoeuvres whispered.

Games helped to relieve the monotony of life in isolated Newark and were always available at the local tavern. Chess and card games such as whist were preferred by the military officers and the élite, and were usually played in the officers' mess or in private homes. In the public houses of entertainment, backgammon, skittles, nine pins, and even billiards were popular pastimes. Gambling with dice and wagering on such prospects as the arrival date of the first ship in the spring from Kingston or the sex of an expected child were common. Although such minor breaches of the law as betting and public profanity were frowned upon by the authorities,[61] they were rarely punished. There would have been great excitement in Newark's taverns in the spring of 1797 when that favourite form of wagering, horse-racing (the first such event in the province), was introduced on the commons, with an official purse of 20 guineas.[62] No doubt many side bets were made in Newark's public houses.

All the taproom's customers, of course, were male. Women travellers could patronize the tavern's dining-room and formal parlours; otherwise, they would be seen waiting impatiently outside the taproom's front door.

FOOD AND DRINK

All these activities were nourished with plenty of food and drink. From most accounts of the period and well into the next century, the food served in Upper Canada's inns was generally unappetizing. Yet according to one writer, some of the early commentators, in an effort to make their travelogues more interesting to the reading public, tended to "generalize upon insufficient experience and to emphasize or exaggerate unfortunate experiences."[63] In late eighteenth-century Newark the variety of foodstuffs available was mind-boggling and mouth-watering — sturgeon, white fish, trout, and salmon from the lake and rivers, varied game from the wilderness, livestock, dairy products, fruits, and vegetables from the local farms, nuts and berries from the woods — all apparently available on a seasonal basis at the local weekly market. Indeed, there were some sumptuous banquets held in Newark's inns on special occasions, enjoyed by the lieutenant governor and his retinue.[64] Unfortunately, such repasts were apparently the exception. Dr "Tiger" Dunlop, who served as surgeon at Fort George in the War of 1812, commented that "our inns are bad ... the proverb of 'God sending meat and devil cooks' never was so fully illustrated."[65] the one staple entrée, often served morning, noon, and night, was fried salted pork, usually dished out swimming in its own pool of grease, possibly with fried potatoes and, if you were lucky, peas, boiled cabbage, or turnips. Toast or "cake," often fried in fat, might also be offered. In defence of the innkeeper of the day, however, one must remember that his involvement in a variety of enterprises meant that he had little time for cooking himself. Further, good chefs were hard to find in such isolated communities. Usually his wife and children were in charge of cooking — often in a hot, smoky kitchen in a back wing or in a separate building. All cooking was done on the open hearth. Cooking supplies were seasonal and limited and there was no refrigeration during the summer months; moreover, the cook would never know how many travellers or locals would show up to be fed — often at odd hours of the day and night. The staff, including servants, and in Newark of the 1790s, black and Indian slaves, was also responsible for serving, cleaning, washing, gardening, and stable attending. There probably were some public houses in Newark known for their good food but specific references on the subject have not been found.

For the average British traveller accustomed to a refined table, the inns of early Upper Canada often induced true culture shock. Not only was the quality of the food not up to their standard, but also the manner of serving the food did not meet their approval. One traveller described the despised American mode of service whereby food was placed on the table for everyone to help themselves: "[There was] a general rush from all parts of the house and the neighbouring stores ... instantly the work of destruction commenced — plates rattled, cups and saucers flew about, and knives and forks found their way indifferently into their owners' mouths or the various dishes on the table. There was little talking and less ceremony." The traveller was then confronted with dessert: "Puddings and creams ... were conveyed to the mouths of the different guests with frightful rapidity on the blades of sharp dirty knives. I ventured to ask for a spoon, a request which only drew from 'Miss' a disdainful toss of the head accompanied by the exclamation of 'My! if the man be'ent wanting a spoon now!'"[66]

Of course, many patrons of Newark's licensed public houses, to quote McBurney and Byers, were "singularly uninterested in the food."[67] During the formative years of Upper Canada, "ardent spirits" — that is distilled alcohol — were a very common commodity. At Newark as in other pioneer societies, distilling whisky from wheat was a traditional outlet for grain.[68] Moreover, the cheapest way to transport grain was as whisky. This practice actually contributed to a shortage of grain for flour on the Niagara frontier in the late 1790s.[69] When the distiller could not pay the farmer in ready cash —a common occurrence—the settler exchanged his grain for whisky. What he and his family could not consume the farmer could sell to the local inns and general merchants (who could sell liquor if they possessed a shop licence to do so). In addition, the garbage of the distilling process, "mash," was excellent for fattening livestock, presumably keeping them contented as well! Whisky was often served to the family including the children, at breakfast. For the pioneer confronted with long hours of hard physical labour, alcohol served as a stimulant; most community efforts such as the building "bees" were fueled by the ever-present pail of whisky; liquor flowed at wakes and weddings; court cases held in the local inns were often settled with the assistance of the "ardent spirits"; banquets and dinners were noted for their many toasts. Men of position and even some clergymen were often "under the influence" towards the end of the day. Drunkeness was not considered a sin unless it significantly interfered with one's duty or occupation; moreover, alcohol was recommended in Newark for the treatment of the endemic fever and ague.[70] The prime ingredient of most apothecary remedies of the day was alcohol.[71] A public letter to the editor of the *Upper Canada Gazette* spoke out against drunkeness and wife abuse as

"A Village Tavern," oil on canvas by John Lewis Krimmel, Philadelphia, c. 1813. Although of a slightly later date than the subject period of this paper, this painting accurately portrays the social interaction inside a typical North American taproom of the day. Note the frame bar with punch bowls, decanters, glasses, and mugs all stored on its shelves. The mail stage-coach has just arrived; newspapers, for the use of customers, are available in portable frames on the wall. (Toledo Museum of Art, Ohio. Gift of Florence Scott Libbey)

early as 1799;[72] however, the critics of liquor, responding to the social ills caused by such alcohol consumption, did not become sufficiently organized to form a temperance society in Upper Canada until 1828.[73] A prospective distiller had to apply for a licence for which he paid 15*d*. per gallon capacity of his still.[74] It must have been a profitable business. According to Jarvis's records, William Legget of Newark was licensed for a still of sixty-seven gallons in 1797, and three years later he had two new stills with a total output of 300 gallons.[75] Undoubtedly many local stills were not licensed.

Although supposedly made from the best grains and purest waters, local whisky was probably often made from mouldy rye, frosty potatoes, pumpkins, and so on. The product was frequently sold the day after completion of the distilling process. "Old" whisky meant "aging" for one month![76] Rum, distilled from sugar cane, was transported into the interior of North America in tremendous quantity from Halifax and the West Indies. The common soldier of the British army was issued a daily ration of rum which he could supplement at the canteen, his favourite tavern, or a local merchant's shop. Rum was the common denominator in the Indian trade and was often included in the government's annual presents to the Indians. Brandy, distilled from wine, was enjoyed by British army officers and gentlemen. Gin, distilled from grains and flavoured by juniper berries and other aromatics, was often called in Upper Canada simply "Geneva," "Holland," or "Amsterdam." In Newark and York, gin was often mixed with other ingredients to make "flips" and "gin-slings."

Breweries were usually established near British garrisons to meet the soldiers' traditional thirst for beer. The first issue of the *Upper Canada Gazette* carried an announcement of the opening of a local brewery, and it urged farmers to grow barley for which they would be paid one dollar per bushel.[77] This was encouraged by Simcoe, who hoped that the lower classes would learn to prefer beer over the more potent ardent spirits.[78] The experiment was apparently unsuccessful — only one brewery in the area was advertising ale for sale in 1799.[79] Tavernkeepers learned to make their own beer out of molasses. Another malt liquor, porter, was also popular in British North America, whereas spruce beer was not popular in Upper Canada and was rarely served.[80]

Port, a red wine from Portugal, was a favourite drink of Newark's upper class. By the late 1790s it was a fortified wine — that is, wine with brandy added. Madeira, also a fortified wine imported from the island of Madeira, would have been stocked by the innkeeper for his genteel guests and for special banquets. Claret, a generic term for clear red wines from the Bordeaux region of France, was also available on the Niagara frontier.

During this period, champagne, as either a still or sparkling wine, red or white, was a rare commodity and probably not available in Newark's inns or merchant shops.

Served hot or cold, punch was concocted of rum or brandy mixed with various fruit juices, sugar, and spices. Schrub, a popular drink in Upper Canada, was a mixture of rum, sugar, and lemon or lime juices. Cider (cyder) was also popular. At first it was brought in from Detroit,[81] but once the apple orchards were established in the Niagara region it was produced locally.

Tea was a very popular drink in England during the eighteenth century, but real Chinese tea was expensive in the interior of North America. Hence, "green tea," made from various local grasses and leaves, was usually served — and often not appreciated, especially by the sophisticated traveller. A generation later, one pioneer physician claimed that one half of his practice was owing to "green tea."[82]

There are few references to coffee during this period since it too was expensive. Perhaps those who felt the need substituted the bean of the Kentucky coffee tree, occasionally found in the forests of Niagara. The term "coffee house," at which much more than coffee was served, was used in England to denote those more aristocratic public houses which served as a rendezvous for various professional and social groups to discuss the issues of the day. Surprisingly, there was no coffee house in Newark during the capital years whereas William Cooper was advertising his Toronto Coffee House in the new capital at York as early as 1801.[83] The earliest coffee house in the Niagara area was apparently the Niagara Coffee House (next door to the Yellow House Tavern) operated by Thomas Powis just prior to the War of 1812.[84] References to large quantities of chocolate in local inkeepers' War of 1812 losses claims[85] attest to the popularity of chocolate drinks at Newark.

THE PUBLIC HOUSE

No contemporary sketches or paintings of any of Newark's or Queenston's eighteenth-century inns have survived. Gilbert Field's house on the River Road, although altered, may date from this period. My description of a typical inn of the period, then, is based on that of contemporary North American inns.

Walking along the street one would have easily identified the inns by their tavern signs. Most of Newark's inns were known by the owner's name — for example, Wilson's Hotel — but a few had more interesting names, such as Weir's Sign of the Lyon, Hind's King's Arms Hotel, and Thompson's Sign of the Black Swan. Interestingly, all had very English names, perhaps indicative of the fact that Newark was the capital of a British colony. Some of the early tavern signs were painted by well-known artists eager to supplement their meagre commissions;[86] one traveller noted that it sometimes appeared more effort and money had been spent on the elaborate sign than on the tavern house itself.[87] (None of Newark's early tavern signs have survived, but apparently they were not as heart-rending as the sign of one early American inn, which, carrying the name "Labour in Vain," depicted a white boy trying to scrub white a black boy standing in a tub of water.[88])

The earliest inns were simply private dwellings in which the owners were willing to take in paying guests, but most of the structures built specifically as inns followed a basic simple design. Two front doors usually greeted the potential customer. The central doorway opened into a reception area with access to the dining-room and/or parlour on the main floor and a stairway upstairs. The other exterior door, where one might encounter several angry women waiting for their husbands, was the taproom door. Stepping inside, the customer would have been almost overwhelmed by the smells of wood and tobacco smoke, stale liquor, and perhaps the occasional whiff of frying pork. His ears would be assaulted by the din of many men's voices, the clink of glasses, the crackle of thrown dice, and possibly the faint strains of a single fiddler in the background. As his eyes grew accustomed

"Minuet of the Canadians," engraving by Joseph Stadler (after Heriot), c. 1805. Although this scene depicts a Quebec ballroom of the period, the "assemblies" which were often held in the ballrooms of Newark's inns would have had a similar ambience. (Samuel E. Weir Collection, Queenston, Ontario)

to the darkness of the room, he might discern a few men warming themselves beside a blazing fire in the hearth, perhaps talking excitedly about their recent trip to the Falls; behind them several men might be standing at the bar drinking from pewter tankards or simple glasses, perhaps discussing the price of grain. In the centre of the room the customer might find several tavern tables at which men, seated on Windsor chairs, were busily eating dinner off pewter or earthenware plates. A pair of glass decanters would possibly be sitting on the table as well. In one corner, several men might be hunched down on the floor throwing dice, while in another corner two well-dressed gentlemen, smoking long clay pipes, might be seen discussing a legal document. A door at the back of the room might lead to another games room, complete with billiards table, or to the kitchen. Beyond, a doorway would lead to the inn's yard. There the customer could perhaps find some local boys, already a bit tipsy, practising their militia drills, while to one side of the yard two young men might be seen admiring a handsome stallion "at stand," available for stud.[89] At the end of the yard stood the necessary privies, and the large stables housing livestock, several horses, stage-coach carriage, and, perhaps, in the back corner, a recently painted sleigh, all presided over by the proud ostler. A fenced-in garden would complete the scene.

Back in the main building, after spending a few hours in the taproom treating his men friends, singing bawdy songs, and trading stories, our customer would be directed upstairs to the "ballroom." Tonight, however, there would be no gay dance; instead, the room would be filled with bodies

"Figures in a Tavern or Coffee House," oil on panel by William Hogarth (attrib.). This painting apparently depicts an interior scene in an eighteenth-century English tavern or coffee house. However, one could imagine a similar scene to portray a heated discussion among legislators relaxing in one of Newark's taverns during the capital years. (Paul Mellon Collection, Upperville, Virginia)

sound asleep on straw mattresses. No privacy here! Taking his boots off, the customer would simply curl up on an empty mattress with his clothes on. Foul breath and body odour (after all, a person was lucky if he had one bath a month), snoring and coughing, and sporadic shouts from the taproom below would not allow for easy sleep. The customer might be consoled by the realization that even in the "private bed-rooms" two strangers were often expected to share the same small bed. The innkeeper's family would occupy a few rooms in a back wing. The servants would merely curl up in front of the hearth or, if lucky, they would have a room in the unheated attic.

No sooner asleep, the customer would often be awakened by the intense and almost unbearable itchiness induced by fleas and bed-bugs and, in the summer months, by the high pitched whine of the ever-present mosquito. As one traveller put it, "There was before morning a bug stained floor and a blood marked wall. The sacrifice of insect life was immense. The piled up carcasses of the slain attested the vigilant night-watch of the unfortunate."[90]

In the morning the customer might find a basin of water and a common "clean" rag in the hallway; a public hair brush and comb might also be provided. Soap and tobacco would probably be available for sale downstairs where breakfast, consisting of fried pork, fried toast, and fruit pie, served with a gill of whisky, might be waiting.

THE INNKEEPERS OF NIAGARA

The innkeeper of early Newark, as in other pioneer communities, was one of the most important personalities in the settlement. Not only did he supervise the many activities in his hostelry, but as postal clerk and host to travellers from afar he was the source of much of the news in the isolated community. As mason, church member, and, in many cases, town councillor, he was well known and usually respected. Many of them had other trades to fall back on if business were slow. One early Newark tavernkeeper was a skillful carpenter, crafting fine wooden cases for Simcoe's office; another was a butcher while still another was a respected tailor. As one of the few businessmen likely to be paid in hard cash,[91] they often invested in other enterprises, such as land speculation, stage-coach lines, postal service, ferries, and shipping. Many of the local innkeepers were interrelated. Although most of the tavernkeepers in Upper Canada in the early nineteenth century were Irish or American,[92] the first generation of Newark's innkeepers was predominantly loyalist or Scot, which reflected the ethnic make-up of the community at large at that time. There was one occupational hazard, however — the ready availability of liquor — and many seem to have succumbed prematurely. The Reverend Robert Addison, recording

211

the burial of yet another innkeeper, commented, "a bad profession for any but very sober men."[93] On several such occasions, the innkeeper's widow, with years of experience in the business, successfully took over the running of the inn. (In a male-dominated society it was a remarkable feat for these women to deal with male customers as equals.)

Although that inveterate patron of eighteenth-century British inns and taverns, Samuel Johnson, might have been critical of some of Newark's early public houses, he probably would have agreed on their immense importance in the social life of the capital. As the little settlement grew and prospered, so too did the local inns and taverns, catering to the physical needs of virtually every adult male citizen. The innkeeper of the day was indeed a resourceful and enterprising fellow who probably knew more about life in the capital than did any other member of society.

APPENDIX

The following list in alphabetical order includes all known innkeepers at Newark and surrounding area during the 1790s. I have included the Landing as well, since it was an integral part of the community. It is difficult to trace these men and women who often did not own the property where they kept their public house; hence, title searches are of limited value. Often the property was leased to one innkeeper who subsequently subleased it to another. Early newspaper advertisments rarely give the location of the stands; many innkeepers simply disappeared from Newark — presumably moving on to other more promising locales.

GEORGE ADAMS kept a tavern in Queenston as early as 1795,[94] but also established an inn in 1797 on the Iroquois Road where it crossed the Twelve Mile Creek.[95] He also owned lot 6 in Newark but it is not clear whether he actually operated an inn there.

THOMAS ADAMS was probably the brother of George. He owned lot 84 in Newark. According to Jarvis's lists,[96] he received a licence to operate an inn in 1799 or earlier. He also owned a tavern in Queenston which he leased to JAMES SECORD[97] but subsequently sold to J.D. Stoddard in 1799.[98]

ROGER BRADT was one of the earliest innkeepers in Newark, having received his licence from Jarvis in 1793[99] to keep "an orderly house of entertainment." His inn was possibly located on lot 15 on Front Street.

JOHN DALY received a licence to operate an inn at Newark in 1798[100] and this was renewed in 1799 in partnership with Honora Edwards. He owned lots 21, 22, and 23 on Prideaux Street. He was also a well-known tailor in the capital.

GILBERT DRAKE announced in the local newspaper in October 1800 that he was recently arrived from New York and had taken over the operation of the Lyon Hotel.[101] Four years later he opened a tavern in Queenston, which ke kept until at least 1809.[102]

JOSHUA FAIRBANKS was host to the masons of Lodge No.2 in Queenston as early as 1795.[103] He was involved in one of the Newark-Chippawa stage-coach partnerships.[104] In 1802 he sold his inn to Patrick McCabe.[105]

GILBERT FIELD was the first innkeeper in the area to receive his licence — in December 1792.[106] Gilbert served in Butler's Rangers and established his inn in Niagara Township, lot 15 (which had been originally settled by his parents, loyalists Rebecca and George Field), on the River Road. As early as 1799 Field began construction of his substantial brick house,[107] which still stands today, protected by the Ontario Heritage Foundation. The masons of St John's Lodge of Friendship met at Gilbert Field's tavern from 1799 to 1804.[108] As an innkeeper, Field was reputed to have taken advantage of some of his inebriated soldier-patrons by obtaining their land grants as payment for their bar bills.[109] Probably Field was not the only enterprising innkeeper to take advantage of this situation. Field died in 1814, apparently while his inn was being used as a barracks by the militia.[110]

CHARLES FIELDS obtained a still licence as early as 1793[111] and in 1799 he took over the operation of the Sign of the Lyon on Prideaux,[112] but he probably also operated an inn on his own lot 53 at the corner of Queen and Gate streets. Fields is best remembered for an advertisement which appeared in the local paper in 1802: "All persons are forbidden harboring my Indian slave Sal as I am determined to prosecute any offenders to the utmost extent of the law and persons who suffer her to remain on their premises for the space of half an hour without my written consent will be taken as offending and dealt with accordinglly."[113] No doubt Sal was very much needed to perform some of the many menial tasks in Fields's inn.

JOHN FLACK, who owned lot 24 on Prideaux, was issued a tavern licence at Newark in 1794.[114] He also plied his other trade, that of shoemaker, during the capital years. He eventually sold lot 24 to Thomas Hind, another tavernkeeper.

THOMAS HIND leased Crooks's Yellow House on lot 1 under the name of King's Arms Hotel from 1793 to 1796.[115] There his guests included Alexander Mackenzie,[116] members of the local Presbyterian congregation,[117] and the masons.[118] In 1804-05 he was running a hotel in York.[119] Thomas Talbot apparently took Hind's children as servants to his settlement at Port Talbot on Lake Erie.[120]

Major THOMAS INGERSOLL, a Patriot from Massachusetts, kept one of the earliest taverns at Queenston (which was also known as Ingersoll's Landing or Ingersoll's Queenston Landing).[121] Ingersoll put his inn up for sale in 1801[122] and subsequently leased from the government an inn at Port Credit.[123] He eventually founded the Ontario town which bears his name today. Ingersoll's daughter, Laura (1775-1868), married JAMES SECORD, and together they operated intermittently an inn at Queenston until the War of 1812 when James was wounded and Laura took her famous walk.

FRANCIS KEARNS received his licence in 1799 and kept an inn owned by lawyer William Dickson.[124] The following year he took over the operation of the Yellow House for one year.[125] He was also a butcher in Newark during the capital years.

JOHN KNOX took over Mrs Weir's inn (Sign of the Lyon) for one year in 1798.[126] By 1800 he was operating the Ferry House "on the Beech [sic],"[127] and by 1812 he was apparently running an inn at Stamford. His claim for losses during the War of 1812 provides an interesting inventory of the furnishings of an inn of the period.[128]

WILLIAM LYONS was issued a licence at Niagara in 1800.[129]

JAMES MACHLEM, innkeeper and merchant at Chippawa, also operated Fairbanks' Tavern at Queenston in 1800[130] and was involved in the stagecoach business.[131]

FREDERICK MARKLE operated the Yellow House in 1800[132] and subsequently took on a partner, James Hamilton.[133] They were partners in a stagecoach line between Newark and Chippawa.[134]

MARY McBRIDE received a licence to operate an inn in 1793.[135] John McBride and his wife, Hannah, served as doorkeeper and housekeeper respectively to the Executive Council chambers at Navy Hall, and later followed the government to York, where Hannah was operating a tavern as early as 1801.[136] In 1802 a Jane McBride married John Emery, a recently arrived innkeeper in Niagara.[137]

JOHN MUIR was licensed to operate an inn as early as 1800,[138] probably in Niagara Township.

RICHARD PHILLIPS was issued a licence to operate an inn in 1793.[139]

DAVID SECORD (1759-1844) served in Butler's Rangers during the American revolution, for which he was granted a large tract of land where the Iroquois Trail crossed the Four Mile Creek. There he established several mills, an inn, distillery, tannery, and other enterprises which became the nucleus of the town that now bears his name (St Davids). He was an older brother of JAMES.

JAMES SECORD (1773-1841) was the son of loyalists and operated a tavern at Queenston as early as 1799. He also operated a pot ashery at Queenston. He married Laura Ingersoll, daughter of innkeeper THOMAS INGERSOLL (*see* INGERSOLL).

TITUS SIMONS (1743-1824) served as quartermaster in Peter's Rangers during the American revolution.[140] In 1793 he applied for an innkeeper's licence at Kingston[141] but apparently followed his son, Titus Geer Simons (1765-1829), who had been appointed co-publisher of the *Upper Canada Gazette*, to Newark in 1797. Simons's inn must have been near that of William Wallace as a disastrous fire in 1797 destroyed the stables of both inns. Simons then followed his son to York, where he applied unsuccessfully in 1801 for a licence to operate an inn.[142] In 1802 he and his son moved to West Flamborough.

ARCHIBALD THOMPSON may be the Archibald Thompson who arrived in the Thirteen Colonies from Scotland in 1773, served with Captain Joseph Brant during the revolution, arrived in Niagara in 1779, and was eventually granted land near the great whirlpool.[143] Another loyalist, Archibald Thompson, master carpenter, arrived in Newark *circa* 1794 from Kingston and later moved to York.[144] Archibald Thompson, hotel keeper, owned at least two Newark town lots, 152 and 186. He operated "The Hotel" in Newark, which apparently was more sophisticated than the other inns in town. The Court of King's Bench was held there in the spring of 1797,[145] apparently because there were insufficient jurors in the new capital of York and the court house at Newark was unfinished. While in town for the court sessions, the magistrates also met there to license public houses for the ensuing year.[146] In April, Thompson leased his hotel to JAMES WILSON.[147] The actual location of this hotel is unknown.

ELIZABETH THOMPSON claimed on one of her petitions that her family had rendered important services to the British government during both the French and American revolutionary wars.[148] Widow Thompson owned lots 28 and 30 on Prideaux Street and apparently operated a tavern on at least one of these lots. This may have been the tavern stand known as the "Black Swan Tavern."[149]

WILLIAM WALLACE appears on Jarvis's list as early as 1793.[150] He owned a portion of Robert Kerr's lot 28 as well as lot 29, both on Prideaux Street. Both William and his brother James (married to sisters) were fine carpenters and were commissioned by the lieutenant governor to produce document cases for his offices at Navy Hall.[151] Wallace also speculated in land, purchasing from the Six Nation Indians block 3 of their Grand River lands (consisting of 80,000 acres) for £16,364. Wallace was unable to keep up the mortgage payments and eventually received ownership of only 7,000 acres of the original grant.[152] A mason and charter member of the Presbyterian congregation of Newark, he immigrated to the United States before the outbreak of the War of 1812.

ROBERT WEIR kept the Sign of the Lyon on lot 45 on Prideaux Street. Weir was one of the partners in the unsuccessful private scheme to develop an iron works near Chippawa.[153] Robert died in 1797 and the inn was operated by his wife for at least one year before being taken over by CHARLES FIELDS.[154]

HENRY WEISHUHN, tavernkeeper at Queenston[155] and farmer in Stamford, was also involved in the unsuccessful scheme to develop an iron works at Chippawa.[156]

JAMES WILSON, apparently unrelated to Charles or JOHN WILSON, took over the operation of "The Hotel" from ARCHIBALD THOMPSON in April 1797[157] and hosted the inaugural meeting of the Law Society of Upper Canada.[158] He may be the James Wilson, early settler of Barton and Ancaster, who along with Richard Beasley and John Baptiste Rousseau purchased block 2 of the Grand River lands from the Six Nation Indians,[159] which was eventually sold to a large group of Mennonite immigrants from Pennsylvania.

JOHN WILSON (1772-1837) was a son of Irish John Willson, a loyalist from New Jersey and a younger brother of Charles Wilson, first innkeeper at the Falls.[160] John kept an inn in Niagara Township, presumably on the River Road for which he was granted a licence as early as 1800.[161] Later he operated a hostelry, The Exchange, on lot 70 at the corner of Queen and Gate streets in Newark. This has caused confusion concerning the actual site of the first meeting of the Law Society of Upper Canada at "Wilson's Hotel."[162] John Wilson's first wife, Jane Adams was probably related to GEORGE and THOMAS ADAMS. Wilson's second wife, Ann McFarland, was a daughter of John McFarland of the River Road.

NOTES

I would like to express my appreciation to L. Gula and G. Molson, Niagara-on-the-Lake Public Library, P. Kennedy and P. Fortier, National Archives of Canada, J. Ormsby and N. Butler, Niagara Historical Society, and the staff members of the Archives of Ontario, the Metropolitan Toronto Library (Baldwin Room), the Niagara Falls Public Library, and the Library of the Law

Society of Upper Canada for their assistance in the preparation of this paper. Special thanks are owed to my family for their patience and understanding.

1   James Boswell, *Boswell's Life of Johnson* (London: Macmillan and Company, 1929), 21 March 1776, 341.

2   Elise Lathrop, *Early American Inns and Taverns* (New York: Arno Press, 1977), viii.

3   Andrew Burghardt, "The Origin and Development of the Road Network of the Niagara Peninsula, Ontario, 1770-1851," *Annals of the Association of American Geographers*, 59, no.3 (September 1969), 417-40.

4   Ernest Cruikshank, ed., *Correspondence of Lieut. Governor John Graves Simcoe ...* (5v., Toronto: Ontario Historical Society, 1923-31), 4:352.

5   John Jackson, *St. Catharines, Ontario, Its Early Years* (Belleville: Mika Publishing Company, 1976), 128-9.

6   *Upper Canada Gazette or American Oracle*, 20 January 1798.

7   "Canadian Letters, Description of a Tour Thro' the Provinces of Lower and Upper Canada, 1792-1793," *The Canadian Antiquarian and Numismatic Journal*, 9 (July-August 1912), 132.

8   Metropolitan Toronto Library, Baldwin Room (MTLBR), William Jarvis Papers, "Licences, etc.," S109, B-52.

9   John Cozens Ogden, *A Tour Through Upper and Lower Canada* (Litchfield, Conn.: 1799), 100.

10   Ernest Cruikshank and A.F. Hunter, eds., *Correspondence of the Honorable Peter Russell ...* (3v., Toronto, 1932-36), 1:9.

11   Ernest Cruikshank, *The Story of Butler's Rangers and the Settlement of Niagara* (Welland: Tribune Printing House, 1893), 8.

12   Isaac Weld, Jr, *Travels through the States of North America, and the Provinces of Upper and Lower Canada during the years 1795, 1796 and 1797* (2v., London: 1799), 2:opposite 118.

13   "Canadian Letters," 93.

14   Mary Quayle Innis, ed., *Mrs. Simcoe's Diary* (Toronto: Macmillan, 1965), 30 August 1795, 165.

15   George A. Seibel, *The Niagara Portage Road. A History of the Portage on the West Bank of the Niagara River* (Niagara Falls: City of Niagara Falls, 1990), 34.

16   *Upper Canada Gazette*, 26 May 1798.

17   Niagara Historical Society, Municipal Records, Niagara District, 1793-1899, Folio 6, 1798.

18   Margaret McBurney and Mary Byers, *Tavern in the Town: Early Inns and Taverns of Ontario* (Toronto: University of Toronto Press, 1987), 103.

19   Emily Cain, *Ghost Ships, Hamilton and Scourge: Historical Treasures from the War of 1812* (New York: Beaufort Books, 1983), 33.

20   John Ross Robertson, ed., *The Diary of Mrs. Simcoe* (Toronto: Wm. Briggs, 1911), 228.

21   For an excellent description of the *Onondaga* and its role in Upper Canada's history, see Malcolm MacLeod, "Simcoe's Schooner *Onondaga*," *Ontario History*, 59, no.1 (March 1967), 23-36.

22   Robertson, *The Diary of Mrs. Simcoe*, 29 April 1793.

23   Cain, *Ghost Ships*, 26.

24 Weld, *Travels*, 2:73.

25 Ibid., 2:83, 91.

26 A succession of British army officers, trained in drawing and watercolour painting at Woolwich, England, and several other European artists passed through the area during this period. The first American artist was John Vander Lyn, who arrived in the Niagara area in 1801.

27 For a more thorough discussion of Niagara's falls and their significance in the eighteenth and nineteenth centuries, see the essays by Jeremy Adamson and Elizabeth McKinsey in *Niagara, Two Centuries of Changing Attitudes, 1697-1901* (Washington, DC: Corcoran Gallery of Art, 1985), 11-101.

28 John Maude, *Visit to the Falls of Niagara in 1800* (London: Richard Nichols, 1826).

29 Cruikshank, *Simcoe Correspondence*, 3:68-9.

30 W. Kaye Lamb, ed., *The Journals and Letters of Sir Alexander Mackenzie* (Cambridge: University Press, 1970), 455. The editor incorrectly states that the Hend's (Hind's) Tavern was at York in 1794.

31 Niagara was the entry point for a few late immigrating loyalists. Mrs Simcoe describes the "terrible passage" of two families (Davis and Ghent) who arrived on 2 gunboats from the Genesee River, having emigrated from North Carolina. No doubt they recuperated at one of Niagara's inns before moving on to their grant of land. John Ross Robertson, *Diary of Mrs. Simcoe*, 17 August 1792, 136.

32 Cruikshank, *Simcoe Correspondence*, 4:351.

33 Patrick Campbell, *Travels in the Interior Inhabited Parts of North America in the Years 1791 and 1792* (Edinburgh: 1793), 147.

34 MTLBR, D.W. Smith Papers, Garrison Orders Book of John Smith, 1793-95, entry for 17 August 1794.

35 Janet Carnochan, *History of Niagara* (Toronto: W. Briggs, 1914), 201.

36 Cruikshank, *Simcoe Correspondence*, 2:282.

37 Ernest Cruikshank, ed., "Records of Niagara 1790-1792," Publication of the *Niagara Historical Society*, 41 (1930), 118.

38 "Canadian Letters," 142.

39 For a good history of the four Freemason lodges in the Niagara area during this period, see John Ross Robertson, *History of Freemasonry in Canada* (2v., Toronto: Hunter, Rose, 1899), 271-7, 339-532.

40 Robertson, *The Diary of Mrs. Simcoe*, 29 July 1792, 125.

41 *Upper Canada Gazette*, 21 December 1796.

42 *Laws of the Province of Upper Canada*, 34th. George 3, C 12, AD 1794.

43 The taxation of liquor in Upper Canada was a source of conflict between the appointed Legislative Council and the elected House of Assembly. The council wanted to place a higher tax on the "more democratic drinks" of whisky, rum, and so on and increase licence fees on stills and taverns. The assembly wanted a higher tax on wine (a beverage favoured by the upper classes). The final act was a compromise.

44 National Archives of Canada (NAC), RG 1 E 15B, (Board of Audit of the Executive Council, Government of Upper Canada), 3, 1796.

45   MTLBR, William Jarvis Papers, "Licences, etc.," S109, B-52.

46   Archives of Ontario, MV2553 (Rogers Family Papers), William Jarvis to John Peters, 4 August 1794.

47   Cyril deM. Rudolf, "St. Mark's Early History," Publication of the *Niagara Historical Society*, 18 (1909), 4.

48   Archives of St Andrew's Church (Niagara-on-the-Lake, Ontario), Record Book of the Presbyterian Congregation at Newark, Folio 1, 30 September 1794.

49   Archives of Stamford Presbyterian Church, (Niagara Falls, Ontario), Subscription to pay the annual salary of the Reverend John Dun, 1 October 1794.

50   NAC, MG 23 G5 (Shepherd-White Papers), Diary of John White, 30 November 1793.

51   *Upper Canada Gazette*, 18 March 1797.

52   Cruikshank, *Simcoe Correspondence*, 1:205.

53   Benjamin Lincoln, "Journal of a Treaty held in 1793 with Indian Tribes north-west of the Ohio, by Commissioners of the United States," *Massachusetts Historical Society*, Collectories 3rd series, 5 (1836), 123-4. See also NAC, MG 23 H1 (Jarvis-Peters Papers), 2, Hannah Jarvis to Birdseye Peters, 19 June 1793, and Robertson, *The Diary of Mrs. Simcoe*, 4 June 1796, 315.

54   NAC, MG 23 H1, Diary of John White, 8 February 1793.

55   Cruikshank and Hunter, *Russell Correspondence*, 2:121.

56   McBurney and Byers, *Tavern in the Town*, 52.

57   *The Laws of the Province of Upper Canada*, 37 George 3, C13, 1797.

58   Law Society of Upper Canada, Minutes of Convocation, 17 July 1797.

59   Cruikshank, *Simcoe Correspondence*, 4:196.

60   Cruikshank and Hunter, *Russell Correspondence*, 1:272.

61   *Upper Canada Gazette*, "Proclamation for the Suppression of Vice, Profaneness, and Immorality," 18 April 1793.

62   *Upper Canada Gazette*, 28 June 1797.

63   Edwin C. Guillet, *Pioneer Inns and Taverns* (5v , Toronto: 1954-62), 1:36.

64   No account books of any of Newark's early tavernkeepers have survived. The account book (1795-98) of York's earliest innkeeper, Abner Miles, records charging each guest at a St John's dinner 16 shillings. See MTLBR, Abner Miles Day Book 'B,' 1795-96.

65   Guillet, *Pioneer Inns and Taverns*, 4:132.

66   Ibid., 1:29-31.

67   McBurney and Byers, *Tavern in the Town*, 151.

68   Bruce G. Wilson, *The Enterprises of Robert Hamilton: A Study of Wealth and Influence in Early Upper Canada, 1776-1812* (Ottawa: Carleton University Press, 1983), 81.

69   Cruikshank and Hunter, *Russell Correspondence*, 3:112.

70   Weld, *Travels*, 2:91-2.

71   For an excellent review of pioneer drinking habits and the rise of temperance in Upper Canada, see M.A. Garland and J.J. Talman, "Pioneer Drinking Habits and the Rise of the Temperance Agitation in Upper Canada Prior to 1804," *Ontario Historical Society Papers and Records* (OHSPR), 27 (1931), 341-62.

72 *Upper Canada Gazette,* 21 September 1799.

73 McBurney and Byers, *Tavern in the Town,* 123.

74 Cruikshank, *Simcoe Correspondence,* 3:3.

75 MTLBR, William Jarvis Papers, "Licences, etc.," S109, B-526.

76 McBurney and Byers, *Tavern in the Town,* 6.

77 *Upper Canada Gazette,* 18 April 1793.

78 "Canadian Letters," 130.

79 *Canada Constellation,* 7 December 1799.

80 "Canadian Letters," 130.

81 *Canada Constellation,* 18 December 1799.

82 Guillet, *Pioneer Inns and Taverns,* 3:202.

83 Ibid., 1:70.

84 NAC, RG 19 E5(a), (War of 1812 Losses Claims), 3743:228 (Thomas Powis).

85 Ibid., 3741:78 (John Emery). See also 3743:248 (Elizabeth Thompson).

86 Lathrop, *Early American Inns and Taverns,* 168.

87 John Howison, *Sketches of Upper Canada* (London: 1821; reprint 1966), 39.

88 Lathrop, *Early American Inns and Taverns,* 198.

89 In the *Niagara Herald,* 23 May 1801, appeared the following advertisement: "Prodigal will stand at the Lyon Tavern, in Niagara, every Thursday ..."

90 McBurney and Byers, *Tavern in the Town,* 159.

91 Hard currency such as British government notes, half-joes (Spanish golden coins), guineas, dollars, quarter dollars, English shillings, and copper pence were scarce in the capital of Upper Canada. Most business was transacted with 'bons,' which were small squares of paper or card on which were printed promissory notes for various sums, usually issued by the more prominent merchants. American currency was not accepted. See "Canadian Letters," 158-9. Many of the local clientele settled their accounts by barter of goods or services.

92 McBurney and Byers, *Tavern in the Town,* 13.

93 Record Book of St Mark's Church, Niagara, burials by the Reverend Addison, 21 December 1819, James Rogers (innkeeper).

94 *Upper Canada Gazette,* 10 June 1795.

95 Jackson, *St. Catharines, Ontario, Its Early Years,* 128-9.

96 MTLBR, William Jarvis Papers, "Licences, etc.," S109, B-52.

97 *Canada Constellation,* 4 October 1799.

98 Ibid., 13 September 1799.

99 MTLBR, William Jarvis Papers, "Licences, etc.," S109, B-52.

100 Ibid.

101 *Niagara Herald,* 24 January 1801.

102 Robertson, *History of Freemasonry in Canada,* 1:506.

103 Ibid., 501.

104 *Upper Canada Gazette*, 26 May 1798.

105 NAC, RG 19 E5(a), 3743:233 (Patrick McCabe).

106 MTLBR, William Jarvis Papers, "Licences, etc.," S109, B-52.

107 Alexander Servos, *Historic Houses*, Publication of the *Niagara Historical Society*, no.5 (1914), 10-12.

108 Robertson, *History of Freemasonry in Canada*, 1:506.

109 Bunker Sharp, *Mother Says* (St Catharines: Niagara Peninsula Branch of the Ontario Genealogical Society, 1982), 22.

110 NAC, RG 19 E5(a), 3728:1 (heirs of Gilbert Field).

111 MTLBR, William Jarvis Papers, "Licences, etc.," S109, B-52.

112 *Canada Constellation*, 23 August 1799.

113 Robertson, *History of Freemasonry in Canada*, 1:508.

114 MTLBR, William Jarvis Papers, "Licences, etc.," S109, B-52.

115 *Upper Canada Gazette*, 14 December 1796.

116 Lamb, *The Journals and Letters of Sir Alexander Mackenzie*, 455.

117 Archives of St Andrew's Church, Record Book of the Presbyterian Congregation at Newark, Folio 1, 30 September 1794.

118 Robertson, *History of Freemasonry in Canada*, 1:501.

119 Edith G. Firth, *The Town of York, 1793-1815* (Toronto: University of Toronto Press, 1962), 250-1.

120 Ibid.

121 Robertson, *History of Freemasonry in Canada*, 1:502.

122 *Niagara Herald*, 18 April 1801.

123 McBurney and Byers, *Tavern in the Town*, 159.

124 MTLBR, William Jarvis Papers, "Licences, etc.," S109, B-52.

125 Ibid.

126 Ibid.

127 Ibid.

128 NAC, RG 19 E5(a), 3750:849 (John Knox).

129 MTLBR. William Jarvis Papers, "Licences, etc.," S109, B-52.

130 Ibid.

131 *Niagara Herald*, 25 April 1801.

132 MTLBR, William Jarvis Papers, "Licences, etc.," S109, B-52.

133 *Niagara Herald*, 31 January 1801.

134 Ibid., 25 April 1801.

135 MTLBR, William Jarvis Papers, "Licences, etc.," S109, B-52.

136 Firth, *The Town of York, 1793-1815*, 99.

137 Record Book of St Mark's, Weddings at Niagara by the Reverend Addison, 7 October 1802.

138 MTLBR, William Jarvis Papers, "Licences, etc.," S109, B-52.

139 Ibid.

140 Firth, *The Town of York, 1793-1815*, 164.

141 NAC, MU2553 (Rogers Family Papers), 1793.

142 Firth, *The Town of York, 1793-1815*, 99.

143 Ernest Cruikshank, ed., "Petitions for Grants of Land 1791-1796," *OHSPR*, 24 (1927), 116-17.

144 "Thomson, Hugh Christopher," *Dictionary of Canadian Biography*, 6 (Toronto: University of Toronto Press, 1987), 772.

145 NAC, RG 1 E 15B (Audit Reports for the Executive Council of Upper Canada), 4.

146 *Upper Canada Gazette*, 18 March 1797.

147 Ibid., 17 May 1797.

148 NAC RG 19 E5(a), 3743:248 (Elizabeth Thompson).

149 Robertson, *History of Freemasonry in Canada*, 1:497.

150 MTLBR, William Jarvis Papers, "Licences, etc.," S109, B-52.

151 NAC, RG 1 E 15B, 3, 1796.

152 Charles M. Johnston, ed., *The Valley of the Six Nations* (Toronto: University of Toronto Press, 1964), 97, 162.

153 Cruikshank, "Petitions for Grants of Land 1792-1796," 51-2.

154 *Canada Constellation*, 23 August 1799.

155 *Upper Canada Gazette*, 6 April 1798.

156 Cruikshank, "Petitions for Grants of Land 1792-1796," 51-2.

157 *Upper Canada Gazette*, 17 May 1797.

158 Law Society of Upper Canada, Minutes of Convocation, 17 July 1797.

159 Johnston, *The Valley of the Six Nations*, 97, 162.

160 Pearl Wilson, "Irish John Willson and Family, Loyalists," *OHSPR*, 31 (1936), 228-42.

161 MTLBR, William Jarvis Papers, "Licences, etc.," S109, B-52.

162 Law Society of Upper Canada, Minutes of Convocation, 17 July 1797.

CHAPTER NINE

HEALTH, DISEASE, AND TREATMENT IN EARLY UPPER CANADA

Charles G. Roland

The Niagara peninsula was one of the earliest settled parts of Upper Canada. During its first years, its future was uncertain, its present replete with problems and difficulties. In the first rank of these were the effects of disease and injury. A consideration of some aspects of the medical history of early Upper Canada, therefore, throws light on the formative years of the Niagara area and the colony as a whole.

The subject is vast, and so some selection has been necessary. Modes of therapy have been emphasized because these were part of the daily lives of first-generation Upper Canadians. Of the multitude of diseases to which our ancestors were heir, malaria has been covered in some detail because it is both significant and often ignored. Surgery also needs emphasis because the more minor aspects were ubiquitous; everyone was bled at some time, and few settlers would have failed to encounter boils, lacerations, or fractured bones. And finally, childbirth and its attendant dangers are outlined: childbirth is the beginning of everything, but two centuries ago in Niagara it was too often an ending as well.

THERAPY

Treatment of disease — the use of remedies — seems to most patients to be the epitome of the practitioner's function. Since we all are potential patients,

223

we all are intensely interested in how an unhealthy person can be helped towards health once again. It has ever been so. The following discussion examines how our forebearers in this country, whether we are descended from Amerindians, Inuit, or people who came to this continent as immigrants, sought to alleviate the ills of the flesh.

Amerindian Medicine

When Europeans arrived in North America, Upper Canada was the home of several Indian peoples, including the Neutrals, Hurons, and Mississauga. It seems that the North American Indians were then generally quite healthy, although controversy surrounds this generalization. Likely the truth lies somewhere between the extreme positions — "noble savages" or supine, disease-ridden lower species. The Indians and Inuit had been in North America for a very long time and had active viable cultures dependent on arduous toil, whether hunting or growing food. This kind of life could scarcely have existed if the hunters and the farmers were not basically healthy. If their life spans were, on average, short, so were those of Europeans at that time.

There is no question regarding the fate of the Indians after contact with Europeans. The native peoples were affected catastrophically by diseases that seem not to have existed on this continent previously, or that existed in much milder forms. The ravages of infectious diseases and the inroads of alcohol abuse may have been more effective than were armies in permitting early European domination of the continent.

In the seventeenth century, when the French were beginning to explore what is now Ontario, the Indians had an intact medical system that had sustained them for centuries. Disease, using that word broadly, was seen as being one of three types.

There was what I shall call *banal disease*. This constituted a group of minor disorders that were seen by the Amerindians to be self-limited or trivial and that were ignored or were treated by the individual or any unskilled person with simple means. I refer to minor headaches, upset stomach, bruises and bumps, hangnails, scratches, and similar occasional bouts of disease.

The second category was one containing quite specific problems that the Indians treated empirically, usually calling in a local expert for that purpose. The midwife is the classic example, but many tribes also had members of proven skill in the challenging art of bone-setting; they would be called upon to care for difficult and complicated fractures and dislocations.

When disorders in either of these categories were treated, the methods used often included botanic remedies and the use of physical methods such as massage and the sweat-bath.

Finally, there was the category of serious disease. This is where the so-called "medicine man" or shaman played his role. These individuals usually, though not invariably, were men. We do the "medicine man" an injustice when we use that term, for he was far more than the counterpart of our physician. Medicine, to the Indians, was and is a component of religious life in the broad, mystical sense. Illness and disease were evidence of dissonance between the sick person and the spirits and gods who exist in profusion. The spirits can create disease as a primary event, the consequence of the patient breaking some taboo, or disease can be visited upon a person by the spirits in response to mortal activity — in other words, someone who knows you can solicit the gods to make you ill.

If diseases are caused magically, then magic must be used to combat them. A medicine man worth his salt has good magic at his disposal, derived from tradition and a lengthy and arduous period of apprenticeship. The magic that the medicine man learns from his master, or that is revealed to him by some sort of mystical intercession, represents the expertise he can offer to the sick. He makes use of this magic in a variety of ways. He knows chants that can combat certain disorders. He possesses objects that contain the essence of his magic and act directly on the patient. And he knows means of physical therapy.

There has been major misunderstanding of the role and the activities of the medicine man, against whom there was much prejudice on the part of the early settlers, and especially of the priests, who were quick to recognize direct competition. This prejudice has coloured most subsequent efforts to look at Indian medicine until recent decades.

For example, there is the accusation of legerdemain. When Europeans were permitted to observe healing ceremonies, they noticed that often the medicine man would suck on an area of the patient's skin, or cut the skin, and then "draw forth" an object — a small stone, or a piece of bone — as if drawing it from within the patient. But the observers had earlier seen the medicine man secrete the object in the palm of his hand. Their conclusion was that a deception was being carried out: the medicine man was trying to trick the patient and family into thinking that he had drawn some foreign object out of the body.

But they judged too quickly, on the basis of too little knowledge. The medicine man tricked no one. The patient, and his family, knew that the object was in the medicine man's hand. It had to be. The object was a magical one taken from his medicine bag and possessing special properties that he judged would be useful in treating the patient's disease. After providing the other elements — dances, chants, burning of aromatic leaves, and so on — the medicine man brought the magical object close to the affected part of the patient's body. The object would then attract the evil spirit within the body and cause it to give up its hold on the patient. If it did so, the patient would be healed. A kind of religious magnetism took place. This is a theory of disease that is different from our own, but it is rational (though not necessarily correct) and it is not trickery. Moreover, it seems to have worked remarkably well.

Despite the existence of this elaborate and functional system, rooted in perhaps hundreds of generations of tradition, the Indians and Inuit, and their indigenous medical systems, could not cope with European infectious disease. This was the rack upon which the medicine men were discredited and the aborigines broken. The native peoples were remarkably susceptible to a wide variety of these diseases, and they were affected by them much more severely than were the Europeans. Measles, mumps, chicken-pox, whooping cough, and scarlet fever caused high death rates among the Indians, much higher than in the newcomers to their lands. And the major diseases, most particularly smallpox and tuberculosis, were catastrophic.

Treatment of Internal Diseases in Upper Canada

Efficacious therapy for serious disease was possible only infrequently in the first generation of settlement in Upper Canada, just as was the case elsewhere. In general, medical theory was based upon beliefs that were becoming increasingly difficult to uphold, beliefs in an ancient system known as the humoral theory, which would be shown to be largely erroneous by the end of the nineteenth century.

Whether treatment was provided by a family member, a quack, or a medical practitioner, it was chiefly empirical. An important specific agent was Peruvian bark, which was unquestionably effective in controlling attacks of malaria, a common disease in Upper Canada that was the chief ailment included under the label of "fever and ague."[1] A few other agents were useful, too: opium was known for its pain-killing power as a medicine as well as for the temporary delights it could bring to the healthy; and the common English foxglove had been found in the 1770s to have great effectiveness in treating certain kinds of dropsy or edema — an action of foxglove that we know now derives from the plant's content of digitalis. Ointments containing sulphur or mercury were effective against a number of skin diseases, and systemic mercury could cure syphilis (though the dose required was perilously close to the toxic level and therapy had to be continued over many months). With these few exceptions, most drug therapy fell somewhere in the spectrum between inert and dangerous.

Before considering the various components of therapy individually, we should appreciate the fact that for patient and practitioner they rarely were used separately; treatment commonly was a combination of physical measures and drugs, often several drugs (where the word "drug" encompasses all substances taken orally for the express purpose of improving the recipient's health). To illustrate this point, here is a letter written by an army surgeon in Newark (Niagara-on-the-Lake) to a private patient at York, laying out a course of therapy based upon the doctor's prescriptions of the disorder complained of:

> I am extremely sorry to find you are like to have a relapse of your former disease — From the symptoms you now describe & what formerly took place during my attendance, I have no doubt in saying it is owing to the fullness of the vessels of the Brain, & which will be removed by bloodletting & Cathartics applied immediately. However, in order to prevent a recurrence of the disease I would advise you to have a Seton put into your neck and continued for some months, upon healing of which it will be necessary to get your head shaved & in future wear a wig. This last to you, who value your hair, will seem hard, but I hope you regard health the greatest of blessings more than appearance — in order to prevent a relapse I would advise you to use a good deal of exercise, leave off reading in bed & indeed anything that obliges you for any long period to have your head lye on your neck *as in writing* — your stove, have it removed from so near your Desk. — As I know you can always pass your evenings in Society, pleasantly, I should advise you to cultivate it, & to enter into every amusement you possibly can ...[2]

Here is exemplified the complete prescription. The drugs are unspecified cathartics; the physical means include bloodletting, application of a seton (an object inserted into the skin to permit discharges), and even shaving the head and the wearing of a wig; the advice is broad-ranging and includes admonitions to improve the lifestyle in several ways. The physician, an experienced practitioner who attained high rank in the medical service during the War of 1812, works at keeping his patient's spirits raised.

Let us now look at some of these specific modes of therapy. The first will be bleeding, that messy panacea of the late eighteenth and early nineteenth centuries about which so much has been written.

Bleeding – How can we explain the enormous enthusiasm for bleeding that characterized therapy in the western world in the eighteenth and first half of the nineteenth centuries? Consider the following well-known example, a case history of almost two hundred years ago. George Washington (a man whose fame was very familiar to all citizens of the Niagara area in the 1790s!) died at Mount Vernon on 14 December 1799. He had become ill the day before with a sudden severe inflammation of the tissues of the opening to the larynx, accompanied by pronounced swelling and fever. He died within

Dr James Macaulay (1759-1822), oil painting, artist unknown. Born in Scotland, he came to Niagara as surgeon to the Queen's Rangers in 1792. He later followed the government to York, where he was the first physician. (Metropolitan Toronto Library, John Ross Robertson Collection, T14924)

twenty-two hours despite the attention of several physicians.

In the course of his final illness, Washington was bled repeatedly, and an estimate of the amount of blood removed by his medical attendants is that it exceeded eighty ounces (the total amount in the average adult human body is 190 ounces). So he was deprived of more than 40 per cent of his entire blood supply, in less than twenty-four hours, in the midst of a very severe illness.

Yet it is true, and must be emphasized, that the treatment Washington received was technically correct given the state of medical science of the day. He was not mistreated. He did not fall into the hands of quacks. How could this take place?

Internal medicine follows different basic principles in the 1990s than it did up to about the middle of the nineteenth century. This is why we find old methods of treatment for internal diseases peculiar. But to understand outmoded therapy, we have to make a philosophical shift. Indeed, to understand the rationale for bleeding, we must go back to the time of the Greeks, to about 450 BC. The Greeks provided the beginnings to many aspects of life in the western world, and nowhere is this more true than in medicine. They made the fundamental leap to discard magical theories of disease in favour of rational theories.

As has every culture, the Greeks worked very hard at understanding the mysteries of their world. What is the earth? What is life? How did we come to exist? Where did we come from?

After a great deal of speculation, they concluded that the structure of all matter could be expressed in terms of four qualities. These qualities were HOT, COLD, DRY, and WET.

The mind of mankind seeks order and organization. That kind of seeking drove the Greeks to conclude that the world is the product of no more than four qualities. But this is only a beginning to a theory of the world. How do these elements interact? What forces bind them together or separate them, under different circumstances? The Greeks concluded that combinations of adjoining qualities produced what they termed "elements." Thus, when COLD and WET combine, we get the element WATER, WET and HOT produce AIR, HOT and DRY explain FIRE, and DRY and COLD produce the element EARTH. That these elements exist, and can thus be observed and measured, is evident.

What we have here is the beginnings of a theoretical explanation of the structure of the world, based not on religion and magic and mysticism, but on observation and rationality. Greece gave us this way of looking at the world twenty-five centuries ago, and the method still works. How does medicine fit into this schema?

We can now leave behind the general philosophers, who try to decide what makes the entire world tick, and narrow our scope to the medical philosophers. Their self-appointed task was to try to throw some light on the questions: Of what does the body consist? How does it work? How and why does it fail?

They built on the general system of the Greeks. They concluded that the tissues of the body were constructed from the same elements as was everything else, but that for each element in the world at large there was a corresponding element or "humour" in the human body. Thus they saw PHLEGM as a humour, corresponding to WATER and the product of COLD and WET; YELLOW BILE was related to FIRE and was the product of DRY and HOT; BLACK BILE was related to EARTH, coming from the conjunction of COLD and DRY; and BLOOD was seen as the humour related to WET and HOT, an extension of AIR.

And this, enormously oversimplified as it is, is the basic explanatory model that was in use for about twenty-five hundred years. It was based, first of all, on observation. Blood exists. That was known from earliest times. So does phlegm, as we all are reminded every time we have a cold or a "runny nose" from any cause. Yellow bile was less obvious but also was found in the abdomen when it was opened by accidental causes. Black bile is difficult to explain and must simply be taken on faith.

Given these four substances, these "humours," all of which existed in the body, we now have a theoretical basis for explaining how the body works and why it goes awry at times. The Greeks were great believers in a sound body. They emphasized the role of exercise in maintaining health. They saw that food and drink and exercise all were needed, and all in proper balance. They created the concept of health as being the expression of a state of balance in the body.

Thus, the healthy person is one in whom there is a proper balance, a proper admixture of humours. Disease occurs when there is imbalance: where one or more humours is present in too great a quantity or too little. That is the peg upon which disease theory hung for two dozen centuries. And it will be the explanation for that bizarre case history I mentioned before.

George Washington had a severe inflammatory infectious disease of the throat. That is, he had the classic symptoms of fever, redness, swelling, and pain. As we all know, patients ill with this kind of sickness are usually flushed. In the most simplistic terms, here was the rationale for bleeding according to humoral theory: (1) there are four humours: blood, phlegm, yellow bile, and black bile; (2) in health there is balance, in disease imbalance, of these humours; (3) in inflammation the patient is flushed — that is, he has an excess of blood in the system; and (4) given these three "facts," the correct therapy is to remove sufficient blood to put the system back into balance.

All of this follows logically. It explains why George Washington, along with the inhabitants of Newark, Upper Canada, and millions of others, were bled for inflammatory illness. The fact that he was bled repeatedly (and that his death may well have been hastened by this bleeding) emphasizes the fundamental defect in the theory. He was bled repeatedly because his illness did not disappear. He continued to be ill, and feverish, and flushed. As long as this was true, bleeding continued to be the "correct" treatment. The humoral theory had gone as far as it could go. In the absence of knowledge about bacteria and a wide variety of other subjects, no progress could be made. When we did acquire the new knowledge, in the nineteenth and twentieth centuries, the humoral theory was abandoned.

Puking and Purging – The principle behind the use of these two treatments was the same as that for bleeding: it was believed that, in most diseases, some humour or combination of humours existed in the body and that this excess must be removed for the patient to be restored to health. If the seat of disease was thought to be in the stomach itself, pukes (the common term of the time and not merely an indelicacy on my part) might be used alone; if the disease was thought limited to the lower bowel, then purges might be used. But in many disorders the two methods were used simultaneously, frequently leaving the unfortunate patient not only ill but also in a severe dilemma with respect to evacuative priorities, as the agents administered usually worked vigorously and frequently.

All manner of drugs were given to effect vomiting and purgation. Botanical substances were used in great profusion. Among those practitioners who believed that anything worth doing was worth doing thoroughly, the metallic drugs were particularly favoured — mercury, antimony, and the like.

Calomel (a mercuric substance) was so universally applied as a depletive drug that it, and to a lesser degree the other compounds of mercury, can be considered the symbol of therapeutics at this time, in the same way that penicillin might have been regarded about 1950. When Dr Solomon Jones, a loyalist physician in eastern Upper Canada, ordered shipments of drugs from Montreal, he routinely included requests for calomel and for corrosive sublimate of mercury, along with such other stand-bys as opium, laudanum, terebinth (turpentine), aloes, castor oil, and powdered cantharides.[3]

Calomel was seen as the great cure-all. It was administered to Elizabeth Russell, the half-sister of Receiver General Peter Russell, as part of the

231

treatment for her dropsy.[4] Years before, Peter Russell had given it to servants and dogs alike during an epidemic in the Niagara peninsula.[5]

Nor did all attempts at therapy depend on standard items from the pharmacopoeia. Even European-trained practitioners tried methods that sound medieval at best. For example, in 1783 the von Riedesels lost their youngest daughter from some diarrheal disease after being treated by Dr H.A. Kennedy of Trois-Rivières. His therapy included the following: "He

Peter Russell, (1733-1808), watercolour by G.T. Berthon. When he lived in Niagara, he was inspector general of the province. On Simcoe's return to England in 1796, Russell became administrator. (Metropolitan Toronto Library, John Ross Robertson Collection, T15064)

had some old hens killed and removed the entrails, which were cooked without being cleaned. Of this he gave her clysters every half hour, which at first seemed to infuse new life into her, but she had already lost too much of her strength, and we had the sorrow of losing her ..."[6]

Physical Remedies – This category encompasses the application of heat or cold, as well as massage and similar measures. Our information on such methods is scanty. The Indians used physical methods regularly, but how extensively their techniques were copied by or influenced the settlers is uncertain.

Dr Robert Kerr (1755-1824), oil painting, artist unknown. Born in Scotland, Kerr came to Canada in 1776. He served as surgeon to the King's Royal Regiment of New York. After the war he lived in Kingston and then Newark where he was surgeon to the Indian Department and conducted a private practice. Kerr served as judge of the Surrogate Court, member of the land board, and deputy grand master of the Provincial Grand Lodge of Masons. He married Elizabeth, dauhgter of Molly Brant and Sir William Johnson (Metropolitan Toronto Library, T14843)

There is considerable evidence, however, to show that the settlers were interested in the existence of springs of all sorts. These often were assumed to have therapeutic properties, sometimes because of mineral or other contents, sometimes — in the case of heated springs — because of the temperature.

There are several references to a spring or springs in the Niagara area. The earliest of these that I have found is to a mysterious "loud volcano" mentioned in connection with Dr Robert Kerr in the 1790s. Whether this was a spring or rather some noise associated with Niagara Falls is not clear.[7] A more definite reference is contained in a long letter written in 1794 describing the various settlements of Upper Canada. The writer refers to a "natural curiosity":

> a spring about two miles above these [Niagara] falls ... — emitting a gas, or inflammable air, which when confined in a pipe, and a flame applied to it, will boil the water of a tea-kettle in 15 minutes: — Whether this may hereafter be applied by machinery to useful purposes, time will determine. It was lately discovered in clearing away and burning the brush under the bank of the river, to erect a mill, and was observed after the brush was consumed to burn for days together, to the great astonishment of the inhabitants ...[8]

The Duke of La Rochefoucauld-Liancourt, an early traveller to Upper Canada, knew of this spring also, and his account adds a little information about its nature. He describes it as a "sulphureous spring": "On the approach of a fire-brand the vapour or steam kindles, assumes the colour of burning spirit of wine, and burns down to the bottom. Much time will probably elapse, before an enquiry shall be instituted, whether this spring be endowed with any medicinal powers ..."[9]

Elizabeth Simcoe, wife of the lieutenant governor, made a picnic expedition to see the same spring on 14 August 1795, just two months after the French aristocrat's visit to Upper Canada. She was disappointed, though that did not prevent her from enjoying both her picnic and the sensation of resting in a tent with the lulling sounds of Niagara Falls in the distance. "I went to see it [the spring] today, but it had not been cleared out for some time & the Cattle having trod in it & made it muddy it did not deserve the name of the burning Spring."[10] Twenty-five years later, another active observer, Dr John Howison, visited and found that no particular use was being made of the spring.[11]

Springs of this nature, though not a major part of Upper Canadian therapeutics, nevertheless illustrate how readily the inhabitants made use of locally available products or phenomena as "cures." This propensity is perhaps displayed most prominently in the use of plant products of all kinds.

Botanic Remedies – The search for remedies was endless. Every plant was seen as a potential therapeutic agent, and a large number proved to have vigorous, though not necessarily curative, effects.

The Indians possessed a rich lore of active botanic remedies, and these seem to have been used regularly by early Upper Canadians. Many native remedies were accepted with enthusiasm by Europeans. Sassafras, for example, was widely used against venereal disease, first by the natives, then by Europeans in North America, and ultimately by Europeans in Europe. The use of sassafras became so intimately associated with syphilis and gonorrhea that English gentlemen felt called upon to give up drinking tea made from sassafras flowers, socially, for fear they might be labelled as harbouring venereal disease [12]

Maidenhair fern acquired an enormous reputation as a hemostatic in uterine bleeding and to alleviate labour pains. The export trade in this drug was flourishing as early as 1687, when the Baron of Lahontan observed that "the Inhabitants of Quebec prepare great quantities of its Syrup which they send to Paris, Nants, Rouan, and several other cities in France." The price varied according to the grade of the plant, the care taken in preparing it, and the quantity available at Quebec. "The Indians went into the bush about the first of August and travelled far above Montreal in quest of it." [13]

Elizabeth Simcoe frequently mentions such agents as the Cardinal flower, which, she had been told, the Indians use medicinally, [14] and also says, with respect to her husband, that "Capt. [Joseph] Brant's sister [Molly Brant] prescribed a Root — I believe it is calamus — which really relieved his Cough in a very short time." [15] And the son of an early loyalist settler in the Niagara district remembers the use of Indian lore also: "We none of us experienced much sickness, but whenever any illness occurred we had recourse to medical roots found in the woods, the virtues of which we acquired by our intercourse with the Indians ..." [16]

Households would attempt to keep a supply of the common necessaries for medicinal purposes, since pharmacies and apothecaries were uncommon in the early days. There was an apothecary at Newark in 1796, but, even so, general stores were the chief commercial source for drug products of all kinds; for example, John Dolsen's store in Dover East carried stocks of opium, Peruvian bark, epsom salts, sulphur, and similar products. [17] We have some idea of what substances were thought appropriate from a letter Hannah Jarvis, wife of Provincial Secretary William Jarvis, wrote to her father. She requested him to bring her: "Bark in Substance & Tincture —

Rhubarb Turky & India, in the Root — Castor Oil — Sulphur — Magnesia — James's Powders — Camomile Flowers — Senna — Tincture of Rhubarb — Antimonial Wine — Camphoric Spirits of Wine — prepared Lint w'd be very useful — these are things that come very high here and what cannot be done without, in such a sickly country — do not spare in getting the above

Advertisement for J.W.A. Hurst's Apothecary. Upper Canada Gazette, *30 November 1796. (Ontario Legislative Library, Toronto)*

articles — and let them be of the Best Quality ..."[18]

Note that all the items on this list are botanically derived except for sulphur, magnesia, James's powders (which contains antimony) and antimony itself.

Hannah Jarvis was a firm believer in the efficacy of castor oil (also derived from a plant), describing it to her father as "the best and most Powerful of all Medicine ... I would not be without it on any account ..."[19] Nor was she alone in her faith. When Peter Hunter arrived to take over the reins of government in 1799 he landed at Quebec in "a very bad state of Health owing to a bilious Complaint — The Medical Men talked despondingly ..." They became discouraged too easily, however, for a dose of castor oil cured him.[20]

Much of what was used to combat disease came from local sources. Elizabeth Simcoe, while exploring in the Stoney Creek area, found a veritable pharmacopoeia of remedies:

> Ginseng, a root which the Merchants tell me they send to England & in some years has sold at a guinea a pound,[21] Sarsaparilla — Golden thread — the roots look like gold thread. When steeped in brandy they make a fine aromatic tincture & liquorice plant; consumption vine, a pretty Creeper. Green's daughter was cured of a consumption by drinking tea made of it. Poison vine in appearance much like the former but differs in the number of leaves, one has 5, the other 7. Madder, toothache plant, a beautiful species of fern, Sore Throat weed, Dragon's blood, Adam & Eve or ivy blade, very large, which heals Cuts or burns, droppings of beach, enchanter's nightshade, Dewberrys, Wild Turnip which cures a cough — it is like an Arum.[22]

How effective were such supposed remedies? I think it can safely be said that very few of these agents have been tested scientifically in modern times. Consequently, what we know about them derives largely from sources that give us information about what our predecessors *believed* the various remedies did.

Elizabeth Russell, in the draft of a letter to a friend in Ireland, mentions her personal use of a native remedy for dropsy, or edema. Not only did she use it, but so had a high government official, making it plain that although the "pagan" medico-religious system was unacceptable to most Europeans, remedies that seemed to work were in a different category: "I have been taking an extract of an Herb which cured Sir James Craige [*sic*] (the late Governor General) of a dropsy with wh. he was affected for several years. *It is a remedy found out by the Indians.* It has been try'd several times on others with great success. This plant grows in great abundance in the woods here so that I can easily procure it and make a decoction myself of it ..."[23]

Perhaps significantly, the sentence in italics was struck out in Russell's draft letter. Was she ashamed to admit to her friend that she was using an Indian remedy?

DISEASE AND INJURY

The above comments on therapy provide a necessary background to a discussion of some of the actual medical problems faced by the inhabitants of Newark two centuries ago. Though not all can be alluded to here, malaria requires attention because of its surprising prevalence.

A phrase that appears again and again in the letters and diaries of this period is "fever and ague." It may be no exaggeration to say that it was *the* disease of the times that was both ubiquitous and serious. Nearly everyone in the province seems to have suffered from the disease, including babies. It was not uncommon in sickly seasons to see infants at their mothers' breasts trembling in a fit of the disease. Moreover, those afflicted with ague had bouts repeatedly, often for years. Nor was it a mild disease; it incapacitated its victims for hours to days at a time, and it not infrequently killed them.

What was fever and ague? Usually it was malaria. The word ague will be used here, but that encompasses instances of fever and ague, intermittent fever, so-called Lake fever, autumnal fever, and others. Fortunately for our understanding of this small component of the general category of fever, uncomplicated malaria is a relatively certain diagnosis because of the remarkable periodicity of the disease. It affects its victims one day, leaves them symptom-free for a day, or two days, and then returns, repeating the cycle two or three or a dozen and more times: when we read that in 1795 Elizabeth Simcoe had fits of "ague" on the 27th and 29th of April and the third, fifth and seventh of May, we can be sure that she had malaria.

Malaria had long been prevalent throughout the Thirteen Colonies, and certainly reached Fort Niagara, across the river from the future Newark, no later than 1778. In that year John Butler, serving with Butler's Rangers near Tioga in upper New York, was struck down by a bout of ague so severe that he had to "seek relief at Niagara."[24] Two years later another loyalist soldier was so ill that he had to be tied to his horse during a march to the same fort.[25]

During the 1790s, every settlement in Upper Canada seems to have had ague. Newark was riddled with it. Hannah Jarvis once wrote to her father that the "Ague and Fever are so prevalent that whole Families are confined at once ..."[26] The disease was noted at Fort Erie in 1788.[27] Farther north, up

Lake Ontario, Kingston did not escape, despite its self-serving (and erroneous) boast to Lieutenant Governor Simcoe in 1792 that a Kingston location for the capital would be better than Newark, since the former was healthy, the latter sickly.[28]

Some families acquired their ague as a new disease in Upper Canada. Peter and Elizabeth Russell arrived at Newark late in 1792. By October 1793 Elizabeth wrote that their servants (local Upper Canadians) had suffered much with ague, but "Peter and Mary have hitherto escaped and I have had but a slight attack of it."[29] Only two months later, Elizabeth had a severe bout of the disease.[30] Apparently she had acquired her infection that summer. She had a miserable time in 1794, suffering greatly with the disease — so much so that she gave some thought to returning to England.[31]

In June 1794 Elizabeth reported that "Mary had now had a severe attack of ague, and a servant was two-thirds of his time ill with the same disease, but her brother remained unaffected."[32] Finally, and inevitably it seems, a year later Peter Russell was "attacked with a bad fever and ague, which shook him very much."[33] Thus, in less than three years, these four persons in one family, none previously having had ague, all fell victim to it. Peter Russell's diary is also filled with references to ague, the disease making serious inroads on 2 April 1794, when he noted that "all my Servants now Sick, my Sister obliged to cook dinner ..."[34] Eleven years later, Elizabeth was still dosing herself for the disease.

In ague, dosing customarily meant taking bark, the so-called Jesuit's bark or Peruvian bark from the cinchona tree, which contained a substance that later was extracted and labelled "quinine." Most general stores carried bark and other medicinals; physicians kept supplies too, of course.

According to La Rochefoucauld-Liancourt, when the Indians had ague they might take the advice of the physicans employed by the Indian Department—Dr Robert Kerr or his colleagues—but they were more likely to take draughts which they prepared themselves.[35] The Indians had many remedies, though in this instance it is doubtful if any could have had the efficacy of bark, which was and remains a specific. Perhaps it was the Indians who guided Elizabeth Simcoe in her preparation of a local recipe; she recorded that sassafras buds, infused to make a tea, produced a beverage that removed her symptoms.[36]

There is no evidence of preventive measures in the province, other than William Berczy's belief in the efficacy of alcohol; he reported giving the men in his party "some spiritous liquors which is inevitably necessary in a country where it is destructive to the health for those who must chiefly work in the open air to drink constantly raw water alone, the newcomer especially being subject to the Ague ..."[37]

Berczy's belief in the danger of drinking raw water was not widely shared. He also noted that in the Niagara area in 1794 ague was prevalent, "particularly before the woods are cleared out, and the air more purified."[38] The miasmatic theory was an attempt to explain this evident relationship, supposing that the putrid exhalations from a marsh constituted a miasm or heavy gas that either gave rise to or carried the agents of disease.

The association of mosquitoes with swamps was evident to all. But until late in the nineteenth century, these pesky creatures were seen as merely an irritation. For Upper Canadians, the mosquito was a painful fact of life, an annoyance to be endured by all. Mrs Simcoe once noted that she could scarcely write her diary because "my hands ... are always occupied in killing them or driving them away." And just a few days later the mosquitoes were so numerous that smoke would not discourage them.[39] So aggressive were they that both Attorney General John White and Peter Russell commented on their abrupt return to Newark in May 1793. On the second day of that month, Russell recorded in his diary that "Muskitoes [sic] begin to be troublesome for the first time." (Three weeks later they had become "very troublesome.") And on 3 May White observed that "for the first time this Season I was much annoyed by musquito."[40] Happily, by 1850 malaria had largely disappeared from Upper Canada.

Other diseases that ravaged Newark and similar communities in the 1790s included smallpox, diphtheria, measles, mumps, scarlet fever, erysipelas, and tuberculosis. The so-called "childhood diseases" that are usually quite benign today seemed much more severe then. Childhood was the most dangerous period of life. The likelihood of surviving from birth to one's fifth birthday was no better than 50 per cent.

Tuberculosis was called consumption in the nineteenth century and was a major killer of that half of the population tough enough, or lucky enough, to survive past the age of five. It was an insidious killer, infectious to others long before the patient realized that he or she was seriously ill. Nevertheless, the disease was mostly ignored, public fears centring on the more spectacular epidemics such as smallpox or diphtheria.

Because of the effects of all these diseases plus accidents, life expectancy was only about thirty-five or forty years. And because of this, the occurrence of cancer and other diseases associated with the older years was low. This was, perhaps, just as well, since surgery would have been of little help to patients suffering from cancer.

Announcement, Upper Canada Gazette, 8 February 1797. This is probably one of the first examples of preventive medicine in Upper Canada. (Ontario Legislative Library, Toronto)

Small-Pox.

AS the innoculation for the *Small-pox* is this day commenced at Queenſton, and the ſeaſon of the year very favorable, the ſubſcribers propoſe innoculating immediately, in the town of Newark, and throughout the county of Lincoln, on the moſt reaſonable terms.

§§§ The poor innoculated gratis.

ROBERT KERR,
JAMES MUIRHEAD.

Newark, Jan. 25. 18

SURGERY

Today we think of surgery as including a multitude of operations on the limbs, the surface of the body, and within the abdomen, chest, and head. In the 1790s these last three areas were out of bounds. Much sad experience had shown the uniformly high mortality that followed when the abdomen, the chest, or the head were opened, either by injury or by a surgeon. For this reason, a large number of disorders that we now think of as "surgical" — gallbladder disease, appendicitis, tumours, ruptured organs: the list is a long one — were then either categorized as "medical" or were obviously beyond any therapy.

Why were the body cavities forbidden territories? Indeed, why was so little surgery done generally? The answer is simple and is encompassed in the words *pain* and *infection*.

Before 1846, when a dentist and a surgeon in Boston combined to bring surgical anesthesia into the world, patients who were operated upon had the ordeal of pain added to the fear customarily associated with serious disease. Various drugs, including liberal doses of ethyl alcohol in any of its various forms, were used to try to alleviate this pain, but none was particularly effective. One consequence was that elective surgery was performed with great rarity. Those who had conditions that were not life-threatening and that did not include a component of unbearable pain usually chose to live with their disorder rather than face the agony of the knife. A regular part of the surgeon's equipment was a group of strong men who would attempt to hold the patient steady while the surgeon did his work. Anyone who could avoid surgery attempted to do so.

Pain was a certainty that deterred those patients who had a choice. The rest had their operations and, in general, had horrible pain. The common practice of urging someone in a difficult situation to "bite the bullet" comes directly from the experience of battlefield surgery in olden days. The bullets or balls used in muskets were of soft lead and routinely were given to soldiers to bite down on, to help them bear their pain while having a wound probed or a limb removed. The fact that some people suffered more than others in surgery partly reflects individual variations in pain threshold. Shadrack Byfield, for example, when his arm was amputated in 1814 at Fort George, reported that the operation was "tedious and painful, but I was enabled to bear it ..."[41] One has the impression that this young soldier — he was twenty-five when he was shot — was an unusually tough man.

Another consequence of this palpable suffering was the premium that was put on the surgeon's speed: the sooner finished, the sooner pain began to recede. A good surgeon was, almost by definition, a speedy operator.

Besides pain, the other factor limiting extensive or invasive surgery was infection. The stereotype of the old-fashioned surgeon in blood-stained clothing, gripping his scalpel in his teeth while he tied a ligature around a spurting artery, is not unduly exaggerated.

Certainly, the surgeon often was dirty. Any surgeon who washed his hands regularly was displaying personal fastidiousness. Most surgeons went from patient to patient without regard to such niceties, and there is much evidence to show that at least some of them rather prided themselves on the accumulation of blood, pus, and other human debris on their operating clothes.

Since the infective properties of germs were unknown, want of cleanliness can perhaps be understood, but the consequences were horrible. A precise comparison of statistics is not feasible because of great differences in the kinds of data collected, but even gross figures are impressive. One surgeon reported mortality from simple fractures (those in which there was no open wound connecting with the fracture) in civilian practice as 9 per cent, and from compound fractures (those with open wounds) as 42 per cent.[42] In wartime, this last figure could, under the worst conditions, reach 90 per cent.

The surgeons of the 1790s knew only that, when they operated, patients commonly developed pus in their wounds. If operations were done on the surface of the body or on an arm or a leg, many of the patients became better, though by no means all. If the operation was done inside the abdomen, or if the patient had a wound that penetrated the abdomen or the chest, or if the skin of the arm or leg was broken and the underlying bone fractured, few recovered. So operations in these areas simply were not done if there was any choice. Whenever there was a choice, surgeons and patients usually preferred not to take the chance, all knowing how unfavourable the odds were.

Amputation

Amputation was perhaps the classic surgical procedure of the times, and certainly the commonest kind of major surgery that was done.[43] The generally held opinion that serious wounds of the limbs called for speedy amputation often must have meant needless loss of arms and legs. The sheer press of the demands upon his services often forced the surgeon to operate when a more conservative (but time-consuming) therapy might have preserved limbs. After the battle of Chippawa in the War of 1812, William Dunlop, at the time the only surgeon with his regiment, the 89th Foot, had more than two hundred casualties in his care at Fort George. We can sympathize with both his patients and the surgeon, for he wrote that "many a poor fellow had to submit to amputation whose limb might have been preserved had there been only time to take reasonable care of it."[44]

For all of the reasons cited above, surgery had a restricted scope in comparison with the practice today, or even with the end of the nineteenth century. Superficial tumours were removed, abscesses opened, some operations in the genital-rectal area were done if they did not involve entering the abdominal cavity (for example, removing bladder stones and incising anal fistulas), some plastic surgery was attempted, and in some large cities cataracts were operated on by a few specialized surgeons. But primarily, surgery in the 1790s was a response to accidents and to trauma of all kinds. The surgeon often, though by no means always, could offer some assistance in coping with the effects of falls, blows, cuts, and crushing injuries on the human body.

Fractures and Injuries

Of trauma, and its violent effects on the body, there was a plentiful supply in Upper Canada. Many of the new settlers, whether loyalist or later immigrants, lacked skills with tools they were required to use, a fact understood by Alexander McLachlan, who wrote in his narrative poem "The Emigrant": "We were awkward at the axe/ And the trees were stubborn facts."[45]

Such awkwardness undoubtedly explained the plenitude of injuries of all kinds, though not everyone was inept, nor was skill long in coming. The treatment of such wounds as were caused by axes, falling trees, and guns was similar to treatments today, though not so successful. But surgical principles have not changed with regard to these kinds of lesions.

CHILDBIRTH

In the Upper Canada of the 1790s, the hazards of childbirth were so common as to threaten every household, often tearing both new babe and mother from the arms of a young family. Today, some hazard remains in childbirth, both to mother and infant. In Upper Canada, the hazard was far greater. Although we know much about the risks of the birthing process in the eighteenth and nineteenth centuries, we know much less about women's perception of the state of being pregnant at that time. At least among the educated classes (from whom, largely, the written record derives) this was considered an indelicate topic to be treated via circumlocutions, if it need be mentioned at all. The subject of pregnancy was not written about in the sort of explicit, open way that it is today.

Not surprisingly, men tended to be somewhat more casual on the subject. In New Brunswick, Edward Winslow referred jocularly to the fact that "two annual comforts a child and a fit of the Gout return invariably. They came together this heat and ... made me as happy as if the Devil had me. The Boy is a fine fellow (of course) and makes up the number nine now living. My old friend Mrs. Hazen about the same time produced her nineteenth..."[46] William Jarvis was equally casual in reporting to his brother that "my number of Children I expect will be increased to four in the month of Oct. next. I know not of what gender ... but I hope of the masculine ..."[47]

When the event occurred — blessed or otherwise — whatever aid was nearby would be summoned. More often than not, local women served as midwives, usually without benefit of formal training or education other than having survived the experience themselves, though some midwives acquired a considerable and deserved local reputation nonetheless. A Mrs McCall exemplifies this tradition, though she had almost missed being with one of her patients in 1794: "Mr Powell ... volunteered to go in search of Granny McCall with the ox team. After some weary hours watching, the 'Gee, Haw' was heard on the return in the woods, and Mrs. McCall soon stood beside my mother, very soon after the birth of a daughter was announced."[48]

The question of midwifery in Upper Canada during this early period remains mysterious. That midwives existed and performed their necessary duties is unquestionably true. How many there were, and how well they functioned, is unknown. In the earliest days of the province, practising midwifery without a medical licence or degree was technically illegal, yet the law seems never to have been enforced, nor would it have been enforceable. A doctor's attendance during labour would most likely have been relatively infrequent.

Multiple births occurred in Upper Canada, twins being referred to often. The same month that Hannah Jarvis was confined, in 1792, she reports that another woman was delivered at Newark of twins weighing a total of twenty-six pounds; if accurate, this is remarkable indeed.[49] Madelaine Askin assisted at the birth of twins at St Joseph's in 1807, both of whom died — not an unusual event.[50] And in York, by 1811, twins were common in one family at least, a correspondent reporting that:

> The women in this country are in general very prolific. I am intimately
> acquainted with a lady who lives in this place that has had five pairs of
> twins four pair of which are now living also two more children that she

Tools of the Trade. Left to right, back row: pill roller and amputation set. Front row: brass mortar and pestle, cupping glass, and brass twelve-bladed scarificator. (Private collection, photograph, William Severin)

had as single births, and has buried several besides. I think it is sixteen she has had in all and she is now only about seven and thirty years of age. Her husband is about Twenty years older than her. They marry very young here many girls not more than 13 and 14 years old.[51]

Predictably, pregnancy did not always end with happy results. The risks of various disorders was high; though records are scanty, our knowledge of disaster often comes from cemeteries, where tombstones can be mutely eloquent. In one modern study of a small group of early Upper Canadian cemeteries, 41 per cent of all female deaths occurred in the age group 15-45 years, whereas only 29 per cent of males died during these years; the inference that can be drawn is that these are the child-bearing years for women.[52]

On a more personal and immediate level are the frequent references to such family disasters. Neil McLean, of Stormont, Upper Canada, received the following letter in 1794: "Your amiable Sister, and my beloved Wife, Died of Child bed the 28 of Jan'y ... I want words to express the Anguish that tears my heart ... as she Lived, so She Died, with Great meekness and Resignation, to the will of her Creator, a Striking example to me to Imitate ..."[53]

Puerperal fever occurred (a deadly disease that we know now is the result of streptococcal invasion of the uterus), though the incidence seems to have been low in Canada. But when Judge William Dummer Powell was in Detroit in 1792, his sister died of what seems certainly to have been puerperal fever, three days after giving birth, and expiring "without a Struggle."[54]

The causes of maternal death would have included not only puerperal fever but also arrested labour (which may have a number of causes), and disproportion, where the child's head is too large relative to the mother's pelvis. The last commonly is seen in women who have had rickets when children; this vitamin-deficiency disease causes deformity of bones, including those of the pelvis. The general state of nutrition was poorer then than now. Vitamins were not discovered till the twentieth century. Major rickets was common enough, and minor rickets that nevertheless produced distortion of the pelvis probably occurred much more often than it was diagnosed.

But it would be wrong to assume that all childbirth was difficult, even though danger may have hovered very close at all times. Most deliveries would have been routine and thus have escaped comment. We know of one such happy event largely because of the contrast it offered to previous confinements. In 1792 Hannah Jarvis wrote to her father, three weeks after she was delivered, saying that she had never been so well, not having had a single pain after delivery.[55]

CONCLUSION

Thus medical problems in Upper Canada were numerous. Therapy for disease, two centuries ago, was indeed a many-splendoured thing. Our Amerindian neighbours continued to pursue old ways, though with their confidence in them sadly shaken. The settlers relied on botanicals and the use of hot springs, both medicinally and, along with physical methods, for applying heat and cold. Their medical practitioners added the stronger medicinal agents based on metals such as mercury, and made vigorous use of the depletive measures of bleeding, puking, and purging. Surgeons plied their bloody, painful, and often lethal trade. On many occasions the sickroom of the 1790s must have been a ghastly place.

NOTES

The author acknowledges the financial support of the Hannah Institute for the History of Medicine and Associated Medical Services. This support made possible the research from which the present paper is derived.

1   For a full discussion, see Charles G. Roland, "'Sunk under the Taxation of Nature': Malaria in Upper Canada," Charles G. Roland, ed., *Health, Disease and Medicine: Essays in Canadian History* (Toronto: Hannah Institute for the History of Medicine, 1984), 154-70.

2   Metropolitan Toronto Library, Baldwin Room (MTLBR), Alexander Wood Papers, Alexander Thom to Wood, 5 October 1806.

3   Upper Canada Village Document Collection (Morrisburg, Ont.), Solomon Jones Papers, Accounts (medical and stores), 1780-99, bill from Blake & Loedel, Montreal, for 1799 and 1800.

4   MTLBR, Elizabeth Russell Papers, Elizabeth Russell to Elizabeth Kiernan, 12 June 1812.

5   National Archives of Canada (NAC), MG 23 HII7 (Farmar Papers), Peter Russell to Hugh Farmar, 21 April 1794. Contains diary entries for 6 and 17 August 1793.

6   See Marvin Luther Brown, ed. and trans., *Baroness von Riedesel and the American Revolution: Journal and Correspondence of a Tour of Duty, 1776 1783* (Chapel Hill, NC: University of North Carolina Press, 1965), 127.

7   See the letter by P. Campbell cited in E.A. Cruikshank, "Notes on the History of the District of Niagara, 1791-1793," Publication of the *Niagara Historical Society*, 26 (1914), 12.

8   [J.C. Ogden], "A letter from a gentleman to his friend, descriptive of the different settlements in the province of Upper Canada," E.A. Cruikshank, ed., *The Correspondence of Lieut. Governor John Graves Simcoe ...* (5v., Toronto: Ontario Historical Society, 1923-31), 3:195.

9   See William R. Riddell, ed., *La Rochefoucauld-Liancourt's Travels in Canada, 1795 ...,* Archives of Ontario *Report*, 13 (1917), 24.

10 See Mary Quayle Innis, ed., *Mrs. Simcoe's Diary* (Toronto: Macmillan, 1965), 14 August 1795, 160.

11 See John Howison, *Sketches of Upper Canada, Domestic, Local, and Characteristic: To Which Are Added, Practical Details for the Information of Emigrants of Every Class; and Some Recollections of the United States of America* (First published 1821, reprint edition 1970), 111.

12 W.N. Fenton, "Contacts between Iroquois Herbalism and Colonial Medicine," Smithsonian Institution *Annual Report*, 1941-42, 512.

13 Ibid., 517.

14 Innis, *Mrs. Simcoe's Diary*, 82.

15 Ibid., 155.

16 The narrator, James Dittrick, was born on the family homestead between Queenston and Niagara in 1785. James J. Talman, ed., *Loyalist Narratives from Upper Canada* (Toronto: The Champlain Society, 1946), 67.

17 The Dolsen account books exist and are referred to by Fred C. Hamil, *The Valley of the Lower Thames, 1640 to 1850* (Toronto: University of Toronto Press, 1951), 172.

18 NAC, MG 23 HI3, 2 (Jarvis Family Papers), 37, Hannah Jarvis to Samuel Peters, 25 September 1793.

19 Ibid., Hannah Jarvis to Samuel Peters, 27 November 1794, 69-70.

20 William Osgoode to John King, 17 June 1799, William Colgate, "Letters from the Honourable Chief Justice William Osgoode, Part II: A Selection from His Canadian Correspondence, 1791-1801," *Ontario History* (*OH*), 46 (1954), 156.

21 As early as 1786, ginseng was being exported from Carleton Island by the firm of Hamilton and Cartwright. Richard A. Preston, ed., *Kingston before the War of 1812: A Collection of Documents* (Toronto: The Champlain Society, 1959), 120.

22 Innis, *Mrs. Simcoe's Diary*, 184.

23 MTLBR, Elizabeth Russell Papers, draft letter, Elizabeth Russell to Elizabeth Kiernan, 12 June 1812.

24 E.A. Cruikshank, *Butler's Rangers* (Welland, 1893), 51.

25 Ibid., 79.

26 NAC, MG 23 HI3, 2, P3, Hannah Jarvis to Samuel Peters, 12 February 1793.

27 E.A. Cruikshank, "The John Richardson Letters," *Ontario Historical Society Papers and Records*, 6 (1905), 74.

28 The cynical nature of the Kingston claim is evident from the fact that pre-1791 experience with ague there was substantial. For example, the Reverend John Stuart wrote on 1 August 1790 that "my wife and several of my children have had the Fever and Ague almost the whole Summer ..." Preston, *Kingston before the War of 1812*, 166.

29 MTLBR, Elizabeth Russell Papers, draft letter, Elizabeth Russell to Elizabeth Kiernan, 1 October 1793.

30 Ibid., Elizabeth Russell to Elizabeth Kiernan, 27 November 1793.

31 Ibid., Elizabeth Russell to Elizabeth Kiernan, 25 April 1794.

32 Ibid., Elizabeth Russell to Elizabeth Kiernan, 16 June 1794.

33 Ibid., Elizabeth Russell to Elizabeth Kiernan, 23 August 1795.

34 NAC, MG 23 HII7, Peter Russell to Hugh Farmar, 21 April 1794.

35 Riddell, *La Rochefoucauld-Liancourt's Travels in Canada, 1795 ...*, 55-6.

36 Innis, *Mrs. Simcoe's Diary*, 178.

37 MTLBR, [William von Moll Berczy], "Narrative Concerning an Expedition in Upper Canada for Settling a Part of the Province with Germans from Europe and the United States" (ms in 2v.; n.d. but 1812 or later from internal evidence), 1:iii.

38 Ibid.

39 Innis, *Mrs. Simcoe's Diary*, 3 and 11 July 1796, 186-7.

40 For Russell, see NAC, MG 23 HII7, Peter Russell to Hugh Farmar, 21 April 1794, containing copied diary entries, including these for 2 and 20 May 1793; for White, see Colgate, "The Diary of John White, First Attorney General of Upper Canada (1791-1800)," *OH*, 47 (1955), 164.

41 Shadrack Byfield, "A Narrative of a Light Company Soldier's Service in the Forty-First Regiment of Foot (1807-1814)," *Magazine of History with Notes & Queries*, 379-80.

42 J. M. Wallace, "A Statistical Account of Fractures Treated in the Philadelphia Hospital," *Medical Examiner* [Philadelphia], 1 (1838), 20-2.

43 The following paragraphs are derived largely from an earlier article on the topic; see Charles G. Roland, "War Amputations in Upper Canada," *Archivaria*, 10 (1980), 73-84.

44 William Dunlop, *Recollections of the American War*, 1812-14 (Toronto: Historical Publishing, 1905), 53.

45 "The Emigrant" was first published in 1861. This excerpt is from chapter IV, canto 3. See David Sinclair, ed., *Nineteenth-Century Narrative Poems* (Toronto: McClelland and Stewart, 1972), 131.

46 Edward Winslow to Gregory Townsend, 17 January 1793; in W.O. Raymond, ed., *Winslow Papers, A. D. 1776-1826* (Saint John: Sun Printing, 1901), 399.

47 New Brunswick Museum (Fredericton), Jarvis Papers, William Jarvis to Munson Jarvis, 3 July 1792.

48 "Historical Memoranda by Mrs. Amelia Harris," Talman, *Loyalist Narratives*, 120.

49 NAC, MG 23 HI3, Hannah Jarvis to Samuel Peters, 5 December 1792, 26-9.

50 John Askin Jr to his father, 11 November 1807, M.M. Quaife, ed., *The John Askin Papers* (2v., Detroit: Detroit Library Commission), 2:583.

51 MTLBR, Elizabeth Russell Papers, Elizabeth Russell to Elizabeth Kiernan, 30 May 1811.

52 Brian S. Osborne, "The Cemeteries of the Midland District of Upper Canada: A Note on Mortality in a Frontier Society," *Pioneer America*, 6 (1974), 46-55; see 53-4.

53 NAC, MG 24 I3, 9 (McGillvray Papers: Neil McLean Papers), James Lumsden to Neil McLean, 29 January 1794.

54 NAC, MG 23 HI4 (William Dummer Powell Papers), Isaac Clarke to W.D. Powell, 8 January 1792, 1:51-3.

55 NAC, MG 23 HI3, 2, Hannah Jarvis to Samuel Peters, 5 December 1792.

CONTRIBUTORS AND EDITORS

NANCY BUTLER, a former president of the Niagara Historical Society, received a BA from Vassar College, New York, a BLS from the University of Toronto, and a BEd from Brock University. She is a co-author of *Niagara-on-the-Lake: The Old Historical Town*, and as a member of the Niagara Historical Society's Publications Committee she helped to publish *The Battle of Fort George* and acted as an editor of *The Capital Years: Niagara-on-the-Lake, 1792-1796*. She currently teaches English to foreign students at Brock University.

J.M.S. CARELESS, retired professor of history at the University of Toronto, is the author of numerous articles and books. He is chiefly known for *Canada: A Story of Challenge* and *Brown of the Globe*. Dundurn Press published a collection of his essays, *Careless at Work* in 1991.

DOROTHY DUNCAN, a former elementary school teacher, has been curator at Black Creek Pioneer Village in Toronto and has held administrative posts with the Toronto Historical Board, the Peel Museum and Art Gallery, and the Ministry of Culture and Communications (Ontario). She is currently executive director of the Ontario Historical Society. Her publications include numerous articles, children's pamphlets, and conference proceedings for the Ontario Historical Society.

BRIAN LEIGH DUNNIGAN received an MA in history from the University of Michigan. He is currently executive director of the Old Fort Niagara Association in Youngstown, New York, and has written several books and pamphlets on the history of the fort. He has also contributed to the recent reprint of the Niagara Historical Society pamphlet *The Battle of Fort George*.

CURTIS FAHEY, a former editor at the *Dictionary of Canadian Biography*, has a PhD in history from Carleton University. Currently a freelance editor and historical consultant, he is the author of *In His Name: The Anglican Experience in Upper Canada, 1791-1854.*

RICHARD DAVIDSON MERRITT was raised and educated in London, Ontario, where he graduated from the University of Western Ontario Medical School. He completed his residency in ophthalmology at the University of Toronto and is now in private practice in Niagara Falls, Ontario. His research in local Niagara history has produced several articles on early loyalist families. He is currently president of the Niagara Historical Society and, as a member of the Publications Committee, is also an editor of *The Capital Years: Niagara-on-the-Lake, 1792-1796* .

PETER NICHOLAS MOOGK was born in England and received his schooling in the Netherlands, London, Ottawa, Regina, and Toronto. On completing his doctorate in history at the University of Toronto, he joined the Department of History at the University of British Columbia. He has published many scholarly articles and two books, *Building a House in New France: An Account of the Perplexities of Client and Craftsman in Early Canada* and *Vancouver Defended: A History of the Men and Guns of the Lower Mainland Defences, 1859-1949*.

JOY ORMSBY received a BA in history and teacher certification from the University of Manchester, and has taught English and history at Belleville and Trenton. In Niagara-on-the-Lake she has served on the Local Architectural Conservancy Advisory Committee and the Niagara Historical Museum Research Committee. Recently, she edited *Niagara-on-the-Lake: The Old Historical Town*.

MICHAEL POWER received his BA and MA at the University of Windsor and an MLS from the University of Western Ontario. He has published several books, including *A History of the Roman Catholic Church in the Niagara Peninsula, 1615-1815*. He has also written a number of articles for the *Canadian Catholic Review* as well as biographical entries for the *Dictionary of Canadian Biography*. As a member of the Niagara Historical Society's Publications Committee, he has served as an editor of *The Capital Years: Niagara-on-the-Lake, 1792-1796*

CHARLES G. ROLAND, on graduating in medicine from the University of Manitoba, went into private practice in southern Ontario. An interest in the history of medicine led to academic appointments at Northwestern University, Illinois, and the Mayo Clinic and Medical School, Minnesota. Since 1977 he has been the Jason A. Hannah Professor of the History of Medicine at McMaster University, Hamilton. The author of many articles in leading medical journals, he has also published *Secondary Sources in Canadian Medical History: A Bibliography which includes 5000 references*.

ELIZABETH SEVERIN received a BA in English from the University of Toronto. She has worked in costume construction for the Stratford Festival, the National Ballet of Canada, the Canadian Opera Company, and the Shaw Festival. She is currently researching clothing styles for Upper Canada Village.

BRUCE G. WILSON received his doctorate in history from the University of Toronto. Today he is head of the Native, Northern and Land Unit of the Government Archives Division, National Archives of Canada. Among his publications are *As She Began: An Illustrated History of Ontario Loyalism* and *The Enterprises of Robert Hamilton: A Study of Wealth and Influence in Early Upper Canada, 1776-1812*. He is also editor and compiler of the useful reference book *A Guide to Manuscripts Relating to Canada in the United Kingdom and Ireland*.

Index

Royal Scots Regiment, 171
Russell, Elizabeth, 31-2, 135-6, 151, 231, 237-39
Russell, Peter, 29, 38, 231-2, 239-40; estate of, 34; portrait of, 232
Ryan, Charles, 127, 179

St Andrew's Church, 39; bill of scantling for, 119; description of, 120; painting of, 121; prominent members of, 123; records of, 103; Simcoe's attitude towards, 122
St Catherines: Anglican church at, 112
St Clair, Arthur, 68
St David's, 167-9, 173, 189
St John de Crevecoeur, 23
St Mark's Church: burning of, 118; picture of, 117; records of, 103, 112
Sanders, John, 171
Secord, David, 173, 189-90
Secord, James, 174
Sects. See Religion; Dissenters
Servos, Daniel, 137, 140, 162
Servos family, 132, 140
Shane, 150; See also Sheehan
Sheehan, Walter Butler, 15-16, 22, 25; See also Shane
Shipman's Corners, 189
Shipping, 195
Simcoe, Elizabeth Posthuma Gwillim, [14], 59, 110, 112, 131-2, 134-5, 143, 157, 171, 239; and food, 149-50, 161-2; and medical remedies, 234-5, 237
Simcoe, John Graves, 15, 23, 38, 54, 62-4, 68-9, 88, 104, 110, 112, 131, 143, 189; biographical sketch of, [14]; entourage of, 28
Six Nations, 55, 91, 109, 112, 115
Slingerlandt family, 179-80
Smith, David William, 35, 63, 166, 169; home of, 33
Society for the Propagation of the Gospel in Foreign Parts (SPG), 104
Sons of St Andrew, 201
Stage coach, 192-3
Stamford, Presbyterian congregation at, 118
Stewart, Jemima, 175

Street, Samuel, 22, 24, 52, 63
Street, Timothy, 175
Stuart, John, 109, 111
Surgery, 242-4
Surveyors: food of, 148-9

Tavern: definition of, 187
Thompson, Elizabeth, 181
Tice, Christina, 192
Tinling, Lieutenant, 20
Todd, Isaac, 54
Toronto Coffee House, 208
Transportation, Chapter Eight
Treaty of Paris, 18

Upper Canada Gazette, 104, 124, 126, 162, 203, 206-7
"Upper Landing," 74

Vanalstine, Jacob, 139-40

Wallace's Tavern, 201
Walton, Shubbal, 21
Warner, Christian, 106
War of 1812 Losses Claims, Chapter Seven
Washington, George, 228-31
Wayne, Anthony, 69
Weld, Isaac, 38, 75, 95, 116, 195
White, John, 32, 57, 203, 240
Willcocks, Joseph, 179
Wilson, Charles, 192
Wilson, James, 203
Wine, 155-6, 207-8
Winslow, Edward, 245
Women, 93

Yellow House Tavern, 170
York, town of, 31, 192, 197
Young, John, 119

Upper Canada Gazette or American Oracle, *18 April 1793. This is the front page of the first newspaper published in Upper Canada. The printer, Louis Roy, came to Newark from Montreal, having been appointed by the government. Most of the weekly paper was filled with government proclamations and news items from Europe and the United States. However, those individuals who could read would probably have been most interested in the few local advertisements and the infrequent items of Upper Canadian news. (Ontario Legislative Library, Toronto)*